GAWKY

GAWKY

A True Story of Bullying and Survival

RICK PALLATTUMADOM

Foreword by Jacqueline Burnett-Brown, PhD

Final proofread by Melissa Peitsch
Book cover design is based on my previous book cover
by ebooklaunch.com.
Interior book design by Sue Balcer

Ghostwritten by my third writer R. Lee Brown
(First & Second Edition).

First Edition was initially ghostwritten by my very first writer
(Name redacted).

First Edition was ghostwritten by my second writer
Marlyse Goodroad (Main writer).

Second Edition
February 2023

eBook ISBN: 979-8-218-10451-1
Paperback ISBN: 979-8-218-10452-8
Hardback ISBN: 979-8-218-10453-5

I would like to thank my uncle, Felix Padapurackal, for personally
reaching out to me and for contributing to my book's fund.

A special thanks to my cousin Legin John Kandathil (Padapurackal) and
Jaison Manithottiyil for their brotherly love and support.

Thank you for buying this book.

DISCLAIMERS

This is an autobiographical (second edition) attempt to accurately reflect the author's recollections of his experiences over time. The author wrote down his life events to the best of his knowledge, based on his memory, but the chronology of some minor events may be out of order. Some names and characteristics have been changed, some events have been compressed, and some dialogue has been recreated.

Reader discretion is advised. This book may contain disturbing recollections and events.

There may be cultural differences in this book between Americans and Indians, which some readers may find confusing.

The author doesn't want to intentionally defame any characters (or their relatives) in this book, but depictions herein reflect how those characters appeared to him during that time in his life.

Information about Kerala in the first chapter includes material from online sources.

Full disclosure: the author is currently diagnosed with schizophrenia and has psychosis. He has written his autobiography to leave painful parts of his old life behind and move into the future.

DEDICATION

I dedicate this book to my consciousness that kept my mind from fully disintegrating into little pieces during the darkest and most perilous times of my life.

I also dedicate this book to my grandmother, Margaret Joseph Padapurackal, who passed away just two months before the first edition of this book was published. I genuinely regret not being able to go back to India and spend more time with her.

EPIGRAPH

"Find a cause…fall in love…write a book."

—Captain John Carter
John Carter (2012 Hollywood film)

About Life from Gita

Life is a challenge	Meet it
Life is a gift	Accept it
Life is an adventure	Dare it
Life is a sorrow	Overcome it
Life is a tragedy	Face it
Life is a duty	Perform it
Life is a game	Play it
Life is a mystery	Unfold it
Life is a song	Sing it
Life is an opportunity	Take it
Life is a journey	Complete it
Life is a promise	Fulfill it
Life is a love	Enjoy it
Life is a beauty	Praise it
Life is a spirit	Realize it
Life is a struggle	Fight it
Life is a puzzle	Solve it
Life is a goal	Achieve it

CONTENTS

FOREWORD

By Dr. Jacqueline Burnett-Brown (PhD)

Schizophrenia spectrum disorders are a class of psychotic disorders that affect nearly three million adults in the US and 1 percent worldwide. Approximately 40 percent of those diagnosed with a schizophrenia spectrum disorder in the US go untreated. While schizophrenia is most often an inheritable disorder, it can develop in individuals as the result of family conflict, where mixed messages are the means of communication between parents and from parent to child.

Schizophrenia is incurable, but most cases can be managed with medication and therapy.

Schizophrenia generally emerges when individuals are in their twenties. It can come on slowly with mild hallucinations, or it may develop following a psychotic episode. There is still much to learn about this disorder. Currently, we do know that we can no longer think of this as a young adult disease as research has found that it can develop during later stages of life and vary according to gender, race, and culture.

Most schizophrenic individuals have higher intellects and unique interests. However, their thoughts are often disordered, and there is confusion about what is real and what is a product of the disorder. Many find that they experience a disconnect from their families and will often leave, even if this means becoming homeless. It is estimated that 20 percent of homeless individuals suffer from a schizophrenia spectrum disorder. Limited access to psychiatric care and the paranoia that often accompanies schizophrenia mean that most persons living with schizophrenia are living with it alone.

However, having schizophrenia does not mean that there is no hope. There is help and hope with a systematic approach to therapy. The individual with schizophrenia needs his or her family or other support systems to be involved in the therapeutic process. Individuals with a schizophrenia spectrum disorder who have a strong support system experience greater success with medication and therapy than those who do not have a support system.

Cognitive behavioral family therapy has proven effective with families in which one or more members suffer from serious mental illness such as schizophrenia spectrum disorders. The focus is on the family members rather than the individual with the diagnosis. This form of therapy should be used concurrently with the psychiatric care of the diagnosed patient and prescription management.

If you or someone you love shows any of the symptoms associated with schizophrenia, please call your local mental health hotline.

A personal reflection about this memoir:

Reading Rick's autobiography, I felt like I was sitting in the room with him as he unfolded his often tragic, at times triumphant, story to me. His voice is truly clear. You get a true sense of who he is and how he experienced these events that have shaped his life.

This memoir reminds me of *The Kite Runner* by Khaled Hosseini. As you follow Rick, the boy, on his journey from his homeland to the United States, then back again to his home, you experience his fears, his joy, his anger, and his joy again. You get to know Rick. You wish to protect the child he once was—so misunderstood, so tortured by those who did not seek to understand.

When I taught high school literature, I taught my students that the lived experiences of humans on their life's journey have always been the most accurate accounting of history we have. This memoir is one to add to our library shelves and be taught in our schools along with *The Kite Runner* and *A Thousand Splendid Suns* by Khaled Hosseini and *Night* by Elie Wiesel.

About Dr. Burnett-Brown:

Dr. Burnett-Brown served in the United States Navy for a four-year term during Desert Storm, then completed her service on a different sort of battlefield as an educator and continues in post-secondary education as a professor and academic coach to graduate and undergraduate students. Dr. Burnett-Brown earned her PhD with research into the difficulties faced by teachers who felt the oppression of administration regarding teaching through a social justice lens or even teaching accurate history.

Throughout her years teaching, she has continued to work toward her long-term career goal of working with educational and corporate environments, as well as communities to forward the expansion of racial and cultural awareness.

Because of her continued study and work to address racial and cultural disparity in our society, she recognizes that racism and discrimination cause not only divisiveness, but can lead to stress, anxiety, and depression in individuals who are the targets of microaggressions. To that end, she retired from education and completed post-doctorate work in marriage and family therapy and now specializes in bringing healing to families and individuals who struggle with racial-, cultural-, and gender-based discrimination and microaggressions in school, the workplace, and the larger community.

In addition to her certifications as a Georgia educator, Dr. Burnett-Brown is a certified cultural diversity and inclusion professional and is registered as a Georgia-Supreme-Court-approved mediator in domestic, civil, and juvenile mediation and arbitration.

Dr. Burnett-Brown is a member of the International Women in Leadership, the National Society of Leadership and Success. She is an AAMFT Clinical Fellow and has been awarded a certificate in higher education by Harvard's Derek Bok Center for Teaching Excellence.

Dr. Burnett-Brown served nine years as a faculty member of the University of Phoenix, Atlanta Campus where she taught social psychology, cultural diversity, EEOC and culture, and the psychology of learning, developmental psychology. She also served five years at South College, Atlanta, where she taught general and developmental psychology. She currently provides her expertise as a subject matter expert in education, mental health, and cultural conflict. She currently serves as an academic coach to graduate students in education and counseling programs.

Dr. Burnett-Brown serves as an ally and advocate to anyone who has ever experienced any form of oppression.

PREFACE

My name is Rick Pallattumadom. I'm an immigrant from India. I was bullied at a local middle school in America in 2005 and ended up with an incurable mental illness. This book exists because I realized I was at risk of losing not only my way of life, but also any legacy I hoped to leave behind.

But this book you hold in your hands was not created easily.

Before you begin reading, there is something that I feel I have to tell you. What I have written here in this preface is a behind-the-scenes look into my life during the writing process. My hope is that it will change how you read and experience my story.

When I returned to the United States from India in mid-2019, I had just finished the rough draft of my book. I asked my cousin for help since I really didn't know how to proceed with hiring a ghostwriter or editor. I was shy and a little bit concerned because I wasn't very experienced. I was afraid of being ridiculed by a writing professional because of any unintentional mistakes I might have made.

Asking for my cousin's help turned out to be a huge mistake. He was very bad for my mental health, and I eventually realized that he wasn't genuine toward me or helpful with my book. In fact, he proved to be toxic. That was the last thing I needed.

His involvement eventually screwed up my mental health entirely. I was already fragile and underweight—only 140 pounds and six feet tall. My morale nosedived, and I lost the momentum to continue writing my book. Even after we both departed from each other, I abandoned my book at least five times. I got easily discouraged. This drove me to do something crazy, which you'll read about toward the end of the book. I nearly screwed up my life past the point of no return.

I started to work on this project in 2018 when I had high energy after seeing my psychiatrist in America. I had become tired of the way most people I met looked at me while I struggled with the consequences of childhood bullying. I wanted to prove my innocence, to leave my dark drama-filled past, and to move on with my life. I believed that I could do that by writing my story and presenting it to the world.

I wanted to accomplish this before I turned thirty, so I took a giant leap of faith and began writing my story. I did it without hesitation, prior knowledge, or experience. I didn't really plan anything. I never studied writing guides or tutorials. I just started writing and writing, and I never stopped.

You could say that I started to build my book in an unconventional way. I had goals, but I didn't achieve them like normal authors would. Dream and fantasy encouraged me more than reality.

I always believed I have an interesting story to tell. It contains a lot of drama, though some moments are depressing. Sometimes, when I'd think back on my life, I'd see my memories as cinematic moments, and those daydreams fueled my writing. As a child, I watched many Indian and Hollywood films, and I'd always joked about creating a movie or epic tale for the big screen. When I started to write my book, that idea stayed in the back of my mind.

When I learned there were already books written about bullying, I went looking for a book like mine—an autobiography or memoir. Nothing turned up in a quick internet search.

So, I figured if I pulled this off—made an actual book—I could get benefits I'd never had before. That would make my life better in the end, which I needed to believe very badly. For the first time in a long time, I had hope for my future. I believed that my life would get better after I published my book. Writing turned into a full-fledged mission and gave me purpose. It became my new hobby.

I didn't want to live like a victim forever. It was unfair for others to stereotype me because I didn't deserve negative comments. I needed to change their mindset once and for all. I needed to spill everything that had happened in my life in an uncensored format, despite any risk of portraying myself unintentionally as a bad guy because of my unflinching determination and fighting spirit.

My inexperience with speaking and writing English didn't sway me from my goal. I also didn't know how to write an autobiography, and I wasn't familiar with how writing a book worked. But I couldn't let those things stop me. Time was my enemy. I needed to write everything I could remember in a document before I naturally forgot it.

By the time I had serious second thoughts, I had already written over 43,000 words. So, I decided to continue since I didn't want to waste all that effort. I still believed I could do my thing and finish. It was too late to quit. There was no turning back.

I am different now, since I started writing. I am more disciplined, satisfied, have fewer panic attacks, feel positive, and, above all, have matured throughout the process, which I badly needed. I'm not perfect, but my improvements are better than nothing. Most importantly, I have a better understanding about myself, and I have a sense of worth, which reduced my negative psychological symptoms without medication.

This book is designed to bring awareness to all people who may be curious about my story, or dealing with any instances of bullying—not just my family and friends. Although, I think it is a good idea to give them my book too. I want to let them know how childhood bullying made an impact on my life.

I hope you will regard my story positively. You may discover that, sometimes, there are things worse than bullying itself.

I never thought I would write my autobiography, but luckily, I did. I decided to publish despite the risk; if I didn't, my past would haunt me continuously. I hope my book is worth it in the end and will free me from my past that still plagues me. I hope to get some feeling of justice and peace by letting you all read about my life.

INTRODUCTION

This is the story of innocence lost, a life molded by difficult circumstances, and a journey to overcome obstacles in my own mind and find my way in a world that never seemed to give me a break.

Suffering through bullying and painful social interactions gave me PTSD and other mental health issues. In the US alone, over 20 percent of young people report being a victim of bullying. The trauma from bullying caused many of my mental health issues. Through it all, I had no way of knowing that I wasn't suffering alone. Countless other teens endure the nightmare of bullying, too, and find themselves changed in myriad negative ways.

My advice to anyone who finds themselves in a similar situation: no matter what you go through, don't lose sight of yourself. You develop an identity from an early age, an authentic self that only you can be. Remember that when all seems lost; cling to who you know you are, and trust that you *can* find that part of you again as you heal and surround yourself with positivity. *You are the key to your happiness.*

I hope my story offers solace to others and gives hope to those struggling. My journey is painful to share, but it offers lessons and hope for the future. It would bring me great joy to know that someone read my story and felt themselves represented on its pages. If I help even one other person through telling my story, then the journey will have been worth it.

PART ONE
HAPPY-GO-LUCKY KID

CHAPTER 1

KERALA

*It takes a whole village
to raise a child.*
—Nigerian proverb

On May 14, 1992, I was born in Kerala, India, a little coastal state at the southern part of the country. It was formed by merging four regions in 1956, following the nation's independence from the British.

Kerala is known as *God's Own Country* and *Land of Coconuts*. It's a beautiful state, full of beaches, mountains, and backwaters. Everywhere you look, there are plenty of coconut trees. There's always lush vegetation throughout Kerala, even during the hot summer when temperatures rise to nearly 100 degrees Fahrenheit. The foliage can even be seen by satellite, making the state recognizable from space.

Kerala is very close to the equator; thus, it has a tropical climate. Because of heavy rains throughout the year, it is one of the wettest parts on Earth.

According to Hindu mythology, Kerala was retrieved from the sea by Parasurama, a warrior sage. Parasurama, an avatar of Vishnu, threw his battle axe into the sea. The new land that emerged extended from Gokarnam to Kanyakumari, the land of Kerala, reclaimed from the waters.

The people of Kerala are known as Keralites or Malayalis. They commonly speak an Indian language called Malayalam, the language I grew up speaking. (Fun Fact: The word "Malayalam" is a palindrome, meaning that it can be read the same forward and backward.)

Onam was an annual ten-day Hindu festival celebrated in Kerala, a high-energy celebration spent making concentric floral decorations with family and friends. It honors King Mahabali, the kind-hearted demon, who is believed to return to Kerala during this festival. It is quite popular, and people of all ages participate. This festival brings joy and positivity to many.

Famous Portuguese explorer Vasco da Gama was the first to arrive in Kerala back in 1498, linking Europe and Asia for the first time by sea. His arrival in my state is considered a major milestone in the history of the entire world and marked the beginning of a new era. Da Gama had discovered India's first ocean trading route, setting in motion an economic boom for the people of India which unfortunately later led to colonialism, a period which ended poorly for the Indians.

There is an Indian martial art called *Kalaripayattu* or simply *Kalari*. *Kalari* means "battlefield." It is designed for the ancient battlefield with weapons and combative techniques that are very unique to India. It is believed to be one of the oldest surviving martial arts in India with a long history, going back three thousand years. It differs from many other martial art systems in the world in that weapon-based techniques are taught first, and barehanded techniques are taught last. The cardinal principle of *Kalaripayattu* states that the knowledge of the art be used for good causes and purposes only, and not for the advancement of one's own selfish interests.

The British Empire once banned this martial art to prevent any chance of inciting rebellion or resistance by Indians. This situation almost led to the extinction of this ancient martial art, which luckily didn't happen.

Modern-day Kerala is also famous for its ecotourism initiatives. Its unique culture and traditions, combined with its varied demographics, have made Kerala one of the most popular tourist destinations in the world. According to *National Geographic Traveler* magazine, Kerala is named as one of the "ten paradises of the world" and "fifty places of a lifetime."

In the state of Kerala, there is a quiet village called Koodalloor. That's where I first lived, in a white, two-story house which was built shortly before I was born.

The area around our home was unique. Our home sat at the intersection of a four-way road. We had neighbors on all sides of us, except to the left where there was a big, scenic area with a large rice paddy.

The paddy was divided into smaller squares which stretched on for quite a distance. If you looked out around dawn, you could watch the sun rise over the paddy. That view was always gorgeous, especially on foggy mornings.

Living among all that beauty was the Pallattumadom family, my family: my mom Ancy, my dad Joy (a common name for men in my culture), and my older brother Jef who was two when I was born.

I didn't know the meaning of my name, Rick, for a long time. According to Google, Rick means "a stack of hay, corn, straw, or similar material, especially one formerly built into a regular shape and thatched." This, of course, would have meant very little to me at the time, but I later found the irony as there was little "regular" about my life.

I also discovered that my name could mean "powerful ruler" or "brave leader." The name from which it is derived, Richard, was often given to kings. It all sounded very nice, but I wasn't even close to being a proper king or leader. I wasn't confident or strong, able to command a room, or to give out a decree that others would listen to. Basically, I was the direct opposite of everything a king was supposed to be.

My parents baptized me into the Catholic Church when I was a year old and brought me up in the church. I remember finding a community there, surrounded by family, friends, and faith. It was a community I would long for in the years to come when the world seemed dark and lonely.

One year after I was born, my parents had their third and final child, my younger brother Chris. Chris and I were close at first; but as time went on, our relationship changed. I withdrew into myself, and Chris became much closer to Jef than to me.

As a little boy, I played with my brothers and the other children in our neighborhood. Lucas was our loyal leader. Another friend was Tom, who we all called Mowgli. Lucas and Mowgli were older than me. My younger friends—Jericho, Hansel, and his younger sister, Anju—completed our group.

We spent time outside, running around the neighborhood, laughing, and playing games—such as cricket, card games, and hide-and-seek.

At home, my childhood was happy and fun, full of light, laughter, and friendship. School, on the other hand, was not pleasant. As in many other places, education is very important in Kerala. We all attended school beginning at a young age.

Our school was near a small town called Vayala, a long distance from my home. It was a private school, not a government-run school, and there was only one building. It was part of the local church nearby. That school was home to children in grades one through four, lower kindergarten, and upper kindergarten.

There weren't many children at school. In my class alone, there were only seven kids—boys and girls combined. Jef's class had a few more. Chris' class only had four kids, including Chris.

The teachers at the private school were strict. If we made mistakes or misbehaved, they would spank us with a long, thin stick. The spanking itself wasn't hard because we were little children. Still, most kids took their punishments seriously, though it was not unusual for some students to get embarrassed and laugh whenever they were spanked.

Almost all the teachers were okay with the way they were directed to discipline students. Spanking was an everyday occurrence in most Indian schools, private or government-run. Most parents supported teachers in disciplining their kids at schools, even if it meant their children receiving a spanking. Both parents and teachers considered this form of discipline beneficial—but not me.

I didn't like spanking because I was sensitive. If a teacher spanked me in front of other students, I always felt like a bad kid. I hated that feeling.

In rare cases, some teachers would get angry and punish students in unconventional ways. I remember one moment when I got a shove to the head from a new teacher who had recently started at that school. I was in the first grade. I could hear the anger in her voice when she spoke to me. I think she even cursed. She was angry because I hadn't listened closely to her directions.

I was more sensitive than many of my friends. Some endured the spankings with ease; I was afraid. Any discipline I received stayed in my mind and kept me from focusing on my schoolwork. I'd often complain about school at home, at the very least displaying reluctance to attend in front of my parents.

Chris and Jef always received the best marks in their classes, although it was not that impressive since there were only a few students. Despite only having a few kids to compete against, I wasn't first in the class like my brothers. I was always behind when it came to my grades. I was supposed to be good at school, but I was not.

I was one of the quietest kids in school. I usually kept to myself, even during free time and breaks. I always tried to sit at the back of the classroom to avoid any attention from teachers. Sitting in front was risky. Teachers would ask questions of those who sat in the front or call on them to read more often—all things I had no desire to do. If teachers assigned me a spot in the classroom, I always hoped I was placed in the back, so at least I could relax a little. If I had been put at the front of the class, my anxiety would have been through the roof.

I was never interested in studying. No one taught me about the importance of studying and learning new things. Every adult that I encountered would just say things like, "Kids go to school to study. They're supposed to enjoy learning and finding out new things." But I didn't know why they felt like that. So, I didn't have any motivation to do well. It would have been nice to know why I was studying, to have a reason other than just the same generic dialogue. Even that knowledge probably would have improved the quality of my life, and perhaps it could have helped me to improve my life when things got rough.

Though I didn't express my interest in school studies as a child, I knew that later in life I would excel, achieve great things, and become very successful. I would have a prestigious job, become respectable, and have a high social status in the community. No matter what happened, I believed I would achieve that. I anticipated those moments when I was very little, and I was invested in that future, even though I didn't know how to achieve my goals at that moment.

CHAPTER 2

A LITTLE SHY

Once bitten, twice shy.
—Australian proverb

When I was just eight years old, I decided I would never get married. I had watched a lot of Malayalam movies which had not left me with a good impression of marriage. In those films, the husband and wife would often argue. Usually, the husband would slap the wife in the face because he was angry or wanted to teach a hard lesson. That always made me uncomfortable. I felt bad for the women and angry at the men who were hitting them. I knew it was wrong for a man to hit a woman; and to make matters worse, I knew that oftentimes, despite the violence, relationships like that rarely ended in divorce. Usually, the wife needed her husband to provide for her, and she was unable to leave him. Without him, she couldn't care for herself or her children.

Whenever I watched these scenes, I was bothered deeply. The situations seemed mean and pointless. Weren't there better ways for a man to let his wife know he was unhappy with her?

I didn't want that kind of drama and negativity in my life. Not getting married seemed the most reasonable way to avoid it. There were too many risks in a marriage, and I couldn't help but think about them and fear that someday that kind of behavior would be expected of me. I tended to dwell on subjects for far longer than necessary, and this was one of those subjects.

Therefore, I started avoiding girls altogether, becoming shy and uncomfortable around them. I also avoided romance films completely; the scenes were too cheesy and reminded me of what I vowed to never have.

Ironically, later in my life when I needed a light the most, the idea of getting married would be the only thing that kept me from drowning in the ocean of my mental disorder.

Drama wasn't the only reason I chose to avoid girls, romantic films, and marriage. Comparing myself to my two brothers, I never felt attractive or smart enough to warrant a second glance from other people. I wasn't jealous. I just genuinely believed that I was ugly and undesirable compared to my brothers. I would look at the two of them and feel a heavy weight settle in my chest. My habit of comparing myself to others played a major role in my self-esteem issues later as well.

To add insult to injury, I also felt like I had a big ear. Sometimes, Jef and Chris would embarrass me by calling me an *aannacheviyan*, which means "the one with the elephant ear" in Malayalam.

Around this time, my dad decided he wanted my brothers and me to learn how to break-dance. At first, I didn't want to because I thought dancing was for girls. However, I didn't speak up because I rarely said no to anything. Disagreeing with others made me sick to my stomach, and I discovered I didn't feel so horrible if I just went along with whatever suggestion or request was made.

So, I agreed to take lessons.

My older cousin Scott had a childhood friend who was a break-dancer. I had fun whenever Scott came to our home. He was always engaging and was a very social person. He had tons of friends from his school and college, and they all thought he was a superstar. Everybody liked him. Sometimes, he would take me and my brothers to watch movies or go out to other fun places. It was always good to have him around. He was studying to start a career in the medical field.

Scott's dancer friend had impressed my father, and my dad asked him to teach us break-dancing. So, the dancer came to our house to teach us simple dance steps. We gathered on the terrace of my two-story house to learn.

Jef wasn't keen on the idea and didn't even bother to try learning the steps. After a few minutes, he went back inside. Even at a young age, Jef was a very serious person. Dancing did not appeal to him. He had only agreed because my dad had pressured him.

Chris and I kept learning. At first, it was only me and Chris and another friend. Within a few days, all the neighborhood kids—around ten or fifteen total—had gathered with us to learn. My dad paid for everybody's lessons. It was a fun experience, full of children's laughter and bonding.

After we had mastered a few steps, we began learning a dance to the American song "Barbie Girl," which had recently become popular everywhere in India. People loved it, even if they couldn't understand the words. That's how I was. "Girl" was the only word I knew, but I enjoyed the song. It had a fun dance beat and interesting voices.

As we took a break during the dance class one day, I noticed someone in the bathroom near the terrace on the second floor. It's still a mystery to me why I did what I did next. I tried to climb to the edge of the bathroom window. But then to my shock, I realized that it was a girl. I wasn't trying to see her naked; I was actively avoiding girls and was not interested in anything like that. It was just one of those stupid things that kids do. But some of the other kids saw me and laughed. I was embarrassed, and my cheeks burned a bright red. I could barely face them when I climbed back down. I hadn't even been able to see anything, as I wasn't tall enough.

I still can't explain why I did that. Maybe I was excited by all the neighborhood kids coming to our house to study break-dancing. I almost never felt excited by anything; and when I finally did, I didn't know what to do with myself. Maybe I wanted to impress the other kids for some reason? I honestly didn't really *want* to know the real reason, but if I had been just a little older, I would have been in deep trouble.

I never knew whether one of the other kids told my parents about the situation, but the shame I felt afterward was so great that I tried to avoid them for a few days, as well as my brothers and the dance students. I tried to erase that embarrassing memory by watching television.

However, one student told the dance teacher what I had done. Everyone thought I was perverted. To me, being known as perverted felt bad. It made my skin crawl, and it gave me a swirly feeling in the pit of my stomach.

Pervert. It even sounded criminal, like something I could be prosecuted for. Nobody ever actually insulted me directly, but I could tell by the way they looked at me that they were judging my bizarre and idiotic actions.

Though I was only eight, I was mortified by the incident, and I quit dancing. I felt I had no other choice.

The other kids continued with the class and learned the dance to "Barbie Girl." They eventually performed it at an auditorium nearby, and I went to see their performance. It hurt to see all the kids up there, having a good time and dancing to a song I loved. I wished for a few moments that I hadn't done something so silly, that I had continued to dance and just brushed off the embarrassment. But I felt I wouldn't have succeeded even if I'd tried. There was just something about me that wouldn't let the problem go.

Unfortunately, that wasn't the only awkward incident I had involving a girl. One day, while I was sitting in the dining room eating, Hansel's younger sister Anju came up to me. Hansel was a good friend of mine, but I had had some interactions with his little sister. I was suspicious of what was about to happen…and, as it turned out, rightly so.

"I love you," she said in English. She then quickly left.

I was shocked! I couldn't believe what I had heard. She was two years younger than me and practically like a sister. I never thought of her as a girlfriend. There was no way I could believe that was how she really felt!

Then I heard laughter nearby. I turned to see Chris and Hansel snickering, and I realized they had prompted Anju to say that to me. I wondered if they were seeking revenge from earlier in the day, since I hadn't felt like playing with them when they'd asked me.

It was a childish thing for them to do. Back then, I couldn't imagine Chris being involved in a scheme like that. Chris was a good brother; we were close. Looking back, I must admit that Chris really would have thought it was fun to tease me.

Because of their prank, I tried to avoid seeing Anju for a few days. I was a little embarrassed then, although looking back on it now, it was pretty funny.

CHAPTER 3

THE AMERICANA

*The best candle is
understanding.*

—Welsh proverb

My childhood wasn't all embarrassment and shame, however. Around the same time as the "Barbie Girl" ordeal, we went to Veegaland Amusement Park (now known as Wonderla) in Ernakulam District, the most advanced district in the state of Kerala. This trip is one of my fondest childhood memories. I didn't know how to swim, but I loved to be around water. The park had artificial beaches where waves would ebb and flow. It was fun to float lazily on the water, soak up the sun, and relax. I had the best time with my parents, brothers, and a few cousins who came along.

Even though I liked the amusement park, I never wanted to go on any waterslides. I wasn't the adventurous type; I wasn't brave. Jef and Chris loved the waterslides and spent most of their time whooshing down them with enormous smiles on their faces. They craved the thrill.

They asked me to go with them, but even though it all looked like a lot of fun, I wouldn't dare. I was afraid. What if I fell off? What if I got hurt? What if, when we got to the top, I didn't want to go down anymore? There were too many

17

---

things that could go wrong, too many "what ifs" that made my stomach do flip-flops. So, I just sat back and watched other people enjoy their time.

As I grew up, I'd hear stories of America. My aunt Ellie and my uncle Ron lived there, halfway around the world. When they'd left, they'd requested visas for us so we could join them, but the paperwork took a long time. We had no idea how long we'd be waiting. America was the most powerful country on Earth. We didn't know how to envision it, but we knew it was wealthy with a strong military. We wanted to live there too.

America is probably at the top of everyone's list when it comes to the ideal place to live because it is different from every other nation. It's advanced in technology and medicine with new breakthroughs happening all the time, making it more appealing than other countries in terms of quality of life and opportunities to gain wealth. That's why most people around the world try to get in, whether by legal or illegal means.

When I was a young boy, I knew nothing about the specifics of what made America so great. But I already had a strange feeling that America was different from every other place I'd ever heard about.

When I was nine years old, I learned more about America.

I was playing on the floor of my living room when the phone rang. My mom answered. I barely noticed, distracted by the game I was playing. My mother's urgent voice caught my attention.

"Turn on the television!"

"Why?" I asked. "Who's on the phone?"

"It's your aunt Ellie. Turn on the news."

I turned the television on, unsure what could be such a big deal. On the news, they were showing a live video of the Twin Towers burning. Even in India, everyone was watching. We saw the smoke and listened as the newscasters said terrorists had hijacked airplanes and rammed them into the towers in New York. It was a strange feeling. So many innocent people had died.

Over the next year, we continued to hear about America and Osama bin Laden. I learned he had been the mastermind behind that horrific terrorist attack. That was what the American president, George W. Bush, kept saying on the news.

Terrorism was a new, scary word, and I started to hear it a lot more often from then on. You never knew when the next terrorist attack could come. I immediately became scared of that possibility.

Osama bin Laden became well-known in India and around the world. Every kid knew his name. President Bush was the leader during a lot of good things, and Osama bin Laden caused a lot of horrible, evil things.

As kids, we had nothing exciting to do in our spare time other than the usual games of hide-and-seek and cricket. It was up to us to devise new, entertaining games. This eventually led to the creation of a game that was heavily influenced by the current events surrounding 9/11 and Osama bin Laden.

My friends and I would play "Osama bin Laden versus America." We'd run around wooded areas, racing after each other with wooden or toy guns, complete with potassium-fed blank ammunition that one could buy at the carnival in my local church. If we were out of that, we would just use imaginary bullets, making gunshot sounds with our mouths. *Bang! Pow!* This was a fun game to play.

While we waited to get official news on going to America, my life continued as usual. I began to develop interests and hobbies, one of which was computers. My older cousin Josh had a computer, and it fascinated me. Computers were still uncommon in most households, but Josh was studying to become an IT professional. He and his mother, my aunt Marissa, lived an hour away from us. When we sometimes went to visit them, I was always very excited, hoping I would get to play on Josh's computer!

Computers seemed magical to me. During our visits, I finally got my hands on one! It was mesmerizing. The more I learned, the more I was sure that I wanted to go into the IT field. I learned as much as I could, looking up words like Microsoft and people like Bill Gates. I wanted to know all I could about this fascinating new technology.

Playing video games on the computer was a life-changing experience for me. Once I'd discovered them, I dove in and couldn't stop. I played *Road Rash, Need for Speed II, Magic Ball, and House of the Dead*. All of them were incredibly fun! I wanted more time to play them, so I made a deal with my dad: we needed to visit my aunt and cousin at least once a month. Amazingly, he agreed. My brothers would go with us occasionally, but I usually didn't mind. All I wanted was to play on the computer. It helped to pass the time, both in my day-to-day life and while we waited for news about going to America.

When I was ten, I joined a local high school in Kidangoor, a thirty-minute walk from my home. In India, high school starts in the fifth grade. So, every student and teacher that I met was a brand-new face. Only a few students, perhaps two or three, from my old school joined my new high school. Along with 20 to 30 other students, I went to a classroom each day. The students would stay in the same classroom all day, while the different teachers for different subjects rotated through. I later discovered that this practice was completely reversed in schools in the United States.

While there, I met a teacher who taught Malayalam. She was one of the oldest teachers in the school and was also strict. I had to be careful around her. She once spanked me with a small, thin stick on the upper thigh for not doing the homework and not bringing my Malayalam textbook. It wasn't just the pain after the spanking that was scary. I could also hear the sound a few seconds before the actual impact as a wind-like *whoosh*. The anticipation of the strike was worse than the bite of the stick, and after that, I was very cautious to do my work and bring all my materials to class. I definitely did not want to repeat that experience.

Another time, that teacher taught us about the word "mummy."

"Mummy," she said, "means 'dead body.' Think of the Egyptians. They have mummies. From now on, you should use the word 'mother' — in Malayalam, '*amma*' — to speak about your mother. Otherwise, you will be calling your mom a dead body all the time." She smiled at us.

The very concept was funny to me. I had always called my mom "mummy" in English. I didn't think about what else the word could mean. When she taught us about the word "mummy," the '90s Hollywood film *The Mummy* also popped into my mind. I was glad she wasn't trying to force us to change what we called our mothers. She was simply recommending we do it, adding some humor to her class.

That same year, some of my family and friends began talking seriously about going to America. I would get excited when I heard them talking about the possibility. Our community knew we would probably leave within a few years. We were just waiting for the official paperwork to come through. It seemed to take forever, and everyone who knew us was abuzz, wanting more information. Even my Malayalam teacher asked me when we were moving because she was curious.

That was one of the first times I realized that we really were going to leave India. It wasn't just a dream or a fantasy. We would soon leave our home and move halfway around the world.

I was excited. Living in America sounded like an adventure. I had only seen the country through Hollywood movies and in the news. It surprised me, but I was even looking forward to starting school in America. It seemed like fun, a chance to start over. I also knew the teachers in America didn't use spanking to discipline their students. I liked the idea of studying at the American school where I would be free from that type of punishment and embarrassment.

While we were waiting to receive our official paperwork, Hollywood kept American culture very present in my life. We'd watch popular US films like *Rambo*, *Terminator 2*, and *Jurassic Park*. I loved them. Even though I didn't know any English, I could follow the storylines of action films. They were full of life and excitement. I'd stay up late, watching them with my dad. On the weekends, my friends and I would gather in my living room and watch.

I didn't know much about the films or who made them, but I knew they were made in the US. I was very curious about what life in America would be like and often wondered if what I was seeing in these films would come close to my real experience in the new country.

Besides films, we also watched cartoons like *The Jungle Book*, *Aladdin*, and *Tom & Jerry* on the VHS player that my mom had brought from Saudi Arabia when she'd worked as a nurse there. I enjoyed the cartoons almost as much as the films, and they certainly kept me entertained.

CHAPTER 4

INNOCENT AND HOLY

*Appearances make impressions, but
it is the personality that makes an impact.*
—Unknown

Around this time, I met a new classmate named Srijesh. He and I became good friends.

The two of us were opposite in many ways. Srijesh was smart and confident. He loved school, and he talked to a lot of the kids there. When he left, he became quiet and reserved, barely saying anything as we walked home together.

I was the opposite. I kept quiet at school, not wanting to be noticed by other students or the teachers. After school, I came to life, ready to talk and enjoy myself. However, since I was so quiet and timid most of the time, others saw me as vulnerable and easily manipulated. Sometimes, they would try to take advantage of me.

One day, Srijesh and I were walking home from school when another kid our age approached me. This kid went to the same school as we did, and his classroom was near mine. We usually saw each other at school and while walking home, but we weren't really friends. On this particular day, the kid asked if I had any unused notebooks at my house.

"Why do you need them?" I asked.

"I don't have money to buy notebooks for school," he answered, looking at the ground as if he were embarrassed.

I was a bit skeptical, but my unassuming nature took over; I believed him, and I wanted to help.

Srijesh saw I was considering giving him books, and he stepped in. "This kid is trying to trick you. He's got notebooks and money to buy more if he needs them. He doesn't need yours. Don't let him fool you."

I paused for a few seconds and quickly realized that Srijesh was right. The kid was asking me for notebooks so that he could sell them to a local man who recycled books and papers. We often saw this man, loaded down with papers for recycling and other recyclable materials, as we walked home from school. The kid wanted to give my notebooks to the recycling man in exchange for money. Then, he would probably go to the store and get candy. That had happened before.

I evaluated the situation a moment longer, just to be sure. I knew he wasn't homeless, because he had a nice, small house that I had walked past before. His family could afford blank notebooks for school use if he needed them.

If it hadn't been for Srijesh, I probably would have given the other kid some notebooks because I didn't want to seem like I didn't care about others. I didn't want to deny the wrong person, someone who may have genuinely needed help, a notebook or other school-related supply. If I'd denied someone who truly needed help, I would have felt bad later, and I may have kept thinking about the situation. That was part of the constant anxiety and fear I felt.

Thankfully, with Srijesh's help, I realized I was being exploited. That kid had seen me as vulnerable and knew I was in a better financial situation than him. He thought I would fall for his ruse if he applied enough pressure, and he knew he could easily make me feel guilty to get what he wanted. His request seemed fishy, though, and the longer I studied him, the more I could see the dishonesty in his face. So, he ended up walking away empty-handed.

I was glad Srijesh had been with me. He was good at reading other people and had analyzed the situation quickly and helped me avoid any embarrassment. He was a wonderful friend.

The closer we got to moving to America, the more it felt like good things happened to me. For the first time, at my local church during Sunday school, I received a higher grade than all the other kids. Even though my grades weren't good at school, I excelled in Sunday school. I was devoted to God; I had faith in Him.

I never lied in front of others because I was always thinking about Him and something my first grade Sunday school teacher told my class: "Don't ever lie to your parents, your siblings, your friends, or to God. It is a sin if you lie to others. Be honest with everybody. Whatever you do, God always sees you. So, be good, and do good things." I remembered that lesson clearly, and I still think about it to this day.

So, I feared God and his punishments if He caught me sinning. I knew that many other kids did not take our teacher's warning seriously. They always seemed to be lying about something.

Sometimes, my faith and careful adherence to the rules would make others perceive me as weak and incapable. I didn't feel weak, and I was confident in my relationship with God. Whenever my brain started to dwell on what others thought of me, I would do my best to toss those thoughts away. I didn't like negative thoughts, even when I knew my peers and other adults thought of me as a fool.

Everybody knew I wasn't clever like my two brothers. Every adult told me repeatedly not to lie to others, but in reality, I had to lie sometimes in order to get through a few tough situations.

There was one time, sometime before First Communion, we had to do confession in front of the priest. We had to go into a little room with a small partition between us. Then, we would tell the priest what we'd done wrong, and he would give us a penance to do in order to be forgiven.

While I was waiting in line for the other kids in front of me to do their confessions, I grew anxious as I tried to think about what to say to the priest. I knew they expected me to confess everything, but I honestly didn't know what to confess. I tried to remember what I had recently done wrong, but I couldn't think of anything as I was too pure and holy—too afraid of God's wrath—to do anything worth confessing. My priest wouldn't believe I had never done anything wrong, though. That wouldn't make any sense since all kids sin at some point in their lives. I was worried, and my heart pounded loudly in my chest.

So, by the time the last kid in front of me had finished his confession, I had made up my mind. I would make up a lie intentionally to tell the priest and God. I had decided to say that I had stolen a pen from another kid.

I never felt good about the lie. Even though the priest didn't bat an eye, I felt like something had changed. I'd lied intentionally and I lived in fear of what God might do to me. I tried to tell myself that it would be okay, that since I rarely lied, God would forgive me. Still, it was hard to swallow down my fear and anxiety about the situation. I had only wanted everything to go smoothly, but I was afraid that I'd perhaps made things worse for myself.

Along with adhering to as many of God's rules as possible, I also had a hard time saying no to others. My anxiety would get the best of me, forcing me to agree to something I really didn't want to do. For example, once a month after Sunday school, there would be a meeting of the Mission League: Sunday school students, nuns, and priests. Many kids didn't stick around, instead going straight home after class. My two brothers almost never attended these meetings. I would see them sometimes after class and ask them if they were coming to the meeting. They would both look at me and just smile. Then, they would go home along with the other students in one big crowd.

Sometimes, I didn't want to go, but I typically changed my mind quickly whenever I thought about God. I felt that if I didn't go, I wasn't doing my duty. So, I went to all the Mission League meetings. I could have just gone home with no repercussions because they wouldn't ask me later why I didn't come. Nobody would have seen me leaving if I'd gone out with everyone else. But I always decided to attend the meetings. All I had to do was sit in that room and hear what the church officials had to say. Everything was over in an hour or less.

Things weren't always difficult in Sunday school. Along with being cautious in keeping God's word, I was sometimes afforded opportunities I didn't know I needed. When we were preparing for First Communion, they needed someone to read the Holy Bible during the ceremony. My teacher didn't have a hard time finding someone to do it. She looked at me and smiled. I was the chosen one. Anxiety bubbled up in my stomach once more. I didn't like to read aloud, much less in front of a lot of people. How would I survive?

After I was picked, I felt the weight of tremendous responsibility. I thought my teacher had chosen me because she knew I was the most innocent of all the other kids. Looking back now, I wonder if she chose me because my dad was a college professor. Jef had read the Bible during his First Communion, and Chris would be the one reading the following year. Now, I can see the pattern. Then, however, I believed she knew my mind was devoted to God, and I was the right person to read the Bible at the ceremony.

At first, I didn't want to do it because I had never done anything like it before. It would be embarrassing if I made a mistake in front of the typically large crowd. Church, on a First Communion Sunday, was sure to be crowded. But I had enough pride in my faith that I couldn't let my fear sway me. I took on the responsibility with all the strength in my heart, and when that day came, I did my part and finished one of the seven sacraments.

CHAPTER 5

GOING TO AMERICA

Leap and the net
will appear.
—Unknown

In 2003, while we were still waiting for our papers to be approved, the United States appeared in our news again. The US had declared war on Iraq. We watched what happened closely. The American government claimed that Iraqi dictator Saddam Hussein had weapons of mass destruction.

I was confused and didn't know of any connection between Saddam Hussein's WMD and Osama bin Laden's terrorist attack at the Twin Towers. I still have a hard time understanding the connection between the two events. Back then, I was too young to be worried about world events anyway, so I left that up to my parents. I didn't try to find out more than the little snippets I saw on the news. But I worried that the war might delay our plans to go to America and make the process of getting our papers approved take even longer. It already felt like we'd waited an eternity and there was still more waiting to do. So, we kept a careful eye on the situation.

That same year, my cousin Sarah, Scott's younger sister, got married. Some of their other relatives came to attend the wedding. One of those families, Martha and Jay, who brought their daughter and son, lived far away from our village. Their son was three years older than me. His given name was Akilan, but his family and friends called him Jith.

He was just a boy like us, innocent and friendly, who didn't seem to have many friends, so my brothers and I became friends with him. He grew especially close to Jef because they were approximately the same age. We all spent a lot of time bonding and having fun, before and during the wedding. Ultimately, Jith would change the course of my life, but that was still in the distant future.

When I was twelve years old, a new teacher came to our school. She taught English and was very strict, just like my Malayalam teacher had been, but with a different tone and teaching style. She was younger than my Malayalam teacher, and she could speak English better than any other teacher at that school. She was modern and progressive and would encourage us to learn English more than Malayalam. My Malayalam teacher was more old-school and conservative, and believed the opposite. She encouraged us to learn Malayalam more than English.

My English teacher's views, in the end, were probably correct. She believed everyone needed to learn English so they could communicate effectively. English was taught in nearly every country on the planet, and that was how most countries communicated with each other about official business. If we wanted to succeed worldwide, English was crucial. Since my family was planning to move to America within the next few years, I would need to know English to thrive in my new environment.

Still, I could see my Malayalam teacher's point. She didn't like to discourage the old way of life and our traditions. If we lost sight of the past and who we were, we would forget our Indian heritage and our original identity. Our teacher wanted us to be proud of who we were and where we'd come from, not completely toss it aside.

I agreed with both of them because they both made valid points. I preferred to find a middle ground rather than choosing a side. I felt safer when no one could say I had completely shunned their opinion. I felt unskilled or slow at making decisions because I couldn't make up my mind.

Finally, in 2005, my life began to change. My dad had the internet installed in our house, and I had my first in-depth introduction to the Web. When I figured out what it was, I was ecstatic! It was expensive, so I knew he must need it for something.

Very few people we knew had a computer, and those who did were not connected to the internet. I'd never even heard of it before and had no idea what I could use it for. Before, when you wanted information, you visited the library and hoped to find what you were looking for in a book. With the internet, we suddenly had access to a treasure trove of information about anything in the world.

It seemed magical.

This idea drew me in and made me excited. I wasn't allowed to use it often, though, so I'd watch my dad and Jef as they used it. That was how I figured out why he'd gotten the internet: he was researching the US embassy. We'd finally gotten our letter!

My dad followed the instructions in the letter from the embassy and filed for the next steps online. He was paving the way for us to leave for America, something we'd been discussing for years, ever since a few months after Chris was born. I really wanted to go to America, no matter what.

Finally, my family's preparations had paid off. After all my dad's research and filing of paperwork, we received an interview date.

We traveled to a neighboring state in India, Tamil Nadu, to visit the embassy. While in Tamil Nadu, my whole family had to go to a pre-approved clinic to visit the doctor. This was a requirement before we went to the embassy and saw the American interviewer.

They took me into a room, and my mom followed. The doctor looked at me and said, "Go ahead and remove your shorts."

I looked at my mom, baffled.

My mom told me, "It's okay. He has to document officially whether you are a boy or a girl. He'll have to check your private parts, but he will not touch you. They require this before we can go to America."

Reluctantly, I complied. If I wanted to go to America, I had no choice. My face burned with embarrassment. I had not expected this to be part of the process. I thought, *Why in the hell do they need to verify that I am a boy?* It was very puzzling, but I did my best to accept it. They needed evidence, or we couldn't go to the interview, let alone to America. More than anything, I wanted to go.

The doctor quickly looked me over and jotted down some notes on a pad.

Thankfully, it wasn't just me. They checked my brothers next, one by one. After that, we were finally permitted to go to the US embassy.

We sat down in chairs, waiting for our interview. I looked around, watching the other people called up for interviews. My stomach felt twisted in knots. I had no idea what to expect. Were they going to ask me questions? Would they speak only in English so that I couldn't understand? Would they tell us we wouldn't be allowed to go? All the "what if" questions swirled around in my head, making me feel a strange combination of worried, afraid, and excited all at once.

Finally, they called us. Our American interviewer waited behind a counter beside a translator. As we approached him, he greeted us. Then, he started our interview.

He asked my mom and dad a lot of questions about themselves. He asked questions about my brothers and me. Then he turned to me.

He asked, "Do you speak English?"

I nodded. "A little."

"How old are you?"

"Thirteen."

"Do you know where the state of Texas is? The city of Dallas?"

I shook my head, as I had no idea, knowing only enough about America to recognize the word "Texas." I realized that was the state that we were moving to, and I'd also heard that was the home state of President George W. Bush.

Finally, he asked me, "What do you want to be when you grow up?"

I knew they were going to ask this, so I was prepared. "I haven't decided yet," I said.

My dad jumped in. "He wants to become a soldier."

I didn't correct him. Besides going into the IT field, I had always wished to become part of the Indian army. I had always had a sense of patriotism when I was little. When I was in school, I'd even been dressed up by my teacher as a soldier during one of the school programs in the auditorium near the end of the school year. Since we were going to America, becoming an Indian soldier would no longer be an option.

The interview dragged on and on. I thought it would never end, and when the interviewer went back to talking to my parents, I grew bored. I was relieved my part was over, but all I really wanted to know was if we were going to be allowed to go to America or not.

Finally, he told us the news—we were going to America! Everybody was over the moon with excitement and happiness.

We went back home to Kerala and started our preparations to leave for the US.

Since I wasn't sure how much time I had before leaving, my friends and I played all kinds of games like it would be our last chance. At one point, however, Jericho got upset with Hansel and walked off. I said, "Hey, Jericho. Don't go away! This is our last opportunity to play a game. By the time we meet each other again, we might be all grown up, and our lives might be very different. Don't go away." I couldn't blame him for leaving, since he wasn't in a good mood.

Despite my pleading, he left anyway.

I was sad. His friendship was important to me, and I wanted to make sure that when we left for America, we were on good terms. I wished he'd been able to put aside his anger and play with me, anyway. We didn't know when we would see each other again.

***

Finally, the moment of truth came—the day we departed from our home. It was July 2005. I was thirteen years old and about to leave behind the only home I had ever known to fly around the world and start anew. Just like it had at our interview, my stomach did flip-flops. I was excited, nervous, and sad. I'd lived in India all my life, and now we were heading off into the unknown, leaving my childhood home behind, seemingly forever.

A large crowd of our neighbors and friends gathered at our house to wish us well and send us off. They were sad because my family was a big part of our local community. After we left, our house, which sat at a busy intersection, would be completely empty.

Members of the community admired my dad for being a college professor. Not only that, but he was also engaged in different associations and organizations in town and held important positions, sometimes even the president or vice president. He was almost famous in and around our community. Parties on both sides equally respected him, even in a disagreement. I guess being a teacher of zoology—the scientific study of the behavior, structure, physiology, classification, and distribution of animals—had a lot of advantages and perks.

There were tears, laughter, hugs, and a lot of handshaking. I said goodbye to all my childhood friends, not sure when I would see them again. Tears pricked my eyes as we embraced. I didn't like to cry, especially not in front of others, so I held my tears back.

A few of my close relatives came all the way to the Cochin International Airport to say goodbye. When we arrived at the airport that evening, I panicked a little. Somehow, I had never made the mental connection that we were going to fly. I suffered from a fear of heights, also known as acrophobia. During those days, all you heard about were bombings and hijacked airplanes on the news, so I was scared for good reasons.

I didn't know what to do. I was terrified, but I knew I had to be brave. This was the only way for us to get to our new home. Walking through the airport, my legs were shaky, and my breathing grew ragged. I wanted to sit down and find a way to distract myself from what was coming.

We checked our bags and waited to board the plane to somewhere in the Middle East. I got more and more nervous as we waited, looking around and trying to find something to focus on as my heart raced. I couldn't get calm. Instead, I was all jittery, and there was nothing I could do about it.

My palms were sweating as we boarded the plane and took our seats. I sat down next to my brother Chris and peered out the window, wishing I were anywhere else. I wondered if anyone around me noticed my discomfort.

All too soon, we were told to buckle our seatbelts for takeoff. The plane started to rumble as the engines started. My heart pounded in my chest, and I closed my eyes tightly, trying to focus on regulating my breathing.

As the plane accelerated, the engines grew louder. I clasped my hands to my ears and squeezed my eyes shut even tighter. I could hear my blood pumping, and my stomach felt like it was in my throat.

Before I knew it, the plane steadied out and quieted down. I opened my eyes and let go of my ears. I looked around carefully. The plane was flying smoothly, and I didn't feel out of balance or like I was way up in the air. This wasn't so bad. I was finally able to calm down. I leaned my head back and let myself drift off to sleep.

We landed in the Middle East and then went on to Europe before finally flying to Houston, Texas. During the flight to Houston, I slept peacefully.

When I woke up, it was morning. By then, almost everyone had opened their window blinds. There was plenty of sunlight streaming in from both sides of the airplane. It was peaceful, calm, and I wondered why I'd been so afraid the day before. It seemed silly.

After a moment, an older male American flight attendant stopped by my and Chris' seats and placed two small vanilla ice cream cups on my brother's tray table. Assuming one was mine, I reached out and took one.

The flight attendant reached out with a sharp look in his eye and took it away from me, putting it back on Chris' table.

I looked up at him, confused and scared that he was mad at me for taking the ice cream. Then, the attendant reached over and put two *more* vanilla cups on my tray table. He locked eyes with me and smiled. Everyone got two! I smiled back, and he moved on to serve other passengers.

I settled back in, enjoyed my two cups of ice cream, and waited in anticipation for America and my new life.

CHAPTER 6

INTO THE UNKNOWN

If you know the beginning well,
the end will not trouble you.
—African proverb

Just like that, my life in India ended. I was thirteen years old, facing a new country, a new culture, and a new school. Nothing could have prepared me for the culture shock.

I'd studied English throughout my childhood in India, but I didn't have any real-world experience using it. I was uncomfortable with the language, unsure, and timid in speaking it.

We took our final flight from Houston to Dallas, then drove from there to Irving, Texas, where we moved into our new home with family members who had come before us. There were fifteen of us in total, living in a one-story house with four bedrooms and two bathrooms. There was a big living room, a nice dining area, and a spacious backyard. My bedroom was a garage that had been converted into a big room.

One of my family members told me that the governor of Texas had the same first name as me. His name was Rick Perry. That was cool to know and made me feel like I belonged there.

Irving was much different from Kerala. We were expecting most of the people to be Caucasian, but in Irving, most people I saw were Latinx. I didn't know anything about the Latinx culture, but I was just happy to be in the US. I hoped I could find a way to fit in.

I was also pleased to note there was a large Indian Malayali population in and around Irving. It was nice to meet other people who spoke the same language and practiced the same customs as our family. We even went to a church where the congregation consisted entirely of Malayali people, and I started to attend their Sunday school class.

There was a family who lived a few houses down with three boys who were younger than I. Another kid lived across the street from us. My younger cousin Ken, my brothers, and I all became friends with them. Ken and his family had arrived in America a few months before my family immigrated. Jef rarely played games with us, saying he was too old for playing, but the rest of us spent a lot of time together.

We all loved to play with the toy guns our neighbors owned. The older boys in the neighborhood also had very long muskets, like soldiers carried in the old days! They taught us about a new sport—American football. The name was confusing for me. In India, we also played football, but in America it was called soccer. I'd never heard that word before.

The three brothers had bicycles, and they sometimes let us ride them in the street. One day, their father gave us a new yellow bicycle. We thought he was just lending it to us, but he insisted we keep it. He just wanted us to have fun. His generosity touched us, and Jef told him, "Thank you." When we had first arrived in the US, my aunt Ellie and uncle Ron had told us we might need to say, "Thank you" or "Thanks" sometimes, especially when someone did something particularly nice for us. We didn't want to risk offending others and were glad we knew what to say.

When we arrived in America, the one of the first things we learned was about the things neighbors expected of us. We also had to learn how to take care of our house and yard. My uncle Ron said that we would need to cut the grass around our house from time to time, or somebody might complain. If there were enough complaints about one house, the city of Irving might fine the owner.

We could have hired somebody to cut our grass, but Ron brought his lawn mower to our home. We didn't want to waste money since we'd just moved. He showed us how to use the lawn mower safely, and where the boundaries of our property were, so we didn't accidentally walk onto the neighbor's lawn or cut their grass. He explained that the neighbor might not like how we cut his grass and could call the cops on us.

Since Jef was older and bigger, he was in charge of lawn care—though Chris, Ken, and I still had to help him.

Soon, it was time to start school, but I didn't want to go. Everybody would be speaking English, and I had no idea how to deal with that and make everything go smoothly. My English wasn't good, at least not good enough to communicate effectively, and I knew I would stick out like a sore thumb. I was afraid the kids in my new school would judge me. I looked different and sounded different from them. If something went wrong, I would have nowhere to go.

Despite my fears, I joined the eighth-grade class at Lamar Middle School less than two months after I arrived in the US.

I was nervous on the first day. Would I understand what everyone was saying? Would I know where to go? Would

I make friends? I tried to calm my nerves as I entered the school and took deep breaths. I was shown to my first class: science. The teacher was white, and his hair was orange. I'd never seen hair in that shade before.

I thought, *Wow. I didn't know hair could be that color!* I wondered whether it was a natural hair color or if he had dyed it.

School was okay at first. I went to each of my classes, doing my best to pay attention and become comfortable in my new surroundings. There was definitely a cultural difference, though. Kids were curious about me and the things I'd experienced in India, and they were full of questions. They also were not afraid to do things with one another that would not have been tolerated at schools in India.

One day, a girl turned around at her desk to talk to me. "I heard people in India get married when they are just thirteen years old! Is that true?" she asked, her eyes wide with interest.

I laughed. That was one of the craziest things I had ever heard. "No. That does not happen!"

I knew that kids who had never been around someone of Indian descent might ask such questions. The girl was friendly and curious about me and India. I think that she may have gotten her information from the news or from films, places that didn't always portray India accurately. That sort of thing *used* to happen in India. My deceased grandmother, Chachy, had married at age fourteen and had nine children. But it was a very outdated practice in modern times. Most people in India no longer thought this was a good idea.

Another time, I walked by a boy and a girl standing very close to each other on the staircase. I realized they were passionately kissing each other. I was not used to seeing kids my age doing that at school. It was awkward for me. I'd promised myself that I would never date or get married, but I didn't really mind if other kids didn't agree with me. I kept going as if nothing unusual was happening.

***

Soon, the novelty of the move wore off, and I started to make mistakes because of language and cultural differences.

I left my science class once to get a drink at the water fountain. When I came back into class, the orange-haired teacher shook his head at me. "You have to ask for permission before you can leave the room for any reason," he told me.

"Sorry." I was embarrassed. I hadn't known that.

I also had trouble finding my classes. In India, students stayed in one classroom, and different teachers would come to the students. In America, students had to find each teacher's classroom at a given time, according to their class schedule. Each classroom was numbered to make it easier. Once that class was over, students left and went to their next class. I wasn't familiar with this practice, and it was difficult for me to remember what I should do.

Once, in the first week of school, I was searching through the hallways, looking for my classroom. A female janitor was pushing a cart filled with bottles of cleaner through the hallway, her fingers full of gold and silver rings.

Suddenly, a tall lady approached me. "What are you doing in the hallway? Shouldn't you be in class?"

I looked up at her, bewildered.

The janitor smiled at me. "Don't you know who that is?" she asked kindly.

I shook my head.

The tall lady raised her eyebrows. "You don't know who I am?" she asked.

"I'm sorry," I said. "I don't."

She laughed a bit. "I'm the school principal."

I was surprised and embarrassed. But she was kind. We talked for a few minutes before she noticed that my backpack and arms were full of books and school supplies. With a furrowed brow, she asked me, "Where is your locker? You should put some of your books and supplies in there, so you only have to carry what you need for each class."

I told her my locker number and she guided me through the school to stand in front of my locker.

"Do you know how to use your locker?" she asked.

"No."

After more discussion, the principal finally understood why I was making mistakes. As she was kind and wanted to help, she and the counselor assigned me to another Indian Malayali student who spoke both English and Malayalam.

I was expecting a boy to help me. But my principal assigned me a female student. Her name was Daisy. She was a good student with very good grades. She was one of the top students in the Lamar Middle School. The principal knew her very well and liked her a lot.

I wasn't sure how to work with Daisy at first. I had never hung out or interacted with a girl by myself before. There had been girls in the group during the dance lessons in India as well as at my school, but I'd never been by myself around a girl before. I was embarrassed, afraid that Chris might see me with her and tell my family and friends that I was hanging around with a girl. I feared he might think I was Daisy's boyfriend, and I didn't want to be made fun of for something that wasn't true. Chris liked to poke fun at me, and the idea of being teased struck fear in my heart. I hated being the center of attention.

However, I had no choice but to be partnered with her. When my principal got us together for the first time, we greeted each other and quickly moved on. It didn't take long for me to learn that I had nothing to fear with Daisy. She was nice and did her best to help me whenever I needed something.

I also learned I wasn't the only one who'd gotten a partner. They also assigned Chris to a male student who spoke Malayalam.

In the upcoming days, Daisy taught me how to find my classrooms, helped me understand my assignments and schedule, and translated what the teachers were teaching for me.

I was glad to have the help. She was very friendly and made my school experience a lot more pleasant. I no longer had to worry about being in the wrong place or misunderstanding the lessons.

Chris and his partner were also in one of my classes, which made me very uncomfortable. Sometimes, Chris would look at me from the other side of the classroom and smile at me. He thought it was funny that I was sitting with Daisy. I tried to pretend I didn't see him, but it was hard to ignore. The whole situation was unpleasant for me. It made me nervous.

Even with the Daisy's help, I still made some mistakes. Once, while I was in English class, the teacher asked, "Would you like to go to the library to read?"

"No," I said, shaking my head.

The teacher smiled slightly. "You should go." I guess she wasn't really asking me but telling me. I was confused. She had asked a question, but it didn't seem like I had a choice.

So, I agreed.

She gave me directions. "Turn left when you leave the classroom. Then, go up the stairs to the library."

I understood some of what she said, so I nodded and went out the classroom door. I turned right and started to walk, but when there were no stairs, I quickly realized I was going the wrong way. Turning around and passing the classroom again, I glanced in. Everyone saw me and started laughing. I just kept going toward the library. My face was red, and I kept my head down the entire way.

Despite embarrassing incidents like that, I was happy overall.

I had known that coming to the US would be hard, but I believed that my life would be better for it. After a few weeks, I was settling in, getting the hang of school, and feeling hopeful and happy about the future.

Little did I know, everything would soon change, and I would start down a dark course that would last for years.

PART TWO:
A NEW UNLIKELY ERA BEGINS

CHAPTER 7

BECOMING A TARGET

*A pain that pricks the conscience
is more effective than a lot of whiplashes.*
—Hebrew proverb

One day, I went into the locker room to change my clothes before gym class. There were no adults in the locker room, and the small office nearby was empty.

As I approached my locker, a boy came up and shoved me. I banged hard into the lockers, the racket echoing through the room.

I was stunned, looking at the boy with wide eyes. Everyone stopped talking and turned to watch us.

I righted myself, then pushed him back. I didn't want him to think he could mess with me without consequences. When I turned around to go back to my locker, he shoved me again.

I turned, ready to keep fighting. I didn't know why this kid was shoving me, but I didn't want it to continue, especially since I hadn't done anything to him. He had no right to push me around. However, a tall Indian student stepped in.

"Don't do it," he said. "If you push him back, this will only get worse."

I looked around. All eyes in the room were on me, waiting to see what would happen next. I nodded, realizing we had quite an audience, and backed off.

The boy who pushed me shrugged and walked away. I don't know if he no longer cared about fighting me because I hadn't pushed him back again or if the tall Indian student had intimidated him. I was relieved to be left alone and hoped that would be the only incident. So, I turned back to my locker to continue getting ready for gym.

I wasn't happy about what had happened, but I felt like it was probably just a fluke. I tried not to think about it anymore. I knew that if I puzzled over it for too long, I'd wind up getting stuck in a spiral of confusion and worry.

Looking back, I think that boy just thought I was an easy target. I didn't know English, so who could I tell about the problem? Since I wasn't big and muscly, I couldn't fight back. He could probably tell how passive I was by my body language. Maybe he knew I had come to America recently, making me the new kid on the block.

Most of the other students knew how to socialize. It looked like that came easily to them; they were comfortable and confident. That helped to deter potential bullies. I rarely found anyone else like me, another kid with no confidence and anxiety related to socializing. No one else acted like they couldn't fight for themselves or stand up to bullies. It felt dangerous to be the kid everyone knew was defenseless. If it was obvious to me, then I was sure that other kids could tell I was weak with few social skills.

Somehow, out of all the other kids in school, that boy became interested in me and chose to pick on me. It felt like I had a big, red target painted on my back, or a sign on my forehead that read, "Bully me." I hated feeling like that. I was doing my best to learn and succeed, but it was hard. On top of all my academic struggles, I was still struggling with the fear and anxiety in my head, and they kept constantly holding me back and ruining my self-esteem.

For the first few weeks of school, my family dropped me off and picked me up. However, one day after the school day was over, my dad waited outside the school for Chris and me. He told us, "From now on, you are getting on the school bus to come home."

I didn't like the idea at first. I couldn't help the little niggle of worry in my chest. The bus was huge, loud, and full of kids I didn't know who talked and laughed about things I didn't understand. What if they made fun of me or, worse yet, picked on me?

I hesitated to get onto the bus. But my dad told me, "It's okay. Don't worry about it. You will be fine." Then, he took me by the hand and helped me get inside. Chris too. Every other student was already inside, and I didn't want to keep the bus driver waiting.

Sitting down in one of the first seats, I felt my stomach twist up in knots. We hadn't even ridden anywhere yet, and I already hated the bus. There were too many kids, all of them staring at me because I wasn't like them. I was obviously from a different country, I couldn't speak to them, and I was almost visibly shaking from nerves and fear. I folded my arms across my stomach and sank down as low in my seat as I could, doing my best to make myself small. With no escape until we reached my house, I wanted to stay away from everyone else and out of sight. There was less of a chance that someone would try to pick on me that way.

I always sat toward the front of the school bus. At the back, the kids were wild and reckless, hollering and goofing off.

A couple of days into riding the bus, a group of kids who sat a few rows behind me took an uncanny interest in me. I knew immediately that they didn't want to be friends.

I felt a slap on the back of my head followed by a roar of laughter from the group of boys behind me. One of them was the same person I'd encountered in the locker room a few days before.

I didn't know what to do, so I said nothing. I chose not to react. I ignored it, doing my best to pretend it didn't happen. Inside, though, my mind was screaming at me to get off the bus and as far away from the boys as possible. I felt like I had no way out. The bus was an oversized vehicle with kids packed in like sardines. I felt like the walls were closing in on me; I was sweating, and my heart was pounding. I wanted off, but I couldn't get off until we got home.

They started jeering at me, calling me names in Spanish and English, and hurling insults at me. I wasn't familiar with the words they were saying, but I knew they were bad, inappropriate for everybody to hear.

I told them to stop, but they hit me again. There was an entire group of them, and they fed off each other. Every time they hit me or insulted me, the entire group would laugh and a different one would strike next. They thought it was hilarious, and they continued to make fun of me as we drove.

I wanted to hit him and his two friends or push them back like in the locker room the other day, but before I decided to raise my arm to fight them back, I thought about getting disciplinary actions from the school authorities or my parents for physically fighting them. I thought, *I may get into big trouble for doing that.* I thought about getting labeled as a bad, spoiled kid with behavioral issues. So, I decided to not to fight back or defend myself.

I didn't know what to do and had no other choices. After I got a beating, I decided to call them "dog" in Malayalam. In my understanding, when you get called "dog" in Malayalam in India, it's referring to a street dog (alone or in a group) that may have rabies or may be risky to encounter.

Most of the times, I would see these dogs on the side of the roads, especially at night. Stray street dogs, sometimes treated as worthless, are not safe—at least, that is the stereotype that is given to those poor dogs in India.

But when some Indians get emotional and out of balance or out of control, they might use that term "dog" to insult someone. Even if someone likes a dog, he will still call those rude and offensive people a "dog."

But anyway, after I called those bullies on the bus that word, they clenched their fists and proceeded to beat me in the head a few more times, which hurt. I still didn't respond to those attacks because of the fear of disciplinary actions from school and from my parents. All I did was use both hands to deflect the attacks which would eventually end.

As soon as we reached my stop, I rushed off the bus. My head hurt, my heart was pounding, and a dark cloud hung over me. I hated what had happened on the bus, and I never wanted it to happen again.

I hoped that it was just a one-time thing, that I was just their target for that day and that would be it. But, as I suspected deep down, it was only the beginning.

Every time I got on the bus, the same group of boys would start in again. They would hit, push, and insult me, egging each other on. It seemed they could sense my fear and enjoyed using it to continue harassing me. It made them feel powerful. The bullying almost exclusively happened on the way home. For some reason, the group was less likely to pick on me if we were on our way to school.

Whenever I was being bullied, I was utterly alone. Nobody helped me. The bus driver was oblivious. None of the other students intervened, not even my own brother Chris. He ignored it and refused to help; I was on my own. The problem was, I had no idea how to help myself.

Chris was tougher than I was. Nobody bothered him. Other students realized he would never stand for being picked on and would fight back. Chris carried himself confidently, striding down the school hallways with authority. Everyone knew he was tough and that he would respond in kind if they tried to mess with him. Yet, for mysterious reasons I never knew or understood, Chris never stood up for me or defended me against the bullies.

If I had fought back that day in the locker room and had showed that I was not to be messed with, then maybe my bully and his cohorts wouldn't have picked on me again on the school bus. But based on my response in the locker room, however, they assumed I wouldn't fight back, and I probably wouldn't tell anybody about their bullying. They felt they could do whatever they wanted and get away with it.

I also wondered why the bus driver didn't interfere. He always seemed to be busy driving. I wasn't even sure if he heard everything that was going on. I hoped he would notice since there was a big mirror inside the bus, and I always sat close to him—just one or two rows behind the front seat. But he never said anything or stopped the bus.

I didn't know if I was allowed to say anything to him or try to get his attention when they picked on me. I didn't want to cause trouble and end up making the bus driver mad at me. Chris and his friend once got into trouble because another kid tried to mess with them from behind. That time the driver saw something was going on and he took Chris' and his friend's school IDs. He told them that they would only get their IDs back if their parents came to the school, even though Chris and his friend hadn't caused the problem.

So, I feared to ask for help or interact with the driver, believing that I would get into trouble.

Day after day, the same bullying happened again and again. It didn't seem like they would ever stop. I wondered what would happen to me if they never quit picking on me. Would something even worse happen? Would they beat me up, leave me lying bruised and bloody somewhere? What had I done to deserve to be picked on like that? Was I unworthy of friendship? I felt broken inside, like someone had taken a sledgehammer to me, shattering me into a thousand pieces that bullies could kick and stomp on, crushing me further. I saw no end in sight.

I didn't know what to do. I didn't know who to turn to. Nobody had warned me I could become a target for mean kids. I couldn't tell my parents about the incidents because they would consider my inability to stand up for myself shameful. I was supposed to be strong and independent, able to tell other kids that I meant business. I knew that they likely wouldn't take anything I told them seriously, probably thinking that I was just lazy based on prior discussions we'd had about me not enjoying school. That thought was discouraging to me, and it kept me from ever telling them what was happening.

It seemed better if I struggled alone, so I wasn't a burden to anyone and wouldn't endure further torment at home.

I was defenseless. Too scared to fight back and too timid to seek help, I withdrew. I wanted to disappear. I wished that the ground would open and swallow me, that I had an invisibility cloak, or someone who could make me vanish without a trace. I tried to make myself as scarce and small as possible, constantly sitting with my shoulders hunched, my head slumped toward the ground, my eyes downcast, and my arms wrapped securely around me in a feeble attempt to protect myself from the world.

Anything would be better than the ongoing torment I was facing.

CHAPTER 8

THE CHANGING

If the heart is sad,
tears will flow.
—Ethiopian proverb

My entire demeanor changed as time went on. I was no longer the happy-go-lucky kid who had run through the woods in India, playing with my group of friends. I became quiet and withdrawn, speaking even less, spending more time in my head, and pondering questions about who I was and why this was happening. The sparkle that had been in my eyes went completely out. It was like I'd become a robot, no emotion, invisible to anyone who looked at me. I was numb, unable to feel anything.

I stopped enjoying everything. Nothing I did brought me any peace. I wasn't motivated enough to even watch TV. Everything felt like it took too much energy, and I had no desire to try. My bullies always seemed to lurk over my shoulder, even when they weren't around. At night, I dreamed of them. I would wake up in cold sweats, my heart beating a loud rhythm in my ears. I looked around my room with dread, wondering what dark corner they might leap out of. I dreaded going to school. Then, through the school day, I dreaded going home. I couldn't concentrate on my work. I stopped eating and sleeping.

The boy who once dreamed of a future as a soldier or an IT professional was fading away—replaced by someone sad, lonely, and scared. I didn't even recognize myself anymore. When I looked at a picture of me from years before, it didn't match who I saw staring back in the mirror. That little boy had light and life in his eyes. Now all I saw was a broken spirit, crying for help.

I didn't have the guts to defend myself. I didn't want to fight anyone; that wasn't my nature. I never liked hurting another person. I could never intentionally beat someone up, no matter how badly they treated me. I didn't know what to do; no one had ever taught me about these situations.

School buses were the perfect environment for bullies. There was only one adult to supervise all those kids. No one paid close attention to their behavior, so the bullies had no worries about getting caught. This was the reason I was bullied on the bus most often. At school, there were almost always teachers around, teachers who wouldn't stand by while one student bullied another. They would speak up and stop the bullying. On the bus, no one could see what they were doing or make the bully stop.

A bus driver's job is to pick up or drop off students, driving them safely to school or home. For the most part, they don't have time to watch the kids behind them because they're busy driving the bus. It seemed rare for a driver to interfere in any situation behind the driver's seat. I had a few drivers before who would stop the bus if the noise got too loud, stating loudly, "If you don't behave, I won't drive the bus. Then, no one will get home on time." If they did pull over, it was only for a few minutes. We'd be right back on the road in no time, and arrival times were unaffected.

Drivers like that made me feel safer than drivers that said nothing. They reduced the chances of bullying by paying attention to times when things weren't right. If I'd had a driver like that while I was being bullied, perhaps the driver would have noticed my struggles and helped me. It would have been nice to have someone witness the bullying and help me stand up for myself.

Or, perhaps, an extra adult on the school bus would have prevented this sort of situation, even if that had cost the school extra money. Students' safety should have been prioritized over school funds/money or expense. An extra adult's presence on the bus would have eliminated this whole issue. The extra cost would have been worth it.

I often thought the school bus was not just a vehicle with which to drop off and pick up students. It was part of the school, too. Kids, especially the nervous and shy ones like me, should have felt safe inside the school bus just as they should inside the school building or on school property. If nothing else, bus drivers should be advocates for students being bullied on the bus and help them find another adult to talk to about the problem.

Victims rarely tell anyone about all the incidents that occur because the victim is afraid that the adult won't know what to make of the situation or how to fix it. Sometimes, kids don't have proper social skills to deal with these types of situations, and that's exactly what happened to me.

Not long after the bullying started, I wanted to just stay home from school. One day, I simply refused to go, which of course confused my family. I thought about telling them what I was experiencing, but I didn't. I was ashamed. I didn't want them, or anyone, to look at me as weak and too spineless to stand up for myself. I had no idea how they would react, and I wasn't willing to find out.

My parents assumed I was just lazy. They remembered my complaints about school in India, when I didn't want to go because I was afraid of being paddled. I was never great at school, but my brothers were both brilliant. School came easily to them, and they never complained about it. It was different for me. My parents, however, didn't recognize that. They felt that my experience should be the same as my brothers; what came easily for them should come easily for me. I didn't know how to explain my struggles to them; whenever I thought about what to say, I would sweat, and grow more and more nervous. It was unlikely they'd ever believe me and even more unlikely that they'd sympathize with me and try to help. I knew I had no choice but to buckle down and try to survive, taking everything one day at a time.

On top of the bullying at school, all was not well at home either. Maybe if I had been happy outside of school, I could have processed the bullying better. Maybe it wouldn't have been quite so devastating.

Around the time that the bullying began, I had a falling-out with my cousin Zoey that shook me to my core and made me grow even more depressed.

When I first moved to America, everything seemed fine. Then, Zoey and I started to have disagreements. At first, it was just small things. She always had a good relationship with my brothers but seemed irritated by me. I didn't know what I was doing wrong, so I tried to shrug off her irritation as being caused by something else. Eventually, it escalated. It seemed like I couldn't do anything right in her eyes.

One day, Zoey, who was four years older than me, was driving Chris, Ken, and me to a park to play soccer. I walked to the two-door car and got in the front seat since I was older than Chris and Ken, and usually the older person sat in the front.

Zoey grabbed the door before I could close it. "No," she said. "You sit in the back."

I thought she was joking and tried to laugh it off.

"I'm serious," she said. "Get out. It's my car. You're sitting in the back."

Chris and Ken looked at each other awkwardly. Nobody knew what to say. Zoey glared at me.

I sighed and got out, moved the front seat forward, then sat in the back. I didn't understand why she was so angry, but it never worked well to get upset back or try to reason with her. It was better to do what she asked and avoid as much of her anger as possible. She drove us to the park. I tried to ignore the tension in the car.

When we got to the park, we played soccer. Ken failed to follow the rules, and I called him out on it.

Zoey became irate. She yelled at me for correcting Ken. I was shocked by how angry she was. She went on and on for several minutes, her face growing red as she paced back and forth in front of me. She kept waving her arms around everywhere like a madwoman. The fight was intense.

After she calmed down, we went home.

When we reached the car, I opened the door and pushed the front seat forward so I could sit in the back again. Zoey reached out and stopped me.

"No," she said, a malicious smile on her face. "You sit in the front."

I realized she was treating me like a dog on a leash. She was making me look like a fool in front of Ken and Chris, asserting her dominance over me. She wanted to prove to me she was older and could force me to buckle to her every whim.

Quietly, I sat in the front seat, fuming silently.

On the drive home, I didn't speak. It was a small thing, her forcing me to change seats. But it reminded me of feeling powerless and alone. All the emotions and feelings I had about the bullying I was experiencing at school rushed toward me at once, and I felt for a few minutes like I was drowning. I just wanted to go back to the way things had been before the bullying, when my life was peaceful, when there was no one picking on me.

When we pulled up to our house, Zoey turned to us. "Nobody say anything about what happened at the park. Just act normal," she told us.

We all agreed and went inside, acting as if nothing had happened.

From that day on, things were weird between me and Zoey. She was distant, rude, and belligerent. Somehow, that attitude and behavior started to affect my relationship with some members of the Pallattumadom family. They all became upset with me and never seemed to want me around.

After Ken witnessed the issues I was having with Zoey, he started developing a grudge against me too. He treated me like his cousin was treating me: cold and mean. Again, it started with small things—a disrespectful comment here, an eye roll there. Finally, he started avoiding me and ignoring me completely.

One day, Ken was in a bad mood. When the game we were playing didn't go his way, he went to find his dad, Roy. After a moment, Roy called for me. I heard him from my spot in the living room, and I was a little worried. I wondered if Ken had told his dad what was happening was my fault. Was

I going to get into trouble? My stomach was doing flip-flops, but I went to him, anyway.

Uncle Roy lashed out at me. He told me not to bother his kid and to stay away from him. Just like Zoey had, he ranted and raved, his face turning red. He started huffing and puffing from the effort of speaking with his hands and pacing as he yelled.

I felt sad, and told him, "I didn't do anything."

Uncle Roy didn't care what I had to say. He went back to his room without another word. It was then that I realized they wanted nothing to do with me. They viewed me as a pest, an annoyance that they didn't want to deal with.

Uncle Roy's personality was much different than most of my other relatives. When Ken told him stories about my behavior, my uncle was *supposed* to ask me what was going on between us without causing a scene or raising his voice. He was *supposed* to help Ken and me work out our differences in a healthy, calm manner. That was how the rest of my family handled such situations. But he *did* make a scene, and my parents weren't there to see it or to defend me. So, he got to act however he wanted, regardless of what he was supposed to do.

There may have been a reason he acted out in such a childish way. Ken was Roy's only child. Naturally, he was very protective. He didn't want anything to happen to his son and wouldn't risk anything happening right under his nose. So, he was immediately suspicious of anyone Ken claimed was causing problems for him.

I hadn't expected that kind of reaction from Roy. He could have at least looked for the facts and contemplated whether I was actually hurting Ken.

I certainly wasn't. I wasn't capable of harming Ken emotionally or physically. In fact, I liked Ken, and he had been
like a younger brother to me. I had known him since he was
a baby. He had been a joy to be around.

When Ken and I spent time together, I was playful and
joking. However, because of the bullying I was not feeling
well and wanted some time to relax and clear my thoughts.
Unfortunately, Ken took my behavior the wrong way, especially after the way he'd seen Zoey treat me. As a result, I had
to endure Roy's yelling. On top of that, my uncle made it very
clear that he didn't think I was as good or as capable as my
brothers. He thought I was immature.

In the end, I decided to stop interacting with Ken. Roy
had demanded I stay away from him, so that's what I did. The
whole situation was weird and sad. I thought, *How did this
happen, even though we all came to America to start a new
life? Life was supposed to be good!* It puzzled me. I'd thought
that, in America, everyone would want to look out for each
other and try to make everyone's lives easier. After all, that
was what America was all about! However, everything was
growing worse by the day, and I was the one taking the brunt
of the negativity.

I was devastated. It was one thing to be suffering at school
but another to be ostracized by my own relatives. It made the
holes of emptiness, fear, and anger in my soul grow deeper
and blacker, and that fuzzy feeling that always lurked at the
edges of my mind grew bigger, invading more of my space. I
just wanted to get along with everyone.

When I tried to mention the bullying to my parents, they
seemed to realize that I had indeed been a victim of bullying.
They appeared to listen when I described what I was experiencing, nodding along as I told them what was happening

every day. But despite this, they still made light of my concerns. They told me to leave those incidents in the past, stand up for myself, and to forget about what had happened. I had no idea why they did that. They were my parents. They were supposed to support me and try to help.

I felt like I was worthless to them. My bullies were winning because my parents appeared to be abandoning me. I realized that my lack of motivation during school in India had come back to bite me in the butt. Perhaps that was what was influencing them. I felt like my parents were treating me differently than Jef and Chris. Of course, I knew that if I mentioned that, they would say that I was just jealous. But I wasn't. I just wanted love and support. It felt as if I would never get any justice.

The pressure in my head began to build. I didn't understand why I had to suffer. Why would no one help me? My peers, my family, myself, and even God disappointed me.

I couldn't count on anyone. I was angry all the time. One day, I took the rosary from my neck—the one that I had worn since I was a child—and threw it on the ground. How could God let me suffer like this? How could He let everyone around me treat me as if I were no better than a bug on a shoe?

I withdrew even further into myself—isolated, scared, and hurt. I needed someone else to understand me. Where was I supposed to find them?

CHAPTER 9
HOPE REKINDLES

*A little spark can
kindle a great fire.*
—Syrian proverb

It seemed like I would be miserable forever. In reality, however, my bullies lost interest in me just a few months later.

At first, I couldn't believe it. I thought they were just plotting new ways to torment me. Maybe they were just biding their time to get me to let down my guard, only to attack again. I wondered if they would try to scare me or jump me to beat me up when I least expected it.

I remained always on guard, watching my surroundings carefully even though I wasn't actively being bullied. I lived in fear for the rest of the year, but the bullies had moved on to another target and completely left me alone. I was relieved that they had spared me from further attacks, but I felt awful for whomever they'd chosen to bully next. No one deserved to be treated like they'd treated me.

But even with the respite from their attacks, the damage was already done. I was never the same after that. I could not sleep, and if I did, I dreamed of being attacked, waking up in a panic. When people would brush by me in the hallway, I'd shrink away from them. I startled easily and found that I had little interest in trying to make friends. Deep down, I felt like I could never trust anyone again. I became more caught up in my head than ever before. I didn't know how to escape it, how to see clearly again, even though I wanted to.

It was only much later that I found out that I was suffering from Post-Traumatic Stress Disorder. Research now shows that bullying is the highest risk factor for PTSD and that teens who endure repeated bullying are likely to carry the weight of it throughout their lives, developing a range of mental illnesses. Since I wasn't in a supportive environment at home and was, in fact, enduring more conflict and teasing with Zoey and Uncle Roy, it became even harder for me to heal. Everything scared me, and I had nowhere and no one safe to turn to for help.

But back then, I didn't understand PTSD or mental health issues. I didn't know that I needed to heal, to find support and help, and to put myself on the journey to recovery. I just knew I was still miserable. I did try to take care of myself and even experienced a few moments of light that kept me going; they reminded me of what it was like to feel like a normal, happy kid. Every day, things got a little better. Every day, I healed a little. A few of my teachers and Daisy, my assigned student helper, helped keep me going.

P.E. class was one of my favorites that year. However, Lamar Middle School split up their P.E. classes by gender. Obviously, I couldn't just stay with Daisy during that class since I'm a boy. So, the teacher would send me to the other side of the gym where the other boys were working out.

One day, the coaches told us to huddle up together. We sat down and listened, excited to find out what we were doing. The coach said that a few of us were going to try wrestling. Each student in the match would have to put their knees down and try to push their opponent outside of a cushioned mat on the floor. Whoever got pushed off the mat would be "out," and the one who stayed on would be the winner.

The coach looked around and chose the skinniest-looking student in the class. Then, he asked that kid to pick a random person to go up against. The skinny kid scanned the room to choose their opponent. After a pause, he pointed his finger at me. I was flabbergasted! Out of all the kids, he'd chosen me. He was smiling. He thought he'd found the right pairing, someone he could beat. Everybody else found this funny.

I had a Malayali friend in that class who had lived in America for his whole life. He spoke a bit of Malayalam. I turned to him. "What do I do?" I asked him. My English wasn't great yet, and I hadn't understood everything the coach had said. He told me I had to wrestle with the other kid. I didn't really understand what was going on, but I met the skinny kid on the mat.

Again, I turned to my Malayali friend. He was laughing.

"How do I do this?" I asked. He explained I needed to try to push the other kid to the edge of the mat. I really didn't like this; it seemed like fighting. I had never enjoyed fighting, even if it was a game. It was too violent, and I was much too passive to enjoy that type of activity.

So, I didn't try to push him. But I also didn't want him to push me to the edge and win, so I planted myself. He tried his best to push me, but I had more bodyweight than he did. He couldn't get me to the edge; I just stood my ground, pressing all my weight into the ground.

The coach watched us, confused. I didn't look like someone who'd be able to win a wrestling match. The other kids found this funny and started laughing.

After a while, it became apparent it was a stalemate. I can't really remember the outcome of the match—either the coach declared it a draw, or I finally gave in and pushed my opponent to the edge. Regardless, it was actually a fun experience—a small, shining light in the darkness that was most of my school days.

Another day, we were playing dodgeball. Surprisingly, dodgeball was one of my favorite games to play. You got to throw soft balls at other kids, so even though you were trying to hit them, it didn't seem violent. It was one of my dream sports to play.

This time, there was only one big ball to play with instead of several smaller ones. I was so focused on playing, just moving along, that it took me a few minutes to realize that it was just me and one other guy left.

In our rules, you didn't just have to worry about getting hit by the ball. The players who were already out could reach out and tag you if you got too close, forcing you out as well. It took a lot of concentration to dodge both reaching, grabbing hands and balls being hurled at you by the other team.

I dodged and weaved, and somehow, I got that ball to throw at my opponent. I grabbed it, lobbed the ball at him, and missed. He sent a ball sailing at me, and I tried to move away. I wasn't fast enough. He hit me, and I was out.

For a moment, I felt sad. I'd wanted so badly to win. I loved dodgeball, and being sort of good at it was something I took pride in. It was nice to know that I could keep up with the other kids and stay out on the floor until the very last second. I wished I'd been able to do a bit better and hit my opponent with the ball.

Then, the part of my brain that always tried to keep me positive took over. I had almost won! I became excited, overjoyed about taking second place out of all the kids in the class—something that had never happened to me before. It had been fun, too! I'd been able to concentrate on the game and not worry about anything else.

Another time, we played a basketball game. We all lined up to take turns trying to score a basket. If you missed, you were out, but if you made the basket, you moved to the back of the line.

The coach played with us. He scored every time, so he kept rejoining the line. One by one, my classmates missed and got out. But I sank every basket. Eventually, it was down to just the coach and me.

My heart was racing, but I was getting tired. My shoulders were sore from throwing the ball. On my next shot, I missed the basket. Then it was the coach's turn. If he made the basket, he won. But if he missed, I would get another shot since we were the last two left.

He missed. I don't know if he was trying to take it easy on me, if it was a fluke, or if he genuinely missed. But I knew that either way, the game was over. I only had to make one final basket to win.

My confidence was so low. *There is no way I'm going to win,* I thought. I was exhausted. I stood in the middle part of the basketball court, a long way from the basket. So, I half-heartedly lobbed the ball with one hand, not expecting to even come close.

The ball soared through the air and landed perfectly in the basket with a satisfying swish. I stared up for a minute, not believing my eyes and ears. It was as if time moved in slow motion, just like it sometimes did in movies.

Everyone erupted into cheers, running over, and giving me high-fives. It felt great! For just a moment, I felt successful, invincible. I had beaten our coach and won the game! For the first time all year, pride swelled in my chest, and an enormous smile took over my face.

***

Shortly after that, I received the news that the counselor and the principal were separating me from Daisy. They said I no longer needed her help, so we didn't have to be buddies anymore.

It made sense; I knew my way around, and my English was stronger. But I didn't want to be separated. She was one of the few people who had been generous and kind to me, someone I relied on every day. I didn't want to lose another ray of sunshine in my life.

Most days, when I came across an intersection in the school halls, I'd see her walking the other way toward one of her classes. I'd watched her, but she didn't notice me. I know that sounds creepy, but I was just searching for familiarity. I noticed her because she had been such a big part of my experience. Watching her helped me feel grounded and more secure in myself. She helped me get through the day.

Overall, my life was in better shape. However, I still struggled at times, and I still wanted someone to talk to about what had happened. On one particular day, I was in my reading class and wasn't feeling well, which was rare. There was a girl sitting across the classroom who was friends with the bullies who had tortured me on the bus earlier in the year. She had encouraged them to pick on me; I'd overheard her urging them on.

I was staring at this girl during class, which made her uncomfortable. I couldn't help staring at her after I remembered the role she'd played in my bullying experiences. She and the bullies were friends. They always left the school bus at the same time, and all lived in the same neighborhood.

She was looking at me too with worry in her eyes. Her shoulders were tense, hugged up to her chin. I wondered if she thought I would rat her out. Our teacher was talking about idioms, and she noticed me looking at the other girl. So, she asked, "Rick, is everything okay?"

I looked at my teacher. Then looked at the girl again. She seemed anxious that I might say something about the incidents on the bus. She probably didn't want to get into trouble or have to explain why she'd chosen me to pick on.

I turned back to my teacher, nodded, and said, "It's nothing. I'm okay." Then, I stopped looking at the girl and concentrated on class. The girl was obviously relieved that I hadn't said anything about her horrible behavior. Her shoulders relaxed, and I noticed her eyes go shut for just a second before she opened them again to watch what the teacher was writing on the board.

If my teacher had pressed further, I probably would have told her everything. The problem was that I didn't know the English words to use to describe what had been happening. There weren't any other Indian students who spoke Malayalam in our class, and Daisy, who had been helping me, was gone, too. I didn't even know the English word "bullying" yet. I thought my bullying incidents were over anyway since they seemed to leave me alone. So, I didn't say anything to my teacher. She was actually my favorite teacher. I would have been comfortable telling her about what had happened, but I didn't know enough English to tell her without being prodded.

At the end of that school year, there was an awards assembly and ceremony. My mom and uncle Roy attended.

The school principal called my name for an award. Everybody clapped as I approached her, and she put something on the left side of my chest on my uniform. It was an accolade, but I didn't know what it was for.

After that, she pointed me to the stage where others who'd gotten the same award were sitting. I took my seat. To my right, I was surprised to see Daisy! She'd gotten the award too. She smiled at me. She said, "Good job, Rick!"

That was the last time I ever saw her. I didn't even thank her for helping me that year—something I've always regretted. I also regretted not telling her about my bullying experiences on the school bus. She might have had some advice to offer or even a few words of encouragement. Unfortunately, I never worked up the courage to tell her. The bullying had stopped anyway, and I thought it was over for good.

I wondered which high school Daisy was going to the next year. I didn't think she would go to Nimitz High School, which was near my home. It would probably be the other high school, I told myself, not wanting to get my hopes up about having a friend at my new school with me.

I continued to grow and heal, though I still carried many symptoms of a mental health disorder with me. But by the end of the year, I finally felt as though things would be all right. I believed I could get better. I'd survived bullying, and I was stronger for it.

On my last day of middle school, I exited through the door at the front entrance. My family was there, waiting to pick up Chris and me in their car—I didn't have to ride the school bus this time. I was relieved that the bullying was over, and I could now concentrate on the future.

But before getting into my family's car, I looked back at my middle school for the last time. I'd certainly had good and bad experiences in that school. I thought, *My worst years are behind me, and I don't have to think about any of that anymore. Just focus on moving forward and staying positive. That's how I'll be happiest.*

High school was just around the corner. I was excited to be attending Nimitz High School. Everyone at Nimitz got a laptop and bag assigned to them from the school for homework. But you could also use it for searching the internet and playing video games online. There had been little time for me to surf the Web and play games since the move to America, and I was thrilled to have a laptop of my own to use for that. Maybe playing games to relax would help me feel more like my old self once again.

Throughout the summer, I grew more and more excited about the new year and the new school, although I dreaded the idea of being the new kid again, having to learn where to go and about all the new students and teachers that would be in my classes and in the hallways. Nimitz promised to be a new start for me, though, so I was keeping my head high and focusing on what I could gain from going to that school, not all the things I was afraid could happen again.

Before the school year began, though, my dad had news for us. He called us all into the living room. "I have exciting news," he said. "An acquaintance of mine from India called me to offer me a good job as a motel manager. We are moving to another city."

I was stunned. I'd survived hell my eighth-grade year, made so much progress, and was finally excited about school. Now, we had to move and adjust to a new home and a new community. I didn't want to believe him and face the reality that we were moving.

It took me a while to come around to the idea of moving again. For several days after my dad's announcement, I was very quiet and withdrawn. I didn't feel like talking to anyone, and I couldn't ignore the feelings of betrayal and mistrust that rose in my chest when I looked at my dad. After not helping me when I'd talked to him about the bullying, he was once again uprooting my life to a new town. I was angry at him, and I wanted to tell him how his new job was harming me and taking away my happiness. The more I thought about it, though, the more I realized my dad hadn't taken the job to hurt me. He'd taken it to help. He wanted to take care of his family and provide us with a good life in America.

So, even though I didn't like it, even though I was still afraid of being the new kid again, even though I felt sick to my stomach and wished a thousand times that we didn't have to go, I accepted the reality of my situation and packed my things to prepare for the next big switch.

We were moving to Denison, Texas, a town eighty miles north, near the Texas and Oklahoma border. The city had some historical significance. It was the birthplace of Dwight D. Eisenhower, the thirty-fourth president of the United States of America. He had been a five-star general and served as a supreme commander of the Allied Expeditionary Force in Germany during World War II. I didn't know much about Eisenhower at first, but my dad told me about him, trying to get me excited about the move. I later learned about him while watching the History Channel. I was fascinated by history, especially anything war-related, so I found it all very interesting. Maybe Denison wouldn't be so bad after all.

My dad told me that somewhere in Denison, they had some kind of museum or monument dedicated to Eisenhower. I thought he also mentioned that his house was there too, the one in which he was born. After hearing that, I realized that this random town that I'd never heard of before could be quite special and interesting. I thought it was cool to learn more about this WWII general and former American president. I knew it would have no effect on my current situation, but that didn't make my fascination with Eisenhower any less enjoyable.

As I began helping my family prepare for our move, at night, I would dream of India. I remembered running through the woods, laughing, and playing with my friends. I remembered what it was like to be happy. I suspected that I'd never have those feelings again as long as we lived in America. My home in Kerala called out to me in my dreams. I wanted to go back more than anything. I convinced myself that Kerala held the key to my happiness, that there had been something there that kept the darkness and haze in my brain away. I had the urge to go back.

I took an oath, making a promise to myself. After high school, I was going to go back to India with my parents to get my life back in shape. I was going to find whatever magical thing there that made me happy, and I was going to find a way to bring it back to America. And I wanted to achieve that by my early 20s, right after high school. I would just have to grind out the next four years in high school. It felt like it would take forever to finish those four years.

I had no choice but to go with my family to Denison and start over again. I had to survive the next four years of high school somehow. Then I could head back to Kerala. The countdown had officially begun.

CHAPTER 10
A FARAWAY PLACE

There will be many chapters in your life.
Don't get lost in the one you are in now.
—Unknown

Right away, our life in Denison was very different from our life in Irving. Denison was a much smaller town, for starters. Instead of living in a house with family, we lived in the motel my father managed. Our living quarters were spacious and luxurious. We had four bedrooms, three bathrooms, a living room, and a small kitchen with a dining area. We had more privacy and space than we'd ever had in Irving. I had not been excited about moving to Denison, but I was happy about the extra space and privacy. I had a place to hide away from my family and the rest of the world, and it was a welcome relief—one I hadn't realized I'd been missing.

Jef and I started at Denison High School soon after the move, while Chris started at a middle school in the area. I was terrified to start school. I couldn't shake the feeling that I would get bullied again. Just like at my old school, no one would know me; I worried that my lack of social skills and inability to speak English fluently would cause the other kids to identify me as an easy target.

In Irving, most of our student population had been Latinx. In Denison, most of the students were Caucasian. There was a small population of Latinx students and very few other minorities. On the first day, however, I did see one other person who looked like me. I quickly learned that he was a Pakistani student named Ahmed.

Indians and Pakistanis had a long history of conflict, engaging in four wars since 1947, when India gained its independence from the UK. We were supposed to be sworn enemies. I'd never seen a Pakistani before.

I didn't think he would react well to me. But Ahmed talked to me. He was pleasant and friendly. We had a lot in common. He was Jef's age with a younger brother my age. We had similar interests. Despite our cultural differences, we became friends.

High school was off to a much better start than middle school. I already had a friend, and nobody was targeting me. I felt safe there. Even with all of that, however, I wasn't excited about my classes or motivated to work hard.

I failed the first semester of my English class with a 68 percent. The next semester, I had to retake that class. My grade rose to a 73 percent, which was higher than I'd expected. I honestly believe that my counselor intervened on my behalf. I've always appreciated that. In most of my other classes, I barely passed with grades in the low 70s.

I found it very hard to concentrate on my work. I couldn't think as I used to. My grades were never as bad at Irving as they were during my first year at Denison. In Irving, I was doing fine. My life, before the bullying, was moving forward in a positive way all on its own. But that had all changed after we moved. I couldn't put my finger on why. I just knew that

I struggled. It hurt, and I constantly compared myself to my brothers and how they were advancing.

My brothers were mostly unaffected. They had been disappointed, of course, to learn that we were moving, but there had been no serious, lasting effects for them. They adjusted to their new environment quickly. Their abilities amazed me. Despite my disappointment, I wanted to do that—to be a chameleon in whatever social situation I was in.

My classes were hard that first year. I didn't have any desire to learn, study, or do homework. My self-esteem was at an all-time low. I didn't even care that I would fail my freshmen year because I felt like I had already lost everything. I had no social life, poor grades, and a family who was closed off and hard to talk to about my experiences. What else could be taken from me?

Years later, I would find out that this was another result of the long-term bullying I had endured. At the time, I believed I wasn't smart enough to do well in school.

Outside of school, I had a lot of mixed feelings. I enjoyed living at the motel and enjoyed the privacy it brought, but I struggled to stay positive around my family. They still didn't seem to notice how distant and reserved I so often was, and I felt abandoned.

By now, someone should have noticed I had withdrawn. If they had, they never commented on it. Instead, they gave me a hard time about my lack of desire to do well in school. They kept assuming I was just not as bright as my brothers. These feelings of loneliness fed into the cycle of silence and shyness at school, too. What was the point of trying to make friends at school if no one at home believed in me?

One day at school, I was sitting in the cafeteria alone. I was eating, minding my own business and looking around the room. All the other students were laughing and talking with their friends as they ate. I noticed a girl looking at me from far off. She was sitting at a round table with a few other girls. She came up to me and asked if I wanted to sit with her and her friends. Apparently, they had all agreed to have me sit with them. They were curious and wanted to talk to me. They'd probably never seen a minority like me before.

I was surprised. I couldn't believe they wanted to hang out with me. But I was too embarrassed to go. I was still struggling with my desire to not get married and stay away from girls. I shook my head no.

She looked surprised and asked again, "Are you sure you don't want to sit with us? There's plenty of room."

I shook my head again.

She shrugged and went back to sit with her friends.

That was one of the biggest mistakes I made that year. I was in the ninth grade at a new school, and I had the chance to make a group of friends. If I had agreed, my entire life could have changed. I could have broken the cycle of loneliness right there, and I might have had a real chance to heal from my past torments. If we'd talked and become friends, I wouldn't have been on my own, in a dark and depressing world with no one to turn to, no one to ask for help.

If I had gone with her and started socializing with her friends at that table every day, it's likely that I would have changed for the better. I could have picked up more words to improve my English, aided by the fact that I wouldn't have felt embarrassed to be talking in front of them. I could have eaten lunch instead of avoiding the cafeteria line and going through the entire school day on an empty stomach. My grades could have improved, and it's likely I would have grown more confident in interacting directly with my teachers and other students. Maybe I could have even healed from being bullied. I could have shared my experiences with the group, and they could have talked me through what I was feeling.

How different could my life have been?

During my first year at Denison, I felt like an outsider. I believed I didn't belong there; looking back, I know those feelings came from the depression I was feeling about our move. My entire high school experience could have been completely different if I'd just taken the leap of faith to sit with the group.

The girl who asked me to join them seemed like a good, genuine person, someone I could safely interact with and be comfortable around. But my fear that my brothers would see me with girls and make fun of me discouraged me from going to sit with her, despite her kind request. This fear fed the feeling that I was only an outsider. Why would they want to sit with me?

***

In the meantime, whenever my family and I visited Irving, I continued to have conflicts with Zoey and Uncle Roy. I didn't want to go, but my family did not leave me any choice. I knew the resentment my uncle and cousin held toward me would persist. Zoey was still cold to me, and Roy still treated me as an annoying pest.

My parents knew about the situation between me and Roy. They knew nothing about me and Zoey, however. Still, my parents had a good relationship with both of them and enjoyed visiting them whenever we had the chance.

During those visits, Ken acted normally around me again, even though we had grown distant during my first year in the US. I didn't know why he started being nice again, so I intentionally tried to discourage him from speaking to me and kept my distance from him. I remembered what Uncle Roy had said, and I knew I didn't want to make him angrier at me.

When Ken tried to talk to me, I wouldn't respond. I think he knew why I acted that way. At least he didn't seem to be bothered by it. I was determined to keep my promise, even after Ken started being nice once again. I didn't want to risk any more drama.

Other than my schoolwork struggles and my issues with family, my first year of high school went fine. I was just happy not to be bullied.

After that year, my family went back to India to visit our extended family. It was weird to go back to India after spending two years in the US. I thought I would be excited about going back. After all, I had made that vow to myself that I would go back to India and find the key to my former happiness. But I found myself unable to get excited. I felt dull and unenergetic. This, I later learned, was a symptom of PTSD. I was still in a state of shock, even after returning to my home country.

We arrived in India and returned to my childhood home. The house seemed smaller than I remembered because I had grown taller.

After we arrived, people around our neighborhood came to see us. My dad gave them all a small amount of money as a celebration of moving to the US for the first time. He gave them cash like Christmas gifts, which everybody liked, and they all gratefully thanked him.

That was one of the reasons people liked my dad—because he offered and was generous with money to those who urgently needed it for things like paying off medical bills. He also gave a sum of money to young people starting college or going to school, especially those who were hardworking and good at studying.

My dad likes to uplift others who want to move up the ladder or want to be successful in life. He doesn't even ask them to pay back the money.

However, his actions could attract the type of people looking to trick him into giving them free money. Fortunately, he was smart enough not to get scammed.

I like my dad's generosity. I like the sincere gestures he displays to others. They can make life a lot easier for those who may be struggling financially.

His generosity inspired me to help other people in need or to give charity to institutions after I get old and become successful. I thought God would reward me for that behavior...plus, I knew I would feel good inside for trying to help others who are truly in need.

Shortly after that, I visited my older cousin, Scott. He was a physical therapist in Kerala. He was living with his uncle Karl, one of my dad's older brothers.

Karl suffered from mental health issues caused by either genetics or environmental factors he'd suffered earlier in his lifetime. I didn't know a lot about Karl's history, but early in his adulthood, he had seemed normal. He had spent some time traveling when he was younger, visiting Germany in the late '70s or early '80s for a few years. He got married, and everyone assumed he would go on to lead a happy life. But he didn't.

Rick Pallattumadom

After a while, Karl's mental health declined. He began to act strangely. He wasn't violent, but problems arose. His behavior put a strain on himself and his family. Eventually, things got so bad that his wife left him. They didn't have any children. From then on, he began drinking regularly and chain-smoking.

Even back when I was only six or seven years old, I had wondered why Karl acted like he did, quiet and distant so much of the time. I wondered what had happened to him that made him want to escape the world as often as possible.

Mental illness was the only thing that made sense to me as a child; I concluded, without anyone else's help, that Karl stayed home because he was not in a good place mentally or he may be afraid of interacting with other folks in public.

The only person I could think to ask about Karl was my dad. Karl was my dad's older brother, so I thought he might have the answers to my questions. I knew it was going to be an uncomfortable thing to ask; my dad didn't really appreciate questions like that. However, my curiosity could not be quieted, so I decided to just ask.

I said, "Hey, Dad. Does Karl have mental problems?"

My dad turned toward me, his eyes wide with disbelief. He got angry but quickly calmed down. I was just a kid, after all. I hadn't meant any harm with my question. Still, I realized I had made a mistake, and I felt bad afterward.

The problem was that, when I had asked my question, I had used the Malayalam word *vattanno*. That word means "crazy" which is often used to shame others or as part of a joke to get under someone else's skin. Since I'd asked seriously, the word came across as hurtful and rude, even though I hadn't meant it that way. I had still been learning Malayalam then and couldn't think of a nicer way to phrase my question.

84

I rarely said things to upset others. I decided not to ask anybody else that kind of question.

Karl had only gotten worse since I'd asked that question and had decided to just stay in his childhood home forever.

A friend of mine named Lev was now staying with Scott and Karl. Lev had hung out with my brothers and me as kids, though he was a few years older. He went by the nickname Mason.

Mason was a professional driver who knew all the roads in Kerala and had a magnetic personality. His trademark was socializing and interacting with others. He had a lot of clients, especially Malayalis, who went to foreign countries and came back for vacation in Kerala. To his clients, he was more than just a driver. He knew the social scene and the area around Kerala well, along with every member of my Pallattumadom family and many other families as well. He was not just a friend but also an asset to help get around Kerala and meet others. Mason's great personality was hard to find in other people.

Mason was also a womanizer. He really knew how to talk to women, and he was charming, flirtatious, and very likable. He knew how to make a woman feel special, which made me a little jealous, even though I wasn't interested in all of that. He didn't do it for sexual favors but to interact with different people. He was quite good-looking, making any woman notice him, especially if he was flirting.

There was a story behind his personality. He intentionally dropped out of high school because his teacher had spanked him quite hard several times. His teacher later apologized to him personally, but it was too late. He quit school and never returned. Then, his family moved him to a different school in a different town. That's why he'd mysteriously disappeared during my childhood. I had known nothing about that.

Now, he was hanging with Scott, a trusted sidekick, helping Scott to help Karl. It surprised me when I realized that Scott and Mason had a very brotherly bond.

Scott, Mason, my brothers, and I started spending time together. We watched Indian films and traveled around Kerala together. For the first time, I learned from Mason how to ride a motorcycle and even drive a manual car. We had a good time, and I didn't waste a moment worrying about the bullying I'd endured. I felt my old energy come back. I was lighter and freer than I had been since I left India. I wondered if I was rediscovering the magic of being happy.

We spent a month there. Our trip ended too soon. Before I knew it, we were headed back to America, leaving late at night. On the flight home, I felt disappointed. I had finally rediscovered happiness, feeling alive in a way that I hadn't felt in years. Now, I had to return to a place where I felt I could never truly be happy.

CHAPTER 11

GRIND AND GRIND

Learning is a treasure
that will follow its owner everywhere.
—Chinese proverb

My sophomore year of school started shortly after we returned to Texas.

School felt boring and uneventful, but I was grateful for that; it meant no more bullying. I flew under the radar, just doing my homework, attending my classes, and trying not to cause any trouble. My freshman year had been fine, and I was determined to keep it that way.

The classwork continued to be difficult for me. Like many bullying victims, I suffered from severe performance decline. I struggled with math especially, getting distracted easily and forgetting how to solve problems. I just barely squeaked by with a 70 percent each semester—which was far from my best work, but I didn't know how to improve. The problems on the page were too difficult to understand with the fog in my brain disrupting my ability to think.

I enjoyed some of my classes, though. Mr. Murphy taught my world history class. He was one of the more popular teachers at the school. He wasn't strict; he was enthusiastic and quite engaging. I felt comfortable in Mr. Murphy's class. I liked his personality right away.

Being in Mr. Murphy's history class changed my perception of the subject. History hadn't seemed as important as math or science before. But as I learned more, I realized that learning about historical events was a good thing. It wasn't just the good parts of history that needed to be taught, but the bad parts too. The only way to keep history from repeating itself, to keep bad things from happening repeatedly, was to learn about them and what caused them.

History proves that people can be evil. Sometimes, because of evil people, bad things happen, and there is nothing you can do about it. But by learning about the mistakes made, when a similar situation presents itself, there is a chance to stop it. History class taught me to focus on learning from my mistakes to keep myself from being bullied again. If I wanted to move on, the only way was to go back to Kerala. The lessons that Mr. Murphy taught us further reinforced my beliefs and made me more determined to get back to India. I just needed to grind out the rest of high school and graduate. Then, I could pursue my goal.

We were required to present one project that year in his history class. When he announced this, I completely panicked. I couldn't do it. The thought of presenting my work in front of other students who might laugh at me was too much to bear. I'd come so far since my nightmare during eighth grade, but I was still stunted. Anxiety overwhelmed me most of the time, and the fear I'd felt about being laughed at or ridiculed in public grew exponentially. It was rare for me to go a day without worrying about others' opinions multiple times.

My solution was to not do the project. I was ready to face the consequences, even though I didn't want to. Surprisingly, when the time came for me to turn in the project, Mr. Murphy didn't give me a zero. He gave me a 70. I guess he realized how timid I was and gave me a free pass. I'd thought he might ask why I didn't do the assignment, and I didn't have an excuse prepared. I was relieved that he never asked, but I felt very guilty for not completing the work. It took me a long time to find peace afterward because of that guilt. I was determined that the next time I faced a similar assignment, I would at least put in some effort. I didn't want to feel like that ever again.

I also took an art class that year. Jef was in my class, which was very uncomfortable for me. We'd never gotten along well at school. We usually just ignored each other, pretending we were strangers. At home, we were fine.

Once I got used to having him in class, I quickly grew to love art. I'd always thought of art as a blowoff class, just as I'd felt previously about history. This class changed that for me. When I was doing the assignments and projects, exercising my creative freedoms, I realized how much better I felt. I could be myself in art; I didn't have to worry what other people thought or said about me. The projects kept me focused; eventually, I realized that art is important too.

One of our assignments was to draw a self-portrait by looking in a small mirror as a guide. I drew my face and was amazed by my own work. I'd done a great job; my picture was a good likeness of my face. I have no idea how I did that successfully, as it was my first attempt. I impressed the art teacher as well. She put my work in the showcase at the library entrance.

I was proud of my work, but the freedom I'd felt to be myself without worrying about judgment in the art room didn't extend outside that class. I was embarrassed by having my art displayed and didn't want everyone to see my face on the wall with my long and foreign last name. What would they think of me and what I'd done? Would that draw more attention to me, making me the target of yet another group of bullies? The thought made me feel sick.

I had some self-esteem issues then. Usually, whenever I responded to others, I would just nod and say one word, "Yes," "No," "Okay," or "Thanks." It was easier for me to say simple words instead of long sentences. I would never dare to say anything longer because it would take me forever to finish, and my voice sometimes sounded funny.

My name was a tricky thing for me as well. For instance, if I joined a new class, the teacher would first try to call out my last name instead of my first name. I didn't know at that time, but on teachers' roll call sheets your last name is listed first, followed by your first name. When they asked me how to say my last name, Pallattumadom, I knew it was very long and difficult for them to say, and I often had to repeat it several times. I didn't like that; I was afraid that both teachers and students might think I was weird. It added another thing to my list of constant worries.

I wasn't proud of who I was or where I came from, and that feeling came on strong in situations where I had to give out my last name. Nobody actually made any embarrassing remarks to me, but I always feared that they might.

In another class called ESL, or English as a Second Language, we watched the movie *Transformers*. I loved it. The CGI was amazing; the Autobots and Decepticons looked very real. It had a good storyline and lots of action which kept me engaged. But what I really loved was the character Optimus Prime. He was a natural leader, able to inspire and motivate those around him with a powerful speech. Driven by kindness, he fought the bad guys and won.

There was a line in that movie that stuck out to me: *"No sacrifice, no victory."* I had a strange feeling that, in order to get my life back on track, I might need to sacrifice the good parts of my life, the parts that I was currently enjoying, or I wouldn't achieve my ultimate goal: to bring back the happiness I'd lost and find myself again. However, it would not be an easy journey.

For example, living in the motel in Denison was peaceful. I enjoyed my privacy. I didn't have to do anything productive; all I had to do was play a few video games or watch television. I did those activities for fun, and I enjoyed them. I didn't have any responsibilities since I was living a life of luxury, even though my mental illness was leading me to believe that everything in my life was going horribly.

I knew that by the time I went back to Kerala, my family would be living in Irving again. The plan was to go back after Chris had finished high school. By moving back to Irving, I would lose the privacy and peace that I was enjoying in Denison. If I needed to live in Irving, I would have to learn better social skills and be successful. I had concluded that the only way to achieve those things was to go back to Kerala and find my happiness. That meant I'd have to give up my way of life in the US.

Later, I watched the *Lord of the Rings* trilogy, an amazing experience. I imagined fighting for Middle Earth, picturing myself in a tremendous battle. The character Frodo resonated with me. He had an enormous burden to bear, carrying the ring that corrupted his mind and the minds of everyone around him back to Mordor to be destroyed. While many friends helped him on his journey, he had to face his burden alone. I could relate Frodo's struggle to my own life. I had endured a long and rough journey. The bullying I'd endured continued to corrupt and change my brain, and no one could help me. Only I could destroy the burden.

I knew that my journey to Mordor was really a journey to Kerala, the one place where I could be truly free, where I could destroy the hold that fear and pain had on my life and emerge into a new world full of happiness and hope.

Watching *Transformers* and the *Lord of the Rings* reminded me of watching Hollywood movies as a child, which I loved so much. Movies had been an escape—a way to shut off my depression and anxiety, and focus on something else for a while. They showed stories of overcoming adversity, of good guys winning and bad guys losing, and of people triumphing in the most difficult of situations. I held on to the belief that, like the heroes in the movies I'd seen, I would one day be able to triumph too.

CHAPTER 12

TIME IS MOVING

There is no hand
to catch time.
—Indian proverb

The summer after my sophomore year of high school, we returned to India to attend Scott's wedding. It was the biggest wedding I had ever attended. Our entire family from all over the world gathered back in Kerala for the marriage.

This time, I was ecstatic. I remembered the summer before—how I'd found myself again, even for just a few weeks. I knew that when we arrived in India, I could feel normal again for a short time.

My time there was perfect. Scott, Mason, my brothers, and I saw movies and went to restaurants, just like the last time we'd come back to visit. The family had a wonderful time, celebrating Scott's marriage, spending time together, and enjoying each other's company.

Once again, I felt my life fall back into place. Gone were the days of bullying, awkwardness, and struggles that had built my life in America. I laughed and had fun, interacted with everyone around me, and found happiness. I was never afraid of what anyone would think of me, or if I'd say something embarrassing, or if someone was lurking around the corner to pick on me. I was truly happy, like I hadn't been in years.

Even so, I couldn't shake the feeling that time was moving forward without me. Everyone that I knew had positive things going on in their lives—and I was stuck, living in fear and anxiety back in the US, waiting for my first chance to bolt back to India for a while. I was struck by the fact that nothing stayed the same; everybody moved on eventually.

All too soon, the summer ended. We packed up and headed back to America.

School started up again not long after we returned. This was 2008, and I began my junior year of high school.

I had Mr. Murphy's US history class. I was happy to be in his classroom again. He was a great teacher, and my time in his room was again enjoyable.

All went well until the time came for another dreaded presentation. I had avoided it the first time around. This time, Mr. Murphy firmly told the entire class that we all had to do the assignment, and he looked straight at me.

I weighed my options carefully. Like the last time, I knew I could choose not to do the assignment and accept the consequences. But Mr. Murphy would probably not be as accommodating this time. I still felt guilty about not doing the work for the project the year before, like I had taken advantage of his kindness. I wasn't sure I wanted to add more guilt on top of what I was already feeling.

This time, the project was different: draw a timeline of historical American events on a long sheet of paper and present it to the class.

I put off my decision until the day before the project was due. Eventually, my guilt got the best of me, and I decided to complete the project. I stayed up all night to finish it.

The next morning, I felt a huge pit of dread in my stomach. I felt a little exhausted from the lack of sleep. My heart pounded in my ears as I moved to the front of the class to make my presentation. Time seemed to slow down. My mouth went dry, and my hands shook as I tried to hold up my paper. Looking around the class, I realized everybody was staring at me. I opened my mouth and in stuttered, broken sentences, tried to remember enough information to recite. My voice broke continually. I did my best to cover up my nerves and anxiety, pushing through the fear I felt. I didn't want Mr. Murphy and the other students to know how much the presentation was affecting me.

Amazingly, I got through it. A wave of relief passed over me, and all the tense muscles in my body immediately relaxed when I got back to my seat. It felt like a miracle. My presentation hadn't been perfect, but I had done it. Mr. Murphy was pleased that I had conquered my fears and given the presentation. He gave me a good grade.

In November of that year, the 2008 presidential election took place. We held a mock election that week at school. Everybody went into the auditorium where the faculty passed out paper ballots. We could choose between John McCain and Barack Obama.

I took my ballot, ready to choose Obama. Nearby, a group of students huddled together. I didn't know who they were; they weren't in any of my classes.

"Dude, pick McCain," one of them said to another.

"Yeah. Definitely." They all murmured in agreement, as though it was obvious McCain was the only viable choice. The entire group nodded and filled out their ballots.

As I watched them, I grew uncomfortable. After students filled out their ballots, they passed them to a nearby adult.

This process didn't offer a lot of privacy, and I was nervous that if I put Obama, that group of students would see. They might make fun of me or bully me for my choice. The last thing I wanted was to be picked on for my political leanings.

I stared at my ballot, unsure what to do. I supported Obama and wanted him to win the presidency. But I remembered my troubles on the bus in eighth grade. I didn't want to do anything to set myself apart from the other students or draw negative attention. With a sigh, I made my vote and passed my ballot to a teacher.

A few days later, Mr. Murphy revealed the results to the school. Most white students had chosen McCain. Most of the Latinx students had voted for Obama. Finally, he announced the results of the Asian population. There were very few of us at the school. Every Asian student had picked Obama except for one. Mr. Murphy paused for a minute, likely wondering who that one person was.

That one person was me. I'd allowed myself to give in to peer pressure and choose McCain. I didn't like that I'd done it, but I also felt relieved that I'd saved myself from being singled out and possibly picked on.

Democrats typically embodied the ideas that young Asians wanted to see in a candidate for president. When I voted for McCain, I almost felt like I was betraying myself. I wanted to vote for Obama, but fear and peer pressure kept me from being honest. I'd thought that the only way to vote without judgment was to betray myself, so I made the safe choice.

After this experience, I knew I needed to become stronger. If I didn't change, I was going to lose my identity and credibility, both from my perspective and the perspectives of anyone who knew me.

In some ways, the year was going well. I wasn't struggling as much with my classes. I was conquering fears and completing assignments. I even found myself interested in more of my schoolwork.

But before long, I began to struggle again. The issues I had, especially the PTSD and anxiety, rose to the forefront. My fear of being rejected, being made fun of, and being bullied kept me from doing my best on my schoolwork. I didn't have the mental capacity to put into both worrying and doing assignments, so I let my schoolwork slide. I didn't understand why these feelings of fear kept coming up. Outwardly, I was okay and happy, but the unresolved issues were hiding at the back of my mind and piling up. All I was doing was waiting for the moment I could go back to Kerala to fix my life. I wasn't truly living.

One day after school, while walking home near the school fence, I saw one student from my ESL class. He nodded at me and said hi.

I didn't respond. I truly don't know why. I just didn't know how to socialize with others. My instinct was to withdraw, not respond with a pleasant, "Hello." So, I didn't react.

Right away, I could see he was offended. He scowled and walked off quickly. My stomach flopped. I hadn't meant to upset or insult him.

The next day, I saw him in the same spot. This time, I knew I wouldn't make the same mistake.

"Hi," I said with a small wave. I gave him a half-hearted smile, hoping it would make up for my rude behavior the day before. He just glared at me and walked on.

I knew then that any possibility of friendship with him was over. After that day, I found a different path to walk so I wouldn't see him again. I was afraid he might retaliate or try to confront me.

That wasn't the only time something like that happened. One day, as I walked through the hallway, I saw my Spanish teacher standing at her classroom door. I nodded my head as a greeting, but she ignored me.

My anxiety took hold. Had I offended her too? Had I upset her? Did she dislike me? I began to wonder if I'd ignored her at some point, the way I had the student from my ESL class.

That was when I realized just how severe my social anxiety issues had become. I wouldn't connect all the dots to realize that bullying was to blame for my issues for many years. I just knew that socialization didn't come easily to me, as it did for so many people around me. I couldn't relate to others or feel comfortable interacting with them.

I was confused and hurt, frustrated by my own actions, and by my inability to either control or overcome them. In addition, I had moments when I wasn't proud of who I was or where I came from. My self-esteem issues became even worse when coupled with my social anxiety.

At the beginning of August, after my junior year, my family and I went to India for one month. While my brothers and I hung out with Scott and Mason and enjoyed each other's company, we watched a newly released Malayalam film called *Puthiya Mukham*—which means "new face."

The film was about a simple, innocent guy who enrolled in an engineering college but got bullied by upperclassmen. The leader of the seniors didn't like the new guy because he thought his girlfriend liked him. So, they beat him badly, and the guy was hospitalized. He eventually healed and came back to school with a new, aggressive personality because the attack had damaged his brain. Eventually, the main character fought his bullies and won.

It was a good film that almost everyone liked. It made me think about my bullying experiences. The main character won in the end, even with his new personality. The only problem was that I didn't get to fight back and win over my bullies in real life; they got away with what they'd done. I hadn't gotten a new personality either, one that would let me heal from my experiences. Sadly, real life was quite different from movies. At least I could fantasize about what could have been and enjoy the movie.

Not long after that, we came back to the US.

CHAPTER 13

GRADUATION DAY

It's good to hope,
it's the waiting that spoils it.
—Yiddish proverb

When school started back up again for my senior year, I was finally excited—not for school itself, but instead excited to be approaching the end of my school experience. Only one more year to go!

I felt more motivated than I ever had. I finally had something to look forward to, to drive me, and to keep me from falling into depression. It paid off. I got better grades in most classes than I had throughout the entirety of my high school career.

That year, a new Indian girl my age started school at Denison High. Her father was an English professor from my dad's college in Kerala. He was a close colleague and friend of my dad's. He got a job at our motel, and her family moved in as well. We didn't have any of the same classes, but whenever I left the school building, she was usually there, ready to head home at the same time.

She tried to talk to me, but I never wanted to chat. I'd never really hung out with girls, and the thought made me quite uncomfortable. So, I completely avoided her, pretending not to see her whenever she would approach or try to say something to me. I feel badly about my behavior now. She was probably lonely and felt like I was someone she could be friends with. We had a lot in common, and she was undoubtedly eager for something familiar, just like when I was in a similar situation a few years before. I wish now that I would have been nicer to her, tried to chat with her, or at least have acted friendlier toward her. She never seemed to hold it against me, though.

During the first semester, I had to take economics. On the first day, the teacher asked me if I was Chris' brother as he had recognized our last name from when Chris was in his class the year before.

Soon, I realized that the economics teacher was the strictest one in the school. He came from a military background and was also the high school football coach. He was intimidating, though he wasn't mean—he just had high expectations of all his students. For most kids, having a strict teacher was not necessarily a bad thing, but it made me very uncomfortable. If I made a mistake or accidentally disrespected him, there was the possibility that he might call me out and cause a scene in front of the whole class. I would have been absolutely mortified.

Being in economics class with him made me wish for Mr. Murphy's class. I liked him and had gained confidence in his class. With this teacher, I was afraid I would lose the ground that I'd gained.

Just as in Mr. Murphy's class, I had a big, dreaded assignment in Government. I had to write ten different essays about something we'd read or talked about in class. There was no way I could complete the assignment on my own; I still struggled with understanding English, and my writing skills were poor. So, I had no choice but to ask my dad for help. He understood stuff like that. Instead of helping me, he did the assignment for me.

I turned it in the next day. The teacher took a few days to grade the assignments, then he started off a class period by handing them back to us so we could see our grades. When he got to mine, he called my name. I was nervous that he would find my work fishy and suspect that I hadn't done it.

Instead, he said, "Rick, you did a pretty good job. Nice work," and moved on to another student's paper. I don't know if he was suspicious or not, but I felt relieved. I'd passed the assignment, and all I had to do now was survive his class until the end of the year.

I continued to struggle with social anxiety. It never seemed to get any better, no matter how much I focused on being polite to other people. Once, while I was washing my hands in the restroom, a student that I knew came in. He said hi to me, and I wanted to respond. It was easy enough to say hello back. However, I froze. I told myself to answer, but I just couldn't.

Fortunately, he seemed unfazed. He just finished his business and left as if nothing had happened.

Still, I felt terrible. I didn't know why I was like this. I wanted to act normally, but I just didn't know how to respond. Whenever someone spoke to me, I would tense up, a response to them right at the tip of my tongue. In those moments, however, opening my mouth and saying the word was impossible. What if they made fun of me? What if they thought I looked or sounded weird? What if responding made me a target for bullying? I knew, deep down, that many of these fears were irrational, but I couldn't keep the thoughts from my head. Despite these social issues, I moved through my senior year successfully.

During that school year, they created a new free time period. They scheduled it before lunch and designed it for the students to go to the secondary cafeteria and do homework. But most of the students didn't do any classwork. They just sat, talking to each other, and had a good time.

I always had work to do, so I would take out my textbooks and complete assignments. A few other students would do the same. Those of us who were actually working would do our best to ignore the loud noises of those who were using their free time to mess around and chat, but it was difficult. Most days, I sat alone at a round table, always in the same place. I only had a couple of friends, but they weren't there at the same time as me.

The other students saw me working on homework during free time and thought I was a nerd. I wasn't. I just wasn't good at studying. I used that time to survive, to work hard enough to pass all my classes. Ever since the bullying in eighth grade, school had become harder for me. I had to put in that extra time and effort. At least no one ever said anything to me or directly made fun of me for working. I still feared that someone would try, however, so I kept my guard up while I worked.

That year, my English teacher Mr. McMahon, from Ireland, was new to our school. He was enthusiastic and engaging. He had a slight accent, one I hadn't heard before. I liked him. He was a fun person.

Unfortunately, we had to read a book aloud in his class, and I didn't like that. Reading in front of the class was one of my worst nightmares. I was embarrassed by the sound of my voice. The idea made me shaky and nervous, and despite my best efforts, I was sure the other students could hear the anxiety and discomfort seeping into my voice. I had a hard time hiding just how uncomfortable I felt. Surprisingly, I didn't get called on to read as often as I'd feared. That was comforting. At least nobody laughed openly at me, which made my few read-aloud experiences okay. Aside from that, I enjoyed his class very much.

I also had to take Speech, a class I put off and dreaded. The thought of standing in front of the class and giving multiple speeches throughout the year struck fear in my heart. I panicked every time, unable to overcome the embarrassment. My mouth would go dry, and I would sweat and shake. The whole idea of the class left me petrified, and I dragged my feet down the hallway each day when it was time for that class.

My speech teacher was very kind. He understood my anxiety and allowed me to come in before school to present my speeches to him, instead of the whole class. This helped immensely. It was still hard to do, but I wasn't nearly as nervous. There was something calming about not standing in front of a group of my peers to present my speech that made me feel just a bit more confident. In the end, I did well in his class.

After school each day, I came home and played video games. It was during my senior year that I decided to make an Xbox account for myself so I could play video games. Previously, I had used Chris' account on our Xbox console. During account creation, Xbox prompted me to choose a username. I had no idea what to pick, and I saw that I could have the system create a random name for me. So, used the Xbox random name generator, hoping something I read would spark an idea for me.

The first few names Xbox suggested weren't great. But on the third or fourth try, I got an unfamiliar but catchy and cool-sounding name: "GawkyPlayer" with four random numbers afterward. Immediately, I liked this name and used it for my ID on my account.

I didn't think too much about the name after I selected it. I didn't even know the exact meaning of "gawky" for the next ten years. For a long time, I assumed that "gawky" was a random word that Xbox had come up with. Later, I realized this random word I had accidentally chosen had become me.

On my last day at Denison High School, I had the same positive feeling that I'd felt when I left my middle school after eighth grade. I didn't have to go to school anymore. Now, I could stay at home and relax if I wanted.

When I left the school, I looked back once again, just like I did when I left middle school. I saluted while facing the high school as a final farewell gesture, just like soldiers would do. I'd had a few unpleasant experiences, but I'd never been bullied at Denison.

Unbelievably, I had survived high school!

The day of the graduation ceremony came. The government and economics teacher was there in his suit, looking at the graduates. Even at that moment, I still worried he knew I hadn't done the last assignment in his class by myself, even though I knew the school year was over and there was nothing he could do. I still didn't feel good about that because I rarely cheated. I couldn't help the fear that settled in the pit of my stomach. Could he still lecture me about it? That would be embarrassing.

I donned a cap and gown and sat with my class, ready to be called by name. I looked around at everyone else who was graduating. My Pakistani friend Ahmed was there as well.

When my name was called, the announcer actually pronounced Pallattumadom correctly.

I felt proud as I walked up to shake hands with one of the school administrators. Mostly, I felt relieved and accomplished. I'd waited four years for that moment. I believed things would get better from there, and I was thrilled about not having to get up early or do homework.

The best part was that I was one step closer to my goal: returning to Kerala, India. Only then would I feel normal again. Only then would I be able to successfully chase my dream of finding happiness again and healing from my trauma.

After the graduation ceremony, I came across the student I'd encountered in the restroom. "Congratulations," he said, smiling.

"Yes. Congratulations to you, too," I replied. We chatted for a moment about our future plans. After that, I asked, "Do you know where I can get my diploma?"

"Sure. It's right back there."

I breathed a sigh of relief, happy that I'd responded normally and that he wasn't holding a grudge from my inability to talk in the bathroom. I thanked him and wished him good luck. He did the same for me. I got my diploma and left the school for good.

Graduation day was great. Finally, high school was over, and I'd come across someone who wasn't bothered by my social awkwardness. I'd even had a positive social interaction with someone who talked to me. I finally felt at peace, and for once, I was looking forward to what came next. Happiness was my next step, and I was eager to capture it once again.

CHAPTER 14

KERALA IS CALLING

He who doesn't look ahead,
gets left behind.
—Venezuelan proverb

Shortly after I graduated, my family bought a new house back in Irving. It was only five to ten minutes away from our first home there, the one we'd lived in when we first arrived in America. But we didn't move back to Irving right away. We stayed in Denison for another two years, moving things slowly and visiting Irving every couple of weeks. We were waiting for the end of Chris' senior year. My parents reasoned that if he had transferred to a new high school in Irving, it would have disrupted his high school experience, so we waited.

In 2010, the year after I graduated high school, I officially became a US citizen. I'd waited five years for that moment. I was very happy and proud. Even though my life in America had been full of struggles, I still took pride in becoming an American. This country was full of opportunities, and I was determined to use them to better my life.

After my graduation, I had very few places I had to go. I wasn't going to school anymore, and I didn't have a job. So, I stayed home a lot. I discovered that the more I stayed home, the more I dreaded going out. It got to the point where

I almost never wanted to leave my house; the idea made me fearful and sick to my stomach.

The only times I left were when I had no choice, like going to a ceremony for my citizenship or seeing the occasional movie like *Inception*. I drew inspiration from films like that. *Inception* helped me to realize that if I didn't get out more and work on becoming the person I wanted to be, I would get stuck where I was, unable to find a way out.

To combat that, I focused on finding a way to get back to Kerala. In my home country, I felt normal. I felt like I could be myself. In Kerala, I was genuinely happy.

I knew I would need some time and cooperation from my family, especially my parents, to pull it off. I couldn't afford to go alone, and I knew it wasn't a good idea for me to live alone. Someone would have to go with me. I didn't think getting them to agree would be a problem. After all, they loved me and would want me to be happy.

The more I thought about it, though, the more I realized that I would have to wait until after the move back to Irving was finalized. There was a lot going on, and though I had promised myself in eighth grade I would head back to India right after graduation, the reality of my situation was that the move just wouldn't be possible. Not yet. So, I kept Kerala in the back of my mind as a goal and focused on a few other things while I waited, like making plans for my future.

I was relieved to be out of school, and I didn't want to just sit at home and do nothing. I knew the best thing would be to improve my life. So, I went to Grayson College near Denison—a big decision for me.

I'd had this idea before graduation, and I knew this was a logical next step to help me move on. Jef had gone to Grayson after he finished high school, and it seemed like a good place for me to continue my education.

I decided to study BOSS (Business Office Support Systems). I wanted to study something related to computers that would, hopefully, not include too many necessary social interactions. It was a two-year program, and if I finished that, I would get a degree.

In order to get the degree, I had to take Accounting. I quickly realized that accounting was an important subject and was surprised by how fascinating I found it to be. I spent my time learning about accounts receivable and payable, assets, balance sheets, cash flows, and equity. The class required a lot of math, which I'd always found to be very difficult. Despite my best efforts, I ended up failing.

I had hoped that my social interactions would get better at college. I would meet many new people and hoped I could teach myself to smile and give simple replies to people who approached me. Unfortunately, my interactions with others continued to be painful and awkward.

One day, I walked into the accounting classroom. A lady my age smiled at me. It was a genuine smile, as if she were glad to see me.

For some reason, I panicked and turned away. Immediately, I regretted my decision. I had made a mistake, just like in high school. I should have said hi, and everything would have been fine. When I turned back to correct my mistake, she had already looked away, stunned. It was too late to fix the problem.

Despite awkward social interactions and tough classes, I remained dedicated to my work. I passed many of my classes with ease, taking on a full load of four classes each semester.

Still, there was a little nagging question in the back of my mind: If I can't learn how to socialize with others, is college even the right choice for me? I only planned to spend a year at Grayson before transferring to North Lake College in Dallas. I hoped North Lake might be a better fit.

That year, I also took my driving test. I passed the paper test but failed the driving test twice. The first time, I drove through a yellow light instead of slowing down and stopping. The second time, I failed to go the speed limit. Every time I failed, I lost more and more confidence.

By the third test, I was flat-out scared. My hands and my feet shook with nerves. My heart raced, and I could hear my blood racing through my head. I wasn't confident I would pass that time either, but I needed to, or it would be completely embarrassing. Most people passed by their third attempt. I was sure someone would make fun of me if I failed another try.

Somehow, I passed. Most of the test passed in a blur, my nerves and anxieties making it too difficult to remember any of the details clearly. After that, I drove my dad's minivan or Jef's sedan to and from college.

By the time I'd passed my driving test, 2012 was fast approaching. According to the Mayan calendar, the world would end in December 2012. There was a lot of hype and hysteria surrounding the possible event. The news reported on it, and there were several movies made that focused on the world ending. Documentaries shown on television talked about the Mayan calendar. Everywhere I looked, someone was talking about the end of the world, and they made the possibility sound real.

I didn't fully understand the evidence in the Mayan calendar behind the world-ending prophecy. The prediction was hard to believe. How could someone know that the world was going to end on a particular day or a particular year? I wasn't sure it would happen, but all the attention it got kept it at the forefront of my mind. I assumed something bad would happen and worried about December. Why else would they continue to talk about it?

***

In early 2012, we officially moved into our new home in Irving. I was excited to move back, despite all the negative things that had happened to me in Irving. I knew that this move put me one step closer to moving back to Kerala. On top of that, most of our family, including Scott, had moved to America by then. Moving to Irving would give us the chance to spend time with them.

Still, I missed the privacy I had in Denison. I liked the peacefulness of isolation.

After we moved back, we started attending a Malayalam church—a different church from the one we'd attended when I was in eighth grade. It had been five years since I'd gone to holy mass.

There were a lot of other people my age at church. I timidly socialized with them, hoping these interactions would help me at college. At first, it felt nice. I even believed that I was getting better at socializing and blending in with the crowd.

Quickly, though, I realized that my social problems were worse than I'd thought. I saw others my age talking, laughing, and engaging with each other, and I wanted to do that too. But each time an opportunity presented itself, I froze. My mouth wouldn't move, my tongue felt like cotton, and it felt like my brain short-circuited.

As a result, I spent a lot of time following my younger brother around. I didn't think it was a bad idea because I hoped Chris could show me how to interact positively with others. Most often, younger people look up to older people, but not in my case. Based on the looks we got, people noticed my tendency to follow Chris around. I worried they thought I was weird. One day, a former police officer from Kerala teased me about that.

He said, "Why are you following your younger brother around?" I could tell by the smile on his face that he was joking, and a few people nearby heard and chuckled too.

I got upset and didn't respond with anything other than a stiff smile. I didn't know how to react. Later, he tried to explain that it was a joke, but it stung me. I was trying to help myself learn how to overcome my social anxiety. I didn't need to be teased for my efforts.

Things like this happened a few times. Other youths would joke around, asking, "Who's the older brother?" Someone else would almost always reply, "Chris is the older brother," even though everyone knew that wasn't true. They just didn't understand why I was the one following Chris around wherever he went. It was a bit embarrassing.

These incidents were isolated, but I knew other churchgoers noticed, even if they didn't comment. Every time I went to church, if Jef wasn't around, I would have no choice but to follow Chris. If I didn't, my only other choice was to stay in one place like a loner—silent, not knowing what to do.

Around that time, Scott asked me to go with him to visit some family. As we were driving back, we were talking about life. I let slip something about the bullying. We ended up talking about it for quite a while. I explained how it had stunted me and made me the way I was. Scott was sympathetic and understanding.

He was one of the few people I told about my bullying. It felt good to let someone in and to be believed instead of shamed or brushed off. He was glad that he had asked me to go along because he'd learned something new about me. His words were a relief to me, and I was glad he'd asked too.

Unfortunately, not everyone was sympathetic. My immediate family still didn't understand my mental health issues, despite the numerous conversations I'd tried to have with them about it. One day, we all got into a huge argument. They blamed me for everything, telling me what I should have done differently to avoid the problems in the first place and how I should have already moved on from the pain. I craved help, sympathy, and basic acknowledgment of my issues. But they wanted me to move on and be normal.

In fact, my dad often scolded me, expecting me to bury my issues and pretend they hadn't happened. They didn't understand how deeply the trauma had affected me. They didn't see the ways I'd already changed as a response to the bullying I'd endured, and none of us knew how much I would continue to change as time passed.

It seemed like my family was intentionally neglecting me, and I didn't know why. They were supposed to care about me and make my life better. Eventually, I got pissed off at them, and my anger led to progressively more serious fights.

One fight sent me over the edge. I wanted my family to acknowledge that I had endured trauma and understand that I couldn't just snap myself out of it. They refused, again placing the blame on me, telling me to get over it and move on with life.

I stormed to my room. As I sat on the edge of my bed, fuming with my arms crossed, I decided not to eat from then on. My dad, mom, and brothers assumed I would give in quickly, but I proved them wrong.

They tried to get me to eat, but I refused. My mom cooked a delicious beef curry, thinking the smell would make me cave. But it did not sway me. I didn't eat for two weeks. After that, I started vomiting. What I was doing wasn't good for me, but it was the only thing I could think of to send them a message.

By the end, I wound up drinking some lemonade. I didn't want to give up or give in, but I could feel my body shutting down. I was in pain, and I knew I had to eat before any serious health problems set in. Those two weeks caused a big change in my physical appearance. I lost a lot of weight, going from a chubby person to a very thin one. When I looked in a mirror, I couldn't even recognize myself. Others noticed too.

Drinking lemonade to break my fast was a symbolic move. In India, drinking a glass of lemonade or a coconut drink would officially end a hunger strike. Typically, these types of strikes took place in public as a way for the wronged party to demand satisfaction from the government, and they wanted everyone to see what they were doing.

I saw events like these on the local news in India when I was a kid. They're not so common now, as the Indian people have found better ways to protest their government's actions. What I did was similar. I held a hunger strike for two weeks to seek action from my parents. That was a horrible experience, and I never wanted to do it again.

By this time, I was twenty years old with no goals other than to return to India. Time was continuing to pass, and I wasn't improving or changing with it. I knew I didn't want to be dealing with my mental health issues when I turned thirty. I thought, *Why am I going to college? It's not getting me anywhere, and I am losing precious time.*

So, I decided to *not* go back to college.

CHAPTER 15

CHANGE OF PLANS

*If you dream of moving mountains tomorrow,
you must start by lifting small stones today.*
—Equatorial Guinean proverb

That summer, my family returned to India to visit family. After we arrived, I followed Chris around, just like at church in America.

Chris and I hung out with Mason and his friends at a school near our church in Koodalloor. One of his friends, Johnathan, took an instant disliking to me. He was a leader in the group and a close friend of Scott's. When he saw me, he instantly thought I wasn't as mature as the rest of the group, likely because I was following my little brother around like a lost puppy. I felt his distrust based on the looks he gave me. I hoped nothing further would happen, that we wouldn't be forced to interact.

We drove to the school so that Chris, Mason, and I could watch people play volleyball on the school grounds. My dad had sold his old car in 2005 when we left for America, so we always used rental cars whenever we drove around Kerala with friends.

On this particular day, I drove, and we parked near the playground. I was supposed to take the car key out of the ignition before getting out and closing the door. But I accidentally left it in the ignition. After a couple of minutes with all the doors closed, the car automatically locked itself. I was standing nearby and heard the familiar *click* of the lock. That's how I realized I had made a mistake.

So, we already looked nervous and angry when Mason jogged over to greet us. "What happened?" he asked, coming to a stop just in front of the car.

Standing by the driver's door, I pointed to the keys still inside. "I locked the keys in the car," I admitted softly, afraid of his reaction.

Johnathan heard my confession since he'd followed Mason out to greet us. As Mason was trying to unlock the vehicle, Johnathan started talking about me. He balled his hands into fists, his shoulders tensed, and his words clipped as stepped closer to Mason, hoping no one else would hear him. He said, "Don't let him drive this car." Unfortunately, he didn't speak softly enough.

Everybody quickly realized he was talking about me. He was not in a good mood, and now it was because of me.

I felt terrible and awkward. He must have known I could hear him. I'd never done anything to him personally, and this was our first meeting. Yet, there he was, angry over something that didn't really have much to do with him. I knew I wasn't the best in social situations, but I didn't deserve to be berated.

Mason didn't react to Johnathan's words. He didn't say anything about me or decide to turn against me because of my mistake. He just dropped the subject, since he knew I hadn't done it on purpose.

Eventually, Mason got a long, thin, steel scale from one of his friend's homes and used that to unlock the door by sliding the scale between the car window and the door.

After that incident, I stopped going to places if I knew Johnathan would be there. I didn't want things like that to keep happening and ruin my mood. Besides, they were just another reminder that I wasn't good at interacting with other people. These hangouts didn't make me happy, and happiness was the reason I'd wanted to come back to India in the first place. I needed to focus on finding myself and ignoring those who tried to get in my way.

Soon enough, my dad and Jef returned to America before the rest of my family. As it came time for Chris, my mom, and me to return, I realized that I had to make my move now. I'd done enough waiting, enough dwelling on the past; I was done with unnecessary drama. It all needed to end, and I needed to leave my past in the past. So, I told my family that I wasn't going back, that I planned to stay in India and build my life there.

My mom didn't know what to do. I hoped she would have a positive reaction to my announcement, but I didn't hold my breath. My parents hadn't reacted well to my confessions of being a bullying victim, so I had definite doubts that they would be okay with me staying in India.

A few days later, Chris and my mom asked me to go with them to a hospital to visit my mom's uncle who was a priest. Their request was not particularly strange. I typically went with Chris or my mom to visit other family member's homes while we were in India. So, I agreed, thinking this was just a regular visit.

After we arrived, Chris left the building. That seemed suspicious. I asked my mom where Chris had gone, but she wouldn't tell me. She only said, "The priest will come in a moment." No matter what I asked, that was her reply.

Her lack of a clear response built up my anxiety. I didn't know why I was there, but I suddenly wanted nothing more than to leave. Nothing good was going to happen there, and I didn't want to see a priest. I went to church and did my best to be good in God's eyes. All the unknowns and frustrations left my heart fluttering wildly and my palms sweating.

After a few minutes, someone called us into a room. I went in first, and a nun asked me to sit down.

I sat down, wary of everyone. It quickly became clear that we weren't there to visit a priest. Something else was going on.

I was being ambushed!

Anger bubbled up in my chest, and my fingers curled into fists at my sides, although I tried not to let anyone see how upset I was. I had no choice but to sit down and see what they all wanted. Anger wouldn't get me out of there any faster.

The nun admitted that my mom had brought me there for an intervention. Also a psychologist, her job was to change my mind about staying in India at my mother's request.

I told the nun that I wasn't going back to America even if the pope himself ordered me to go. I was surprised by my words. Normally, I was never that aggressive, especially in front of a stranger.

We discussed my options for a few more minutes. Then, the nun told me I was free to go. My mom stayed behind to talk to her.

It was only after I left the room and the fog of anxiety lifted slightly that I realized what the place really was. We had come to a mental hospital in Moolamattom. Most Keralites knew about that place. I had heard about it since I was a little boy; it was a common joke in Malayalam films or made in conversation when I hung out with our friends. Characters in movies would tell one of their friends that they might need to go to Moolamattom to fix their problems.

Sometimes, family members would lie and mislead someone they loved in order to admit them to the facility. They would pretend that they were visiting a movie theater or a family member's home, but they were bringing them to the mental facility in Moolamattom.

I'd heard about teens that never listened to their parents, had gotten into drugs, or started using alcohol, who had been admitted to the mental facility. Their families had become so discouraged by their behavior they felt they had no other choice. In those cases, the patient didn't have a mental illness so much as a problem that needed solving. The plan was that talking with mental health professionals would help them find new ways to cope.

When I was a kid, I'd joked and laughed about being sent to that facility. This time, the joke was on me.

As I waited for my mother to finish talking to the nun, a feeling of white-hot betrayal washed over me. Why would they bring me to a mental health facility just for wanting to find myself in a place where I was truly happy? Didn't they want me to be happy? Didn't they care about me and what I wanted for my life? The more I thought about it, the more I realized my dad must have told my mom to send me to a psychologist when they realized I intended to stay in Kerala. This visit had been their plan all along.

Eventually, after much conversation and argument, I agreed to go back to America. I had actually decided days before I told my mom and brother, but had been faking my desire to stay to let them all know how I really felt. Once my family knew that I was serious about wanting to live in India,

I could more easily plead my case to return when the time was right.

Despite still being in India, I knew I couldn't stay no matter how much I wanted it. I needed to prepare both myself and my family first, and I hadn't given my family a heads-up before we left America. We could have further discussions once we were all back in the US and could make proper plans for me to return to India for an extended stay. It had to be that way if I wanted a clean start to turn my life around.

Plus, it would have been unwise to stay without first making the proper arrangements. I knew that and tried to accept that I was going back, hoping it would be a sign of good faith to my father. There could be no mistakes; that was very important.

A few days after our visit to the mental facility in Mool-amattom, we returned to America.

CHAPTER 16

MOMENT OF TRUTH

Plant during good times, so that
during the times of misery you may reap.
—Malayalam proverb

December 2012 came. A few days before the predicted end of the world, NASA made a statement telling the public that nothing bad was going to happen to Earth. There was no sign of an asteroid or other natural disaster and there was no reason to worry about the world ending. That made me feel a little better. I trusted NASA and believed they wouldn't lead the world astray.

So, I went about my business and tried to put the end of the world out of my head. There were still a few pieces of me hanging onto anxiety until the last moment, though. I was overjoyed when the world *didn't* end.

We had a big New Year's Eve party at our church. I had decided that I would not attend church anymore. I didn't see the benefit in church, and, oftentimes, going gave me more anxiety and worry than I could handle. I needed to get my life on the right track, and I had a plan for just how to accomplish that, which didn't include church. So this would probably be my last chance to celebrate with the members, and I partied as if it were my last party ever.

When it officially became 2013, I was sure that I didn't want to be in America any longer. It had been eight years since bullies had turned my life upside down, and I was ready to do something about it. I told my family that I wished to go back to India to build a life. I begged my dad to take me.

I explained that I had no future in America, that I wasn't truly living, locking myself in the house all day to avoid socializing with anyone, pretending that I was fine when inside I was dying to return to India. I had unfinished business to take care of—an impenetrable blockade in front of me. The only way to break through the blockade was to go back. India held the key to who I truly was; and after I'd rediscovered myself, I would return to America and start over there.

Eventually, my dad relented. He knew I would keep asking until he agreed. After I had seriously expressed my desires the last time I was in India, as well as countless times over the previous eight years, he realized I would not let it go. He couldn't ignore me anymore.

He agreed to move with me back to India.

I should have been overjoyed, but I wasn't sure if he was completely on my side or not. Something seemed off. I pushed my suspicions away, hoping for the best. I was finally getting what I wanted, and nothing would stop me, not even my reluctant father.

I didn't ask my mom to make the journey with us because she was still working as a nurse, and I didn't want to disrupt that. Much of the family's income was coming from her. It would be enough to have my dad with me. We could make it on our own for a little while. Besides, my brothers were not going either, and they needed someone to stay with them while they attended college and work.

The news spread quickly through my entire extended family like an intense wildfire. Many came to visit or called to find out why I would want to leave.

After years of keeping my bullying experiences a secret, I shared the truth. I told everyone who asked that I had been bullied at school, that the trauma was still affecting me. I explained I needed to return in order to find myself and find what had brought me joy during my youth.

Even though some were understanding, many still opposed my return to India. By this point, nearly our entire family had moved to America. They didn't want us to go back. They believed our best life was in America.

I knew they cared about me and wanted the best for me, but I also knew that my only chance to return to a normal life was back home in Kerala. I could rediscover myself there, finding who I truly was when I was at my best and who I was meant to be. To do that, I needed to be back in my childhood home, and spend time with my childhood friends and decide how to go from there.

Then and only then would I be able to reconnect with the happy little boy I'd been before our move.

My plan was to attend a local college in India while I was rediscovering myself. It didn't matter whether I got a degree; I didn't need an official piece of paper to rediscover myself. I just wanted to live normally, learning how to socialize with other college students during my daily classes.

I also planned other simple activities, like going to movies and restaurants with my childhood friends Lucas and Mason. They seemingly still had their innocent spirits from childhood, despite now being mature adults. I could benefit from hanging around them. They could teach me how to socialize.

I didn't want to disrupt their way of life, however. I promised myself not to jump in without their permission.

At the end of the day, I wanted to go to social events, make friends, and hang around with people I knew. By practicing, I knew I would become confident and heal from my trauma, returning to life as a fully functioning adult.

I had never planned to live in Kerala forever. I wanted to go back to America after my mission was complete. Once I achieved my goals, I could safely go back to restart my life there and study IT.

I felt no need to explain this to anyone, not even those opposed to my journey to India. What I wanted to do seemed self-explanatory to me, and I owed no one an explanation.

My cousin Zoey came to visit me. I hadn't spoken to her in eight years. She had heard I was leaving and found out about the bullying. She was nice to me while we chatted. I shared my experiences in detail, and she sympathized, telling me she had been bullied at a very young age too. I immediately understood why she had treated me so poorly all those years before.

Since we'd last talked, it seemed, she'd been able to heal. I was sure that she would treat me in a nicer, more understanding way going forward. She had forgiven me for the things I'd done in the past, and most importantly, she'd decided to forget about her bullies and what they'd done in order to move on. After we talked, we made up, and she returned home.

By this time, I had already forgiven my eighth-grade bullies for how they'd treated me—or at least tried to forget them. Their bullying had destroyed my innocence and had made me depressed and overly anxious. Essentially, they'd ruined my life. But somehow, I had to move past all that for the sake of my future. I could only get over what had happened if I thought positively. Forgiving and forgetting my bullies was my first true attempt at healing.

A few days before we were supposed to go to India, my dad got a long call from Jay in Kerala. After he hung up, my dad told me that there had been an accident in my childhood home. A fridge had burned, causing ash and smoke to fill the entire house. My first reaction was to worry that the fire would change my experience in Kerala. Had it ruined anything?

My dad had asked Jay to check on our house before we came back. Jay had gone over, ensuring that everything looked as it should. Before he left, he had plugged in the fridge. When he'd gone back the next day, he'd walked into a house filled with ash.

The fridge was old and in poor condition. Apparently, someone had repaired the fridge poorly at one point and freon gas had leaked and caught fire. The blaze happened at night while everybody was sleeping. It had burned so hot that the ceiling fan in the kitchen had melted and bent out of shape.

We were surprised but felt lucky that it had happened before we'd moved back. If we'd been there during the fire, our lives would have been in danger. We might have died from smoke inhalation while we were sleeping.

This meant I wouldn't be able to start my mission right away. We had to repair any damage to our home first. After we were safe, I could begin. I tried to stay positive. I hoped the fire wouldn't disrupt my plans for long.

Finally, my dad and I were ready to return home. It had been a long time since I had felt this optimistic. I believed Kerala was the answer, that I was finally on the right path.

My real adventure was about to begin.

CHAPTER 17

A CHARISMATIC BULLY

Be careful who you trust,
the devil was once an angel.
—Unknown

Finally, I was returning home!

I was elated. Instead of my usual preflight nervousness, all I felt was joy and anticipation. I couldn't believe what I'd waited for years to take place was finally about to happen.

Before we left for the DFW airport, our nearby family all gathered to say goodbye. We chatted and wished everyone farewell, then loaded our bags into my dad's minivan.

I must admit, despite my excitement, a sad feeling swept over me as we were preparing to leave. I sat inside the minivan—the only place I could get a minute alone—and cried for the first time in a long time.

I'd been living in America for eight years. Despite the hardships, it had become my home. My entire family was there. Now, I was leaving behind my mother and brothers for a chance at a new life. This was the first time I really understood that I wouldn't see my mother or brothers for quite a while, and it hit me hard. Still, I had to press forward without looking back. Fixing my life was my priority. I couldn't stay inside my comfort zone if I wanted anything to change.

We got to the airport and checked in. Boarding the plane, relief flooded over me. Everything was falling into place at last. We were well and truly on our way, and in a less than a day, I would be back in India. I already felt a sense of normalcy again.

Socializing would be much simpler in India. I had things in common with the people there. The cultural and language barriers that had always made my time in the US difficult would no longer be a factor. I could finally fit in, finally be normal.

For the first time since we'd left India, I felt driven. I wanted to do something useful with my life, to set goals and reach them. I dreamed of studying at a college, making friends, and fitting in. I longed to feel free of my burdens and struggles that had plagued me for so long, and I knew the key to my happiness was now just mere centimeters from my fingertips. All that was left was for me to reach out and take what I wanted from life.

When we landed in Kerala, Mason picked us up from the airport. We went to see Jay first, then got our keys to both our house and front gate. Then, we went to Karl's home—my dad's childhood home—to visit him before we checked on our house. When I saw Karl, I noticed something strange. He was too thin. He had always been a little bigger with a little more weight on his bones. I worried about that and tried to tell myself that maybe he had just reduced his food intake. That was probably why he seemed so skinny. I thought, *He will regain his weight after eating more food. I probably don't have to worry about his condition right now.*

After Karl and I had a short chat, my dad and I were finally exhausted and ready to relax, so we went to our home.

When we arrived, I hopped out of the car and hurried to the front gate, unlocking it without waiting for my dad. Then, I shoved the gates open with my right foot and walked onto our property, right foot first.

I opened the gates with my right foot to mimic an Indian wedding tradition. Sometimes, when a new bride comes into her groom's house for the first time after the wedding, she steps in with her right foot first. This symbolizes a new beginning, a newly married and prosperous life, and a new future. That was what I wanted for my future in India: a new, prosperous beginning.

Even though I had come back for vacation a few times over the previous eight years, I wasn't there for a vacation or sightseeing now. I was back to find myself. Despite what others might have thought of me reimagining the wedding tradition, I used it as a good omen. I was focused on getting my life back, and the sky was the limit.

While we inspected our home, my distant cousin Jith came inside. I waved and said, "Hi," certain he saw and heard me. But Jith didn't acknowledge me. It was odd that he didn't reply, but I shrugged it off. Maybe he was focused on something else and wasn't paying attention.

Days later while sitting outside of our house, I saw Johnathan riding his bike on the road. I wasn't sure if we were on good terms after our last interaction, but as I was determined to make the best of each new situation, I raised my hand to greet him.

He raised his hand too, but not to greet me. Instead, he mocked me. He raised his fingers at an angle and made a motion back and forth with a hint of a question in his eyes. This

Gawky: A true story of bullying and survival

was an Indian gesture for shaming others from a distance. The intended target knew and understood the message easily. He was asking, "Why did you come back to Kerala from America again?" He thought I should have just stayed. He'd belittled me the last time I came back to visit and was clearly trying to make fun of me again. I ignored his attempt to hurt my feelings and focused instead on making a life for myself in India.

Our house still needed some repairs after the fridge fire, so we moved into my dad's childhood home with Karl. Jith lived nearby, only a few minutes' walk from Karl's home.

After we moved in with Karl, my dad called on Jith for help with tasks around the house. My dad relied on him a lot. He asked Jith to drive him places or help with minor tasks like picking up materials or doing simple repairs.

I had no problem helping my dad with the repairs; I was very excited and willing to jump in. I needed to get involved so we could move back to our own house, and I could concentrate on my mission. But I lacked the knowledge and maturity to work on those projects; I had no prior experience with house repairs. So, I tried not to complain about Jith. We had only just reunited, and I didn't want to risk our friendship. He was friendly, despite not responding to my greeting. So, I was okay with him helping my dad, but I was still a little concerned.

Before my dad and I had arrived in Kerala, I had asked him not to bring others into our private lives. I didn't want anyone to interfere with my attempts at finding the key to my happiness. I needed to be left alone as much as possible, taking steps forward at my own pace if I was going to be successful.

At first, Jith and I got along fine. I even shared the story of my bullying. He confided that he had also been a victim of bullying when he first went to college. I believed our pasts bonded us and that we would have a wonderful friendship.

But experience had taught me that it didn't matter how friendly someone acted; in the end, they could change for any reason and attack when I least expected it. I'd been burned in the past and didn't want to go down that road again.

After a few weeks, my dad and I traveled to Kaduthuruthy to visit my mom's family. Driving in India was wild and unpredictable, not at all like in the US. People in India were used to it, but it was very difficult for me. Cars drove wherever they pleased without lanes, going as fast as they wanted, weaving in and out of traffic. I was uncomfortable driving to Kaduthuruthy, so my dad asked Jith to drive us.

The trip went well, and we quickly arrived at my aunt's new house, and our family greeted us. As my dad and I talked with family we hadn't seen in a while, Jith stood aside, not talking to anyone. My dad didn't introduce Jith and then went inside to see the new house, leaving Jith and me outside.

I shuffled my feet awkwardly. I didn't really know how to introduce Jith, since I'd never been in charge of introductions before. Shooting him an embarrassed expression, I hoped he would read my face and realize that I wanted to introduce him but didn't know what to say.

After a few minutes, my dad came back and, realizing what had happened, introduced Jith to everyone. I breathed a sigh of relief, confident that the awkward moment had passed. I felt a bit guilty about leaving him hanging, and it annoyed me that my dad had put me in that position. Additionally, I was annoyed at myself for not knowing what to do.

When we left, I confronted my dad in a gentle way. "Why didn't you introduce Jith when we first got there?" I asked.

My dad shrugged, acting as though it didn't matter.

As the mature adult, my dad should have been the one to introduce him. When I glanced at Jith, I saw he looked angry and insulted. I was sure he was angry with my father. If Jith was upset, he would have to work it out with my dad.

After we got back to Karl's that night, Jith, my dad, and I ate dinner, then sat on the porch, talking until it was late. To my surprise, my dad suggested I go sleep at Jith's house. I really didn't want to but agreed; it wouldn't be a big deal. However, the look on Jith's face was malicious, like an alligator waiting for its prey. He just kept looking at me. I didn't understand what was about to happen.

Jith and I walked to his house in silence. When we were almost there, out of nowhere, he spoke. "Why would you insult Anna? Huh?" Anna was Karl's live-in helper.

I stared at him with no idea what he was talking about. "Eh? What?"

"Earlier, you told your dad that after you washed your clothes at Karl's house, they smelled weird. Anna is a hard worker and tries to keep the house clean. You shouldn't insult her like that," he sneered.

I was floored, as I barely remembered that conversation. I had mentioned something about the way my clothes smelled, but I hadn't said anything about Anna that was insulting or sarcastic. "It was just a comment I made in passing," I told him. "I didn't insult her."

He didn't reply but kept quiet. He had said that out of anger and had been holding on to it, waiting for a moment to say it out loud, even if it made little sense.

At his home, I slept in his room across from his bed. I laid there in the dark and stared at the ceiling, wondering, *What the hell just happened?* I had no explanation.

The next day, Jith didn't mention anything about the day before. He acted like everything was normal. Jith seemed fine now. Finally, after much worrying, I decided to let it go. If he wasn't bringing it up, I wouldn't either. Maybe we could move on—forgive and forget.

But I couldn't ignore the gnawing thought that something was off.

Unfortunately, forgiving and forgetting was not possible with Jith. From that point on, our strained relationship grew worse with each passing day. I had only been in India for ten days, and I was already faced with a new bully without a chance to heal from my previous ones. Jith analyzed everything I did, finding the bad in each situation.

He acted like I was the enemy combatant. In essence, he declared war on me, and there was nothing I could do about it. Every interaction led to more bad blood between us.

The more time I spent around him, the more I noticed that something was different about him. His voice had changed in both tone and timbre. He spoke firmly and slowly, deeply, and strong. Only six months earlier, he'd been the exact opposite. Everyone had ignored him before, but now, everyone noticed him. He demanded their attention each time he spoke. I didn't know the psychology behind it, but he had intentionally changed how he spoke to gain respect. I wondered if he constantly attacked me in a misguided attempt to gain the respect of his peers.

The worst part was that Jith played mind games with me. He would be nice one day and pick on me again the next. He insulted me and retreated before I had the chance to react. I hated this more than the mean comments he made. At least I could respond to those.

His behavior perplexed me. He was not the same person I had known when we were kids. People change as time moves on, but these changes were unexpected. He seemed nice when we were around others, but when we were alone, he was angry and quick to take offense.

The last thing I had wanted was an enemy. Determined not to let the situation escalate, I tried my best to ignore him and not fuel the fire. I had come to India with a mission, and I was not going to let Jith derail me.

PART THREE:
HELL BREAKS LOOSE

CHAPTER 18

GETTING WORSE

*Pain of mind is worse
than pain of body.*
—Latin proverb

Jith did his best to shove me off my path.

One day, when he and I were driving back to my home after eating in a restaurant, he suddenly said he needed to see someone. He asked if making a quick stop was all right, and I agreed. He drove us to an unfamiliar building, and we went inside. Leaving me by the doors, Jith went over to two nuns and spoke with them for a few minutes. Then we left.

I didn't know why we were there, but I was suspicious about his motives for talking to them. I was worried that the nuns were part of some evil plan he'd concocted to get rid of me. The rational part of my brain, however, knew that he'd spoken with professionals regarding his feelings about the bullying he'd experienced in college. Perhaps these nuns had been a part of that process? His mother, Martha, was very religious. Maybe he'd needed to see them because of her.

Whatever the reason, I did my best to discipline my brain not to think the worst. That would only lead to more depression and anxiety that I couldn't afford if I was going to continue searching for myself and my happiness.

A few days later, when I left the bathroom after taking a shower, I heard strange voices downstairs. I glanced over the railing and saw Jith and two nuns. My dad welcomed them as if he were expecting them. Were they there because of me? I rushed back into the bathroom and locked the door, refusing to answer when Jith and my dad called out to me.

Luckily, my bathroom had a window looking out over the terrace. When they realized I was not coming out, Jith came by the window. If he didn't see me, he would come upstairs, looking for me. So, I waited for the perfect moment to pop out, and when he saw me, I just smiled. Jith had no choice but to smile back. Eventually, the nuns left, and they never came again.

This time, I didn't stop myself from having racing thoughts. I ran through every possible scenario.

Clearly, those nuns were psychologists sent by my dad to convince me to go back to America. They couldn't be here for any other reason. This is the second time he's done this to me! I can't trust him anymore, but I definitely can't confront him. He will never admit it.

Or…Maybe the nuns were Jith's idea. Yeah…He knows my dad doesn't want me to live in India, and he's sucking up to him again.

He probably thinks it's his duty to help my dad, especially since my dad has taken such a liking to him. He's smart. My dad likes smart. He's mature. My dad likes mature. He's resourceful. My dad likes that too. He probably just wants the social rewards he knows my dad can get for him. He's found ways to impress my dad so my dad will accept him and listen to him. That's the first step in his master plan to put me down and send me back to America.

If he doesn't want me to live in India, then of course he's going to make my life miserable. In order to do that and not lose my dad's respect, he'll have to be sneaky about it. That way, he can still climb the social ladder and exact his plan against me.

On top of all that, it's obvious my dad is trying to undermine me, and he's using Jith to do it. He must have asked Jith to get in touch with the nuns. He wants to go back to America. It all makes sense now...

I didn't see any other explanation. I tried not to worry too much about it. After all, I was already living in India. They couldn't force me to go back until my mission was complete.

I tried to move forward, pretending I didn't have a problem with Jith or my dad. But their actions were tearing me up inside the entire time. I couldn't let my dad know I was leery of him and his allegiances, so I had to bide my time, try to appear neutral, and focus on the task at hand: finding happiness.

But now that was proving much harder than I'd thought.

To make matters worse, whenever my dad couldn't be home with me, he asked Jith to stay with me instead because there was no one else close by. Besides, asking someone else might have made their daily routine difficult, and none of us wanted to be an inconvenience. Jith was already close, and unfortunately, the only one available.

Our beds were in the same room—mine in one corner, his opposite. The first night, I flipped on the switch for the ceiling fan and got into bed. Without saying a word, Jith got out of bed and flipped off the switch.

We had no air conditioner, and after only a few minutes, the heat started getting to me. I got up and switched the fan back on. Moments later, Jith got back up and turned it off again.

Irritated, I moved to another room. I wasn't going to play games all night over the ceiling fan, and I couldn't sleep without it.

I lay there, thinking about Jith's actions. Why didn't he just let me know he didn't want the ceiling fan on? I would have moved to another room right away. Instead, he played mind games to make me irritated. What did he gain from that? Did he just want to establish himself as the smartest person in the house? The last thing I needed was another bullying hell to suffer through. The best solution would be to ignore as many of his behaviors as possible. Maybe he would grow tired and quit trying, like my first bullies in America had so many years prior.

Ever since we were kids, Jith wanted to be an actor. He spent most of his spare time watching movies and working on small film projects. He was talented and even had some modeling success. So, when he asked me to come with him to a video project he was acting in, I agreed. I thought by supporting him, perhaps he'd lay off, at least for a while.

I did everything I could to keep the peace.

We traveled to a hospital where they were shooting a scene in an exam room. Jith played the patient, and another actor was the doctor. The scene went like this: The doctor called his patient in to tell him he had cancer. The patient refused to believe him and left the room. Simple enough.

On our way to the set, we spotted the camera guy preparing. I had brought my camera with me—a slim Canon point-and-shoot style. It was inexpensive, not the highest quality, but I enjoyed photography and took it with me everywhere.

At the shoot, I took a few pictures. Jith grabbed my camera and showed it to one cameraman. "This camera is junk compared to yours, isn't it?" he asked snidely.

The camera guy said, "Of course. It's cheap, not studio quality."

Blood rose to my face. It wasn't the best camera on the market, but I didn't care. I only wanted to take a few photos for fun. Jith, however, used my hobby to insult me, throwing the cheapness of my camera in my face. He pretended not to know anything about camera quality in an effort to embarrass me.

I didn't say anything.

Another time, Jith and I went to a mechanic to have his uncle's old car fixed. Upon leaving and entering the busy roadway, a police jeep passed us on the left. The policeman looked directly at us. Jith spat, "Rick, overtake that police jeep."

Of course, I didn't want to do that. "That police jeep is already going too fast. If I overtake him, there is a risk that he may stop us and cause a scene."

Jith snarled something under his breath, his face red with anger. He hated to be insulted, and the policeman's gaze had somehow insulted him. He wanted me to catch up to the jeep so he could try to insult the officer back. That was Jith's nature. No one ever got away with insulting him. He was always ready to fight and defend himself.

I chose to not overtake the police car. It wasn't a good idea, and I didn't want to pick a fight with anyone.

Not long after, my dad and I discussed what to do about internet. We hadn't set anything up since we'd arrived in India, but we were both ready.

Jith heard us talking about it and told me he had a router we could use if needed. I didn't want to accept any help from him or give him any fuel to use against me. So, I asked my dad to buy a new router instead.

It didn't take long to get the internet set up. Jith was offended when he learned what I'd done. He waited to confront me until we were with a group of friends. "Why did you buy a router?" he said in front of everyone. "I offered you one. You bought one for no reason!"

Everyone around us stared.

Ah...Here we go. When he finished yelling, I told him simply, "It has new features." Thankfully, that shut him up.

The worst part about constant issues with Jith was there was no way to avoid him. He stayed at our house often, helping my dad. He was friends with all my friends. We spent a lot of time together.

The other horrible part was how often he played me. Sometimes, he would be kind to gain my confidence. But any time I let my guard down, he used it against me.

During one of his fake "nice periods," I confided to him that I was struggling with another friendship. My childhood friend Hansel and I were growing apart and it hurt to see him pulling away. Jith asked me to give him my cell phone. I wasn't sure why he wanted it, but I handed it over. Then, I left the room for a moment, and when I returned, he gave me back my phone.

A few minutes later, my phone rang. It was Hansel. I answered it, surprised to be hearing from him.

"Hey," he said. "What did you need?"

"What?" I asked, confused.

"You called me. I'm returning your call."

Jith must have called Hansel so that he would return the call, putting us in an awkward position to talk to each other.

I told Hansel, "I don't know. I think I called you by accident." Then, we hung up. I felt like I was in a movie. That was the problem with Jith. He was always caught up in a fantasy.

A few days later, as I drove us back from the theater, Jith confronted me. "I don't have any privacy or liberty because of you," he accused.

His words struck me as odd, because he'd used the word *liberty* in English, an uncommon word to choose.

"I've lost all my freedom. You need to fix your attitude," he went on.

Even though I was irritated, I did my best to reply politely. "I am working on myself! That's the entire reason we came back to India. It's what I'm doing every day."

Jith's lack of freedom wasn't my fault. My *dad* was the one who constantly called him for help. I even told my dad to stop several times. Before we'd even come to India, I'd asked him not to drag other people into our lives. I had work to do on myself and didn't need the distractions. He hadn't listened, though, and now Jith was feeling stuck.

Jith continued to act like a nice guy, put on a show, and gain my trust. Then, he would go out of his way to make me look foolish.

One night, on the way to visit Karl, who was sick, Jith and I stopped at a restaurant. When we were finished, we went up to the counter to pay. The cashier asked what we had ordered.

I wasn't sure, so I turned to Jith. "What all did we get?"

He ignored me.

"Jith!" I exclaimed. "What did we order?"

Again, he refused to acknowledge me. The cashier looked at us, confused. Jith finally helped sort it out.

When we left, I asked nicely, "Jith, why did you do that? Did you not hear me?"

He didn't say anything and looked away like nothing happened.

I once again looked like a fool.

There was always some minor incident like that with Jith—something that might not be a big deal by itself, but these incidents kept piling up. They never let up.

I was helpless. I couldn't even tell my dad. Even if I did, he wouldn't take it seriously. Jith was pleasant and kind around him. It was all part of the act.

It was frustrating not being able to confront Jith. He would likely have downplayed the events, pretending they were nothing. Perhaps he would make fun of my accusations. He probably would have denied everything, making it seem like I was the one who was wrong and had misunderstood him. That would only make me more frustrated. So, I kept my ongoing issues with him a secret, just like he knew I would.

I continued to question his behavior. Why did he take pleasure in making me look like an idiot? Why did he hang out with me if he was just going to treat me like crap?

After that, things escalated. My dad went to the hospital often, leaving just me at home. One day, Jith arrived at my house with two friends and a bunch of alcohol, like he owned the place. He hadn't asked if he could bring them, yet he ordered me to bring water and soda for his guests like I was his personal servant.

They all sat around, talking, drinking, and having a good time while Jith kept asking me to do things. I did as he asked because there was nothing I could do to get him and his friends to leave.

Another time, as Jith and I returned from hospital, he drove carelessly, constantly zooming over the worst patches of road. We were nearing my house when Jith asked, "Wanna go hang out at church? My friends are there."

I had no desire to hang out with his friends. "No. I'm okay. You can go without me." I was afraid he might try to make fun of me in front of them, as he'd done before.

He shrugged and dropped me off at my house.

Before I went inside, I politely asked, "Please don't run over any potholes or rough spots in the road. My father's car is already damaged, and we don't want it to get worse before we can get it fixed."

Jith felt challenged, and I could see the anger radiating across his face. He drove away far too quickly, driving aggressively.

Later that night, Mason called me. "Hey, Rick. Why did you give Jith the car?"

"Is there a problem?"

"Yes. He's driving recklessly. Don't let him take the car again, or he'll damage it further."

I was confused. How did Mason know how Jith was driving? Then I realized that he must have been at church. Jith had been in a terrible mood when he left, but I hadn't realized he'd be so disrespectful with something of my father's. I presumed his recklessness and bad attitude were because of me.

CHAPTER 19
NOT WITHOUT AN INSULT

Whoever does not respect you,
insults you.

—Moroccan proverb

As time went on, Karl's physical health seriously declined. One day, Anna asked my dad and me to come over right away. My uncle was shaking uncontrollably. Luckily, we were able to get him into the back seat of the car and drove him to the hospital.

The medical staff ran a battery of tests and reported that Karl had tuberculosis, a contagious infection that usually attacks the lungs. The infection could also spread to other parts of the body, including the brain and spine. Karl's diagnosis explained his weight loss and other physical symptoms.

After the diagnosis, Karl required even more hands-on care and attention. We were very worried about him and wanted to pitch in as much as possible.

I put off attending college so I could help. This wasn't a decision I made lightly, but I wouldn't have been able to focus on studying with Karl suffering. I wanted to spend as much time with my uncle as possible before I no longer had the opportunity.

Jith realized this and used my decision as ammunition to continue attacking me. "You're hurting your dad," he told me. "He's disappointed in you because you're not going to school."

I tried to shut him out, to focus on my family and my life. Jith had a way of getting under my skin and was nearly impossible to ignore.

Everything came to a head when Karl took a turn for the worse. My uncle Ron came to visit from the US. He paid Jith to drive him where he needed to go and asked me to tag along. We visited Ron's hometown and went out to eat.

While we were at the restaurant, my dad called Ron. "Karl is not looking good. His health is deteriorating quickly. This could be it. I need you all to come to the hospital."

We left right away with Jith driving. I sat in the front seat, emotional. Things sounded very serious, and I knew that the end was probably near for Karl.

Jith looked at me and smiled. How could he smile at a time like that? I was on the verge of losing my uncle, about to break down in tears. So of course, Jith would kick me while I was down.

We arrived at the hospital, and Ron went into the ICU to visit Karl and discover his condition. Jith and I sat in the waiting area. That was when Jith decided to talk about his past sexual experiences in graphic detail. *Why was he acting so inappropriately? My uncle was fighting for his life, and Jith was talking about sex.*

I just ignored him, refusing to react.

While we waited for an update, I got lost in my head.

I am not at peace. Everything is crazy right now, out of control. It feels like it's swirling all around me, and I have no way to control it. My life is a constant battle with Jith, the very thing that I came to India to avoid. If I'd wanted to live in turmoil, I would have stayed in America. How could I have avoided this? My dad...

It struck me hard that my dad had allowed this to happen. He brought Jith heavily into our lives, despite my request to spend time alone and work on myself. If he had just listened to me, none of this conflict would have happened, and I would have already made progress on my mission of self-recovery.

After we left the hospital that night, my anger toward my father lingered. He still refused to listen to me and continually denied my request to keep our private lives private. How could I be expected to move on with absolutely no help from anyone?

Karl held on for another month, but, eventually, couldn't fight the illness anymore. I was heartbroken when he passed away. I had lived with him for five months, and now he was gone. I broke down crying at the sight of his lifeless body.

His funeral service was beautiful. Karl had moved on, was no longer in pain, and could now rejoice at being in heaven with God. Though nice to think about, each time I thought of Karl my eyes welled up with tears.

I felt I had missed so much of Karl's life. I hadn't known what he was like before he became really sick—before his mental illness took over so much of his life that he became like a zombie. Before we'd left for America, I hadn't spent a lot of time with him. I had just been a child, so I only focused on playing with my friends.

As I sat at the funeral, I was overcome with remorse, wishing I'd known more about Karl before, done more, and spent more time with him. It was too late now. I hated the feeling of regret that took hold of me. I wanted to wash it away, but I didn't know how to handle those emotions.

Family came from different countries to mourn him, including my mom. I was glad that she came; my life always seemed to go a lot smoother when she was around.

We laid him to rest in a tomb at our church. By the end of the funeral, I made an oath: I wouldn't let Karl down by following his fate. I would learn from Karl's life and his situation by having a prosperous and productive life. I wouldn't lose focus on my mission, and I wouldn't let any problems distract me. I still had a great chance that Karl probably never got in his life.

I promised myself that I would never let him down.

After we paid our respects, most of my relatives returned to their respective countries.

Not long after Karl's death, my brother Chris began to call me frequently. We talked about what was going on in my life. Then, our conversations took a turn for the worse. Chris had changed somehow; he was more like a stranger now than a brother. He was studying computer technology at a local college, and he seemed to think he had his life all together. I could tell that he was far more serious and very capable, judging by the way he spoke.

He lectured me about how I should move on with my life instead of holding on to the past. It felt as though he was trying to force me to heal *his* way, not *my* way.

My anger slowly bubbled over.

After many similar conversations, I finally told him, "Whatever happens in the future, don't interfere with my life ever again." He agreed, and we said our formal goodbyes. I then cut all contact with him.

I had mixed feelings about my decision but ultimately knew he would become a distraction to my mission. Besides, he made me feel like an idiot when he spoke to me. Between Karl's death, Jith, my dad, and other sources of stress, I still hadn't really been able to start looking for happiness.

My uncle Jack, who was also Scott's father, came to see me before he returned to America. We chatted for a bit before he asked, "Hey, Rick. Why don't you go back to America with your parents? There is nothing here for you, no future. Everybody is living in America, anyway. Just go back with your parents. It's better there, okay?"

I hadn't expected that. It took me a moment before I could respond, "I will go back eventually. Not now."

He wasn't the last one to make this request.

My parents also asked me to return with them. My dad planned to return to the US with my mom. Since he wasn't a US citizen yet, he had to go back within six months of leaving or face legal issues. I had dual citizenship, so I could stay as long as I wanted.

I refused. If I went back, they might not let me return to India again. They finally agreed I could stay, and my aunt Marissa would move into my house.

So, they returned to America. I stayed. But things had to change. Jith's behavior had gone on long enough, and with my dad headed back to America, I decided to avoid Jith altogether. I had enough of his antics.

Jith invited me out, but I declined. I wasn't rude but firm. I no longer wanted to spend time with him or let him undermine me, destroy my confidence, and distract me from finding my happiness. He eventually realized that the game was over. I wasn't playing along anymore.

It was time for me to end the drama and concentrate on my mission to get my life back.

Unfortunately, another family tragedy soon derailed me. Less than one month after Karl passed away, my uncle Jack died in America because of liver failure.

I knew that I would have to put my plans on hold and head back to the US for the funeral.

Jith wasn't about to let me leave without one more jab. On one of my last days in India, as I sat alone on my bed at my house, Jith sat down on the other bed where he used to sleep when he visited.

I made my position very clear to him. "You know," I said, "I've worked very hard in the past six months to get my life back on track." I don't know if I was hoping for sympathy or respect, but I got neither.

Jith laughed. "No, you haven't!" His voice was icy. "You achieved nothing. You don't even have a job. You have nothing to show for the past six months."

As usual, I didn't reply. I didn't know whether to feel sad about the status of our relationship, angry, or just relieved that, despite the poor circumstances, I would get away from him for a little while. He was like a parasite, taking advantage of a host, constantly draining my energy.

Perhaps by the time I saw him next, he would get over whatever his problem with me was and move on. That was the best I could hope for.

CHAPTER 20

HERE WE GO AGAIN

If it ain't broke,
don't fix it.
—American proverb

Aunt Marissa and I packed and prepared to leave for America. Just before we were going to leave, my distant relative Phil, who we called Uncle V, visited.

"Rick," he said, "you need to move back to America. It's so much better for you there than being here. You don't have to be here!"

I wasn't angry about what he said, but disappointed. Uncle V rarely voiced his opinion about such things. It seemed that no one trusted me to make decisions about my own life. Few people knew about my past, and it wasn't their place to comment on my choices. So, I pretended like I did not hear him.

I felt my dad was partially to blame for my relatives' negative opinions. He had never fully supported my move back to India. He never showed any visible confidence in me, especially in front of others. Everyone thought I was demanding, forcing my dad to come back with me to Kerala. They thought he was weak for giving in to me.

Yes, I did heavily pressure my dad, but I didn't have any other choice. My life would either have been even more miserable, or else would have continued to be a waste just like the past eight years. If my dad had shown the same level of affection for me as he did for my brothers, my relatives wouldn't have made these sorts of assumptions about us.

Ultimately, nobody would change my mind. They could tell me whatever they wanted, but I would not be swayed.

The day Aunt Marissa and I left for America for my uncle's funeral, all the remaining family members and some local people gathered to wish us well and see us off.

Jith came with his mother, Martha, and his father, Jay. Despite my strained relationship with Jith, Martha and Jay had always shown me kindness.

As we had nowhere to cook when our house was being repaired, my dad and I usually went to a restaurant to eat our meals. The food wasn't always good, and eating out that much wasn't healthy for us, especially for my dad. Martha knew about our situation, and she always invited us to her home for food or a friendly talk. She wanted to spend time with us. My dad and I often visited Martha, Jay, and their daughter while I was there in Kerala.

It sucked that Jith had treated me so poorly during those six months while his parents and his sister had treated me kindly, like their own son. We had bonded and grown close. We were all emotional as we said our goodbyes.

Jith was supposed to take us to the airport, but he tried to back out at the last second. He asked Mason to take us, but there was no way for Mason to shuffle his schedule around. So, Jith was stuck. Reluctantly, he agreed to do it as promised. I assumed he was doing it to keep my dad happy. While he didn't like me, he had an obligation to my father, and he didn't want to mess that up.

Mason's younger brother, Lucas, came with us to the airport. We departed from our home at night, as we usually did when going to America. Jith drove aggressively, exceeding the speed limit and our comfort zone.

We came across a bumpy, elevated part of the road, going far too fast. Our car was almost flying. I could feel my stomach rise inside my body. Lucas and I passed looks between us, confused by Jith's bizarre driving.

At one point, I got so uncomfortable I almost threw up. Lucas noticed my nausea and asked Jith to stop on the side of the road. Surprisingly, he stopped, though it was likely out of respect for Marissa. Typically, Jith didn't listen to anybody whom he considered inferior. It was unlikely he would have driven like that if my dad were present.

Once we got back on the road, his unsafe driving habits continued, but no one bothered to say anything to him, since we all knew he wouldn't slow down. He likely was driving that fast in order to finish this unwanted task as quickly as possible and return home.

We survived the journey and arrived at the Cochin International Airport.

Aunt Marissa and I were not sure how to check in. Fortunately, the airport personnel came to help us. They pushed her in her wheelchair which she booked from the airport, and we finally boarded the plane heading back to America.

Our family held Uncle Jack's funeral shortly after we arrived in September 2013. Most of the other Pallattumadom families came from far and wide to pay their respects. We all mourned Jack. He had been the senior-most member of our family. I'd known him my entire life, and I was devastated.

I had a theory about why his health had deteriorated so quickly. Jack had gone to India for a few weeks, back while Karl's health was still good. During that time, he drank a lot of alcohol, and his health had gotten worse. When he came back, however, he stopped drinking for a while, and he got better almost miraculously.

But when Karl had died a few weeks later, Jack went back to India for a second time for the funeral. Karl's death had upset him. He was mentally broken, and I understood his feelings.

Karl's death had really affected Jack psychologically. After Karl's funeral, he'd gotten drunk once more and left for America just days after the funeral. Within a few weeks, his health had deteriorated a second time. His last round of drinking had taken a huge toll on his liver; there was no going back. It was too late.

I was depressed when he died. I felt his absence, like someone was missing. We'd lost a great patriarch in our Pallattumadom family just weeks after losing Karl.

***

After the funeral ended and family went their separate ways, I made plans to return to India. So much had happened in such a small amount of time. Jith was finally out of my hair, unable to bother me since my dad was back in the US and not around to invite him over. I had adjusted to living in India, and those around me had too. All that remained was for me to focus on getting my life back—the reason I had gone to India originally.

I couldn't wait to get back and get started on some of my actual goals. But my life changed again for the worse when

Scott came to visit. I thought this would be a visit like any other. He wasn't just there to chat, though.

When Scott arrived, he spoke about some random family-related topics with my parents. Curious, I came downstairs to see what they were talking about. After a few minutes, Scott talked about my future. He said, "Rick, you should just stay here. There's no reason to go back to India. Your whole family is here. You don't need to go. I know you would rather stay here."

Turning to my father, he continued, "Joy, you don't have to go back to India. Rick doesn't need to go. He can live here."

My brother Chris jumped in. "I said the same thing."

My mom and Jef were both silent. I could see that they weren't going to object to the idea of me staying in the US.

My dad didn't respond, which caught me by surprise. I panicked, worrying that my dad had no intention of returning to India with me. That would be my worst nightmare.

Unfortunately, that nightmare became real.

I realized that coming back to America for my uncle's funeral was the biggest mistake I could have made. But there had been no way to avoid the situation; I needed to come back to grieve my uncle.

When my dad asked me to return to America with my mom and him after Karl's funeral, he made me a promise. "We can come back after I get my US citizenship, Rick."

That was a bad idea. I'd told my dad, "No. I don't want to go. I will only go back once I get my life in shape." I had no way to know that my uncle would pass away soon after, making my decision to return to America sooner than planned.

Many times, I could have put up fights or given in to the pressure of everyone around me telling me that I needed to go home. I never did. Now, though, I didn't know what I was going to do to get back.

My dad was much too credible; there was no way now that others would help me or say he made a mistake. They would think I was the one who was wrong.

My situation reminded me of an old story I heard from one of my family members about my dad's father's cousin.

When this cousin was young, he dreamed of becoming a priest. But his father refused to allow it and pressured him into marrying and having kids. The cousin had no other choice but to listen to his father's wishes. He didn't want to object and cause any problems with his dad. He didn't want to look bad in front of other family members, and he felt like ignoring his father's wishes would not turn out well for anyone. So, eventually, he married instead of becoming a Catholic priest.

When he became an old man, there were problems with him and his wife, causing much drama. He had denied his future because of his father, hoping his life would turn out for the better. Instead of a happy married life, however, he had conflicts with his wife and, later, with some of his kids.

My predicament felt identical to that story. Should I accept my dad's will and give up my mission, moving on with my life? My dad didn't want me to continue my mission, even though he had agreed previously.

My choices were to comply without objection or change his mind. If he remained stubbornly set on me giving up, my life would be over, and I would have to live with those consequences, bad or good. I would have little to no chance of getting back to the happy person I once was if I gave in.

I didn't like that idea, so I decided not to give up. I hoped my dad would eventually honor everything we had agreed upon, and I could safely return to Kerala. I didn't know my dad would use this as a perfect excuse to lock me up in America.

He cheated me by refusing to honor his promise, and I felt betrayed by my dad's silence. He remembered the promise; I could see it on his face, but still decided to do nothing. I didn't know why.

Following Jack's death, my dad was now the patriarch of the entire family. It would be nearly impossible to convince him on my own, and I certainly couldn't expect help from any other family members. Not that I would have bothered asking anyone else to fight my battle for me. I, alone, wanted to convince my dad to stick with the mission.

There were no others to help me except my mom and two brothers. But even then, they weren't willing to do anything except remain silent.

But it seemed like my dad would not accept that. He began to avoid me. Distraught, I would remind him about my mission and how much I needed to go to India to get my life back on track. I asked him repeatedly when we were going back.

I couldn't believe he treated me this way. Why was he denying his own son something he'd agreed to before? Why was he standing in the way of my mission, my one and only chance to heal myself? If he didn't let me go back, then the last six months—not to mention the last eight years of my life—would have all been for *nothing*. I would be screwed over again. This time, my brain and body might not recover from another attack.

My dad's silence only made me more depressed. I already felt down in the dumps, thinking about what I wanted for my life and how close I'd been to getting it. Despite Jith, I felt like I had made some progress in Kerala. Staying in America was not a good choice. I was in danger of losing everything I'd gained if I waited much longer.

Still, he skirted my questions and refused to give definite answers. We argued constantly. In fact, I had daily arguments with everyone in my immediate family, including my brothers. Our arguments often escalated into screaming matches, and our home became a nightmare.

CHAPTER 21

A HOUSE DIVIDED

Unity is strength,
division is weakness.
—Swahili proverb

I lost the next *two years*. I could not go back to India. My dad took two precious years from me, wasted them, all because he refused to listen to me.

Each day was the same. Each morning, over breakfast, I would kindly remind my dad that I really needed to go back. I asked, "Why are you not coming back with me? You told me before you left for Jack's funeral that we would return. Why aren't you upholding your promise? Please, just tell me why. I have to go back in order to move on with my life. Time is quickly slipping by."

My dad ignored me.

That always made me emotional. I felt abandoned and betrayed. No one listened to me or tried to understand why I wanted to go back. They all believed they knew better, that staying in America would serve me well and returning to India would be detrimental to my future.

I eventually realized my dad was not going to do anything to help me, despite my concerns. Each day my anger grew. I would dig up each of my bullying situations, letting them stew for a moment. Then, I'd tell my dad about each one in a long, drawn-out speech that would inevitably lead to a never-ending argument.

This repeated every day, and each time nothing changed. I felt myself drawing closer and closer to the edge of a mental cliff.

Chris and I got into a huge argument late one night. He was defending our dad, and I was having none of it.

"You're causing so many problems!" Chris screamed at me. "I'm failing my math class because of you. I can't concentrate on school because of all the arguing! This is all your fault!"

I was furious with Chris. I wasn't the real reason for his failure in college. "I'm not causing any of this! Your problems are all because of Dad. He won't listen to me!"

Chris had no sympathy for me and didn't give a damn about my past as a bullying victim or the other struggles I'd suffered. Despite everything that had happened to me, he turned against me.

Although my dad never ordered him to defend his decision, Chris felt like it was his duty. I was against my dad's decision, so he had to actively be against me. He aggressively treated me like the bad guy. If my dad had never forced me to stay in America, Chris would never have behaved like that toward me. My dad was influencing him.

Eventually, my dad intervened, and we separated to cool off.

The next morning, I noticed a police SUV in front of our house. I panicked. Was it a coincidence? Or had we fought so loud that a neighbor had called the police? I was sure that had to be the case. Someone had probably been walking by, heard our screaming, and called the police to issue a noise complaint. I worried about the SUV all day, but the police never came to talk to us.

Chris was very aggressive toward me each time we fought. We got into another argument a few days later. He went berserk, picked up my gaming laptop, and hit it on a wooden ledge inside the house. Luckily, my laptop was durable and didn't get damaged.

In a fury, Chris picked up a sharp object and threw it into a nearby upstairs wall. The object almost hit the television screen, missing only by inches.

The arguments also affected Jef. Once, while I was arguing with my dad, Jef became so pissed that he took my video game joystick and ripped it in half. It was an expensive piece of equipment, and he demolished it. These arguments were causing deep rifts between me, my dad, and my brothers. Would it ever be possible for them to be repaired?

What had I done to deserve this treatment from my family? Why was I their enemy? Why did I feel like a stranger to them? We were supposed to be a family!

These incidents swiftly spiraled out of control. My family continued to be upset and angry with me. I worried they would call the police or have someone take me away. It was a terrible living environment, but I didn't know what to do.

If the situation had been about Jef or Chris, it would have been a whole different story. When I was in high school, Jef went to India to study after graduation. My parents allowed that. They certainly didn't like it, but still allowed him to stay there. They even went with him to drop him off at his new college, traveling by train to Manipal in the state of Karnataka, near Kerala.

Jef was the oldest and the most promising son compared to Chris and me. They didn't want to upset Jef for fear that he would find a way to ruin or shame them.

I had told myself two years prior that I wanted to be the person to convince my father to let me go back to India. However, after so much time in a combative family environment, I wondered whether there were any other people my dad might listen to—anyone whose advice he might consider following. The only person I could think of was my uncle Saul, but he had sadly been dead for several years. Saul was my father's oldest brother and had, at one time, been the family patriarch.

Everyone in my family had respected him—not just because he was the oldest member, but because of his character. He was calm, wise, and respectful to everyone. I wished he were still alive. My dad had always looked up to his older brother, and I felt sure that Saul would have agreed with me about the importance of my mission.

However, that didn't matter now. There was no one else in the family that my dad would consider listening to, so I was out of luck. What else could I do but continue to argue?

One day, I got so angry that I hit my boiling point. I threw a chair over the ledge to the lower level. The sound was deafening, and one of the chair's legs went flying across the room. My family threatened to call the police. Thankfully, they didn't, but they did warn me that acting so out of control could warrant a police visit. They tried to scare me, so I wouldn't do things like that again.

It worked and I retreated.

The arguments continued, however, and I grew more frustrated and depressed each day. There was a never-ending cyclone of questions and worries spinning through my head. What if I never got back to India? What if I never got the chance to fix myself? What would become of me if I never found happiness again?

One day, while I watched a movie, Scott came over with his son and someone I didn't know. The three of them walking through the door flipped a sensor in my brain; something was going on.

The stranger smiled. "Hello," he said. "What are you doing?"

I narrowed my eyes. I did not know this stranger, much less trust him. I was right to be skeptical. He was a pastor and psychologist. My dad had asked Scott to bring him over to counsel me and help me with my anger.

I was floored. My family didn't care about my feelings. They only wanted damage control. I was pissed off at Scott and my dad; I left the room, furious.

The psychologist followed me upstairs. "Rick," he said, "I'm only here to help you. Can we talk for a few minutes?"

"No," I answered.

"Your family is worried about you. Will you listen to me? We can work on your issues."

"Why would I do that? I don't want to talk to you." I was firm, and fortunately, he respected my answer. He went back downstairs to talk to my family.

I wanted to believe my family had my best interests in mind, that they only wanted to help. But instead, I was certain they were just trying another way to dissuade me from going back to India.

I was stubborn, though. There was no way I would give up on my mission.

I felt like a bird in a cage. While they might provide me with necessities for life, I wasn't happy. Much like a bird, I wanted to get back to where I knew I was free and happy: India. No pastor was going to convince me otherwise.

CHAPTER 22

THE PARANOIA

You can outrun what is running after you,
but not what is running inside of you.
—Rwandan proverb

During the next two long, painful years in America, I continued to struggle with socialization. Once, while I stood in the backyard, one of my neighbors came out of his house.

"Hi!" he said, smiling and waving at me.

I froze up. I didn't know my neighbor well. We'd never spoken before, and while I saw him outside from time to time, we never interacted. What was I supposed to do? I couldn't think straight. So, I didn't respond. Instead, I turned and hurried back into the house.

Once I felt safe, frustration quickly took over. He was just being friendly, but I had panicked, just like I had done in high school time and time again. I was sure I had offended him. I would have been offended if the same had happened to me.

My anxiety, depression, and fear of judgment kept me from socializing and relating to people. My body had forgotten how to react to non-threatening approaches. My initial response was to assume each interaction would be painful.

It was a vicious cycle that made my anxiety, depression, and fear worse.

Scott visited again, this time by himself. I was upstairs on my computer, still emotional and angry after my latest interaction with the pastor. The last thing I wanted to do was see Scott.

Still, I heard him talking with my dad and went downstairs to prove a point. I started in on my dad with our usual topic, just like I did every day. I raised my voice, egged on by his silence. We were on the verge of yet another argument.

Scott tried to intervene and told me to go upstairs. I refused and raised my voice again. He stood up from his chair.

I then did something I'd never done before in my life. When he came toward me, I became even angrier and shoved him. At almost the same time, he pushed me too. We both stumbled back, surprised at the other's bold move, staring at one another for a moment. I had no intention of beating him up; I was just pushing him for show. It was a display of my displeasure toward him.

I wasn't sure he had the same motivations.

Then, my dad interceded and told both of us to get out of the room. I went upstairs, and Scott went home.

I replayed our interaction over and over in my head. I had made a huge mistake. It was completely unlike me—not what the real Rick would have done. I felt bad and hoped that I wouldn't do that again. I didn't want to make my situation worse. I tried to avoid negative thoughts and feelings, to learn from my mistakes and then move on.

Scott and I didn't talk for a long time, and he didn't visit my home for quite a while. My dad must have told him to stay away. No one wanted to risk any more problems.

A few weeks later, I dropped my mom off at the hospital in Desoto where she worked. When I returned home, my neighbor was once again outside. He greeted me again, complimenting my brother's sports car which I had been driving. I nodded back at him. He smiled, and I breathed a sigh of relief. He wasn't upset over our previous awkward interaction. I still felt guilty and frustrated with myself for the way I'd handled the original situation, which made me more certain that I needed to get back to India, back to where I could rediscover myself and find a way to be normal again.

My family continued to put off our return, ignoring my pleas and refusing to commit. Since it seemed like returning to India wouldn't happen any time soon, I finally decided to make the most of my situation while still in America.

I had always had an interest in computers. It had started with a love of video games, which I'd discovered in the fourth grade. That interest had remained strong. Video games were an escape for me; they distracted me from my life. I couldn't imagine living without video games.

After doing some research, I decided I needed to switch from a gaming laptop to a desktop for the best experience. I dove into learning about CPU, GPU, RAM, PSU, SSD, types of cases—anything and everything related to computers. It felt good to do a deep dive into something—to focus, learn, and grow. I scoured YouTube, forums, articles, and whatever else I could get my hands on.

I bought a new, smaller computer case and all the parts to build my computer through Amazon. I had some trouble with the CPU and spent a lot of time researching ways to fix it, putting a lot of time into troubleshooting. But I gained a lot of experience and knowledge as I channeled my efforts into something worthwhile. I felt accomplished and proud.

YouTube, though good for learning about computers, was also a good place to find other things I probably shouldn't have been watching. Driven by boredom and mild curiosity, I stumbled across conspiracy videos, starting with 9/11, and went down a rabbit hole. After that, I watched videos on the *Titanic*, the US monetary system, aliens, devil worship and cults, the Kennedy assassination, reptilian people, the New World Order, the mysterious pyramid with an eye on the US dollar bill, the Illuminati, alien implants, and so much more.

There were so many questions and theories. Some of them blew my mind. My opinions on many of those topics began to shift. It didn't even matter if the conspiracies were real or not; they changed my outlook. I learned to see from a wide angle, to look at the big picture, and question everything.

My hobby grew into an obsession. I loved watching conspiracy videos and researching theories online. Ultimately, paranoia crept in as well. I worried that the government was viewing my internet browsing history. I thought they might take an interest in me and start monitoring my activities.

One day while I was dropping my mom off at work, I saw a golden Crown Victoria behind me. I didn't think much about it at the time; nothing seemed odd. But the next day, I saw the same car in the next lane. Then, I saw it a third time. The driver even looked at me.

I almost never went outside other than to drop my mom off at work. So, if someone wanted to spy on me, those drives would be their only opportunity.

Since my mind was always on high alert, I often noticed weird situations that other people might not have seen. I made up stories, which may or may not have been true, to go along with the occurrences.

For example, an IT technician came to our home to fix our internet issues. We'd been having trouble with outages, our first problems since moving in. He checked outside of our home where the internet box was installed, then came inside to fix our router. I was anxious about people coming inside. I thought that, if he were a spy, he probably came to check on the target—me—face to face. I worried that he might have even planted a bug or malware somewhere in the router to monitor me more easily.

I wasn't sure if the whole situation was real or not. It felt real, but the rational side of my brain told me he was just a friendly repairman doing his job. Either way, I felt like I was crazy.

Hypothetically, if everything I feared was true, it puzzled me how I could have got their attention. Did it really only take watching conspiracy videos? Surely there had to be more to it than that. I honestly did not know.

Not only did I develop a fear of being watched, but I also came to fear that people I didn't know might know a lot about me. If someone was spying on me, were they also checking my family's phone records? Would they know about my bullying? Were they aware of my arguments with my family? I could only imagine some of the awful things I had said to my family that they could have overheard.

I wondered if the spies thought I had mental problems. Perhaps they believed I might hurt someone. Maybe they believed I was a menace to society. If they were watching me, they certainly knew that I wasn't acting normal.

I didn't know if the golden Crown Vic was, indeed, someone spying on me, a coincidence, or my imagination. Paranoia was definitely taking over. I tried to tell Chris about it, but he dismissed it.

So, I never brought it up to anyone else again.

While my interests in gaming, computers, and conspiracy theories were a welcome distraction, they didn't fix the root problem in my life. I was still sad and angry; I still longed, more than anything, to go back to India. Was it really impossible? Was there nothing I could do?

Then, I saw the movie *Interstellar*. In the movie, CASE—a robot character—tells the main character, Cooper, "It is not possible." Cooper replies, "No, it is necessary" while trying to dock their spaceship to their damaged, spinning, small space shuttle/mothership.

That quote resonated with me. Everyone around me dismissed my goals. It seemed like going back to India was impossible, but my mission was necessary. I had to get back.

Finally, I decided I had put it off long enough. In November 2015, I announced to my family that I was going to return to India on April 1st of 2016, no matter what.

My dad, surprisingly, relented—which was odd, since he hadn't responded about the subject for two straight years. Maybe he'd had enough of this violent and unstable environment.

He agreed to return to India with me.

CHAPTER 23

THE BULLY RETURNS

*If the camel once gets his nose in a tent,
the body will soon follow.*
—Saudi proverb

April arrived, and I did return to India. My mom had resigned her position at the hospital and came with us.

While I was waiting in line at the airport, I noticed a golden Crown Victoria parked a little way behind our vehicle. I was surprised to see that car again. I wasn't close enough to see any detail, but I was sure that it was the same one from my trips to the hospital. Shaking my head to clear out any cobwebs, I tried to keep calm. But the familiar feeling washed over me each time I looked at it.

I knew for sure that it was not a taxi. I couldn't see any driver or passengers inside the car. There were also no people standing near the car or bags beside it. It was just parked there, right behind my family car.

Was someone watching me?

I immediately thought back to my browsing history and all the hours of conspiracy theory videos I'd watched. I wondered if the FBI or other government agencies had found me suspicious and were surveilling me. Maybe my mind was playing tricks on me, but it seemed that I was being watched and followed—a scary thing to consider.

I tried to ignore my anxiety and focus on the mission ahead. I was cautiously hopeful. After putting my goals on hold for so long, I was finally going to get the chance to pursue myself and heal. But people had disappointed me before, so this time around, my hopes were not as high. I was no longer the excited person I'd been in 2013 during my first mission trip to India.

When we arrived in India at the Cochin International Airport, another odd event happened. As I stood near the baggage area, waiting for my parents to pick up our bags, a man in his fifties approached me.

"Excuse me, but I hope you wouldn't mind answering a few questions. Which flight did you just come from?"

I shrugged, not sure of the flight name.

"What country are you from?"

"America."

He nodded once, watching me closely. "Do you live in Kerala? Where?" He wore regular clothes, no uniform. Maybe he was just a random, curious passenger?

His questions became more unsettling. "What do you like to do?" he asked.

"I'm studying," I said, even though I wasn't. I grew suspicious.

"Oh! Where are you taking classes?"

I had a funny feeling in my gut that I should stop answering his questions. Something seemed off to me. I said, "I'm studying somewhere in Kerala."

"Yes, but where?"

"Somewhere in Kerala."

After that, he left. He was most likely part of airport security, but I had no way of being sure. By the time I asked him who he was, he had quickly moved away. He seemed like a regular passenger. But what normal passenger would ask any of those questions? Not to mention, he carried no luggage with him or any visible ID.

He could have seen me on their CCTV camera and thought I was acting suspicious. After all, I was lingering alone near the baggage area. Perhaps they noticed I had averted my eyes from the camera at the counter where they'd checked our passports. Perhaps, since I was a US citizen, they might have thought that I was an American spy. Who knew what was going on in their minds?

It was possible that asking questions was their standard procedure. If he was part of airport security, he just wanted to check me out. The whole situation was weird though, and my mind reeled with possibility after possibility. I was also angry. He'd asked me questions as if I were an idiot who'd give him all the information he wanted.

Finally, my parents retrieved our bags, and we left the airport and went home.

This time, I planned more carefully. I knew Jith would only serve as an unwelcome distraction, causing drama and chaos that would keep me from reaching my goals. I asked my dad not to bring him into our lives, confessing that Jith had bullied me the last time I'd been there. I needed to stay away from him in order to look for my happiness.

My dad agreed.

Yet, shortly after we arrived, Jith came to our door. I was stunned, angry, and completely brokenhearted. My dad had promised to support me. He'd promised not to involve Jith.

My heart thumped wildly with nervousness, and a wave of disappointment flooded over me.

As he walked in, Jith said hi to me. I reluctantly greeted him back. We shook hands.

My racing heart slowed a bit. Maybe he had changed? After all, it had been two years since we'd seen each other, and he seemed to have moved past his issues with me. So, I was optimistic about him. Why not?

I announced I was going to take a shower and left. About twenty minutes later, I came back from my shower to find Hansel's mom, Bethany, talking to my mom.

I gently greeted her, but she didn't hear me. It was slightly embarrassing. That was when I noticed Jith smiling wickedly before he turned away.

That was all it took. He still held a grudge against me! When I'd failed to introduce him to my relatives years before, he'd been embarrassed and insulted. Apparently, he wanted me to feel the same way. He was happy to see me embarrassed. He liked when I was hurt.

I had barely been in Kerala for a few days, and I was already back to feeling disappointed, angry, and very emotional. I had given Jith a chance, only to be stabbed in the back. He had betrayed me, abusing my trust. He had still not grown past his need to make me the butt of each of his pranks!

After a brief chat with my dad, Jith prepared to leave. I was watching him. He still wore a huge grin as if he'd accomplished something big. Even though he came to visit my dad, he'd been prepared to strike at me as soon as my dad turned his back. I knew he'd be happy the rest of the day, knowing he'd gotten in the first jab. He left shortly after.

Finally, it sank in: Jith didn't want to be nice to me. No matter what I did, there was going to be conflict with him if

I was in India. That set me to thinking. If I was going to find happiness, I'd have to face this situation head-on. Jith had made my life miserable before, and he would continue if I let him. I needed to cut him off, keep him from further ruining my fragile mental health.

My anger quickly turned toward my dad. "Why did you let him into our house?" I snarled. "That shouldn't have happened. You promised me you'd keep him out."

My dad didn't say anything as I was furious and emotional.

"That's the whole issue," I continued. "I don't want him to come in anymore, even if he shows up uninvited."

My dad didn't take it seriously. It was almost as if all our previous conversations about Jith's behavior hadn't happened. My dad had no problem continuing to let him in, despite what he'd done.

The next morning, my dad had some unfortunate news for me. "Last night, Bethany's husband Timothy came to our house. He heard you arguing and yelling at me, and he left." My dad's brow furrowed.

I worried that I might have given Timothy a bad impression of me. I didn't want to seem like a spoiled kid, even though I still felt justified. My dad knew that I needed to keep Jith out of my life.

The only time I'd been able to keep Jith at bay had been after Karl's funeral. I'd avoided him as much as possible, staying distant if we had to be near one another. He'd gotten the message without me causing a scene.

But I had been in a better place mentally then. I wasn't the same Rick now as I had been before I ended up stuck in America for two years. That Rick had been excited to take back his life, ready to move on and take on the world. That had all changed. I had been corrupted, which made it harder to accomplish my mission.

The ever-clever Jith realized that I wasn't the same person, that I was very vulnerable to any kind of psychological attack. He knew that my dad and I were not on great terms because of our frequent arguments.

He took advantage of that.

Jith used juvenile tactics to get at me, which became clearer once I'd settled into our house in Kerala. I had brought my expensive computer case to use for gaming. But the PSU (power supply unit) plug was only compatible with American outlets. I had purchased an extension cord with an adapter in 2013 and had stored it on top of a big wooden cabinet in our house. When I went to look for it, I couldn't find it. Instantly, I suspected Jith must have taken it after I'd left in 2013.

I asked my dad to ask Jith where the extension cord was. Of course, Jith denied knowing anything. He said I had probably misplaced it. I searched my home from top to bottom, but it was nowhere to be found. I knew exactly what was happening. Jith was messing with my head. I had no choice but to buy a new, expensive extension cord.

In the meantime, I found the card that had come with the missing extension cord, which had a picture of the cord on it. The next time Jith came over to my house, I showed him the card. "This is the extension cord that I'm missing," I said. "Have you seen it?" I watched his face for clues.

He didn't answer right away and looked guilty. "I don't know...maybe I've seen it. It could be in my house somewhere."

He knew I suspected him but didn't care. He knew I would not ask more questions, even if I knew for certain he had taken it. I was sure Jith would never give it back to me willingly.

There was only one way to find out.

A few days later, I was running errands with Jith's dad, Jay. When we went back to his house, I snuck into Jith's room to see if I could find the cord. Just as I expected—there it was. He had lied to my dad and me.

So, I took it back. The cord was mine, after all.

Back home, I showed my dad the cord and told him what had happened. Jith was a crook and had intentionally lied. My dad, unsurprisingly, brushed it aside as if it didn't matter.

As hard as I tried to avoid Jith, our lives appeared to be unfortunately and constantly connected. He came to our house one day and saw me using my mom's iPhone. iPhones were expensive compared to most other smartphones in India. It was a sign of wealth to have one.

"Oh," Jith said. "Those cost a lot of money, right?" His lip curled, and there was a glint of hate and maliciousness in his eyes. He was judging me; he viewed us as rich and snooty. He'd always been jealous of my family's status. Jith was a hard worker but hadn't had the same opportunities I did.

Another time, he showed up and asked if I had seen his cricket bat. He was concerned because it was expensive. His question confused me. The only bat I had was one that Hansel had given to me in 2013. I'd left it at the house in India when I'd gone back to America, and I'd recently lent it to another friend.

Jith was very sure of himself and insisted that was his bat. He said, "Please get the bat back."

"I will."

He narrowed his eyes and hissed, "You'd better get my bat back." There was anger behind his gaze.

This kind of behavior continually appalled me. Jith was erratic and he could turn on me in a split second, asking nicely one second and spitting fire at me the next. This time, he made his threat in a straight-up thuggish way. All of this went back to the fact he'd felt I'd insulted him two years ago. As a result, he continued to make me miserable with insults and other unkind actions. He even did it in my own house!

Years later, I learned Jith had taken the old bat Hansel had given me from my house, sold it, and bought a more expensive one which he had left there in its place. He hadn't bothered to tell me about that, hoping for an opportunity to seek revenge against me.

Just days later, Jith came to ask me for it again. I told him that one of my friends was using it at a nearby playground, and we could pick it up from him. Jith agreed, and we went to find my friend.

I beckoned my friend over and asked for the bat, letting him know the bat wasn't really mine. He flashed me a confused look but quickly handed me the bat so I could give it to Jith.

Jith carefully looked it over and put the bat on the back seat of his car. He started to drive again.

Instead of going back to my house, Jith took me to a new place, a paddy field a little way from my home. I sighed. He wasn't going to let this go without a little more fun. I kindly asked him to drop me off at my home, but he declined.

"It's fine, Rick. Let's play with some of my friends."

I had to go along with him; I couldn't just open the door and jump out while the car was moving. Why was he forcing me to hang out with him when he so clearly didn't like me?

While he drove, he said, "Hey, Rick. I've been looking for a girl. I want to marry a girl who's living in America."

I was surprised and a little concerned by that. If he married a girl from the US, then he would eventually live there.

But I had my doubts too. No girl would just marry a man who came from a low-income family. He wasn't from the middle class like most American girls. It was unlikely that an American girl's parents would want their daughter to marry someone like Jith.

Jith was trying to elevate his status by marrying a foreign girl so he could be like my father. That was part of why he'd worked so hard to gain my father's trust. If my dad was backing him, he could recommend him as a suitable partner to a well-to-do girl, even if he wasn't exactly in a financial position to court a girl.

I knew he could do it, and I was worried because if he arrived in America, we would definitely cross paths with each other. That was not a good thing for me. He would destroy my mental well-being even further.

A few days later, we had some power outages in our area after a vehicle crashed into a post that supported the power lines. The lack of power and internet frustrated me. I wanted to play a game, but there was no way I could.

"We should just go back to America," I said sarcastically.

The next day, Jith and his mom visited. My mom jokingly told Martha that I wanted to go back to America.

Before she could explain the context of my comment, Jith piped up and said, "Then why not just go back?" He gave me an ugly look. My mom and Martha didn't notice, but I saw him openly criticizing me.

He clearly wanted me gone.

CHAPTER 24

ABANDON SHIP

If the heart is empty,
the rest will soon abandon you too.
—Arabic proverb

After a while, living in India became torture. I'd come there to find sanctuary, to find myself, and the key to my happiness. I hadn't realized that my happiness (or unhappiness) lived in my mind, not in a place.

I became paranoid, depressed, and anxious. My appetite went away. I grew too anxious to go outside or leave my room. I just slept and stayed in bed day after day. The fog in my mind grew thicker and deeper; I couldn't think straight or face the world.

All the charm that I had back in 2013 was lost. I developed symptoms of panic attacks, my most vulnerable moments. These were the first signs of the psychotic disorder I was suffering from; I just didn't know it yet.

One day, sometime in the middle of June, my dad's younger cousin Bren came to visit. He invited us to go to his house. My head pounded at the thought of leaving. I just wanted to go back to bed. But not wanting to be rude, I agreed.

As we were riding to his house, I became very anxious. My breath came out in short gasps, and my chest constricted tightly. Then my dad seized his own chest. My eyes snapped up to him, concerned. He looked at me, clearly in pain.

"Something is wrong," he gasped. "I need to go to a hospital right away."

I didn't know what was going on, but something was happening to both of us. Ben drove us to a nearby hospital.

They rushed my dad in for tests. All they told us was that his blood pressure had spiked. They gave him some medicine and let him rest. Later, they determined he was under strain and experiencing anxiety.

I wondered if that had to do with me.

While the nurses were tending to my dad, my mom noticed my face. I was pale, panting, and had huge drops of sweat rolling down my face. My body seemed to be on vibrate mode. I did not look good.

She worried that the same thing that had happened to my dad was happening to me. She called over a nurse to check my blood pressure. That's when they discovered an erratic heartbeat.

A doctor named Ranny checked on me, then took me into her office. She was also my dad's doctor, the only one on call. She smiled at me. "Your heartbeat is unusual. It's quick and erratic. We don't see that often in a healthy young person. At twenty-four, your heartbeat should be regular and much slower. Is something making you anxious or panicked?"

"I...don't know," I answered. I didn't have the words to explain what had been going on with me, how panicked and worried I'd been recently.

She told me I needed to stay in the hospital for a while. This was no ordinary hospital. It was the Clinical and Research Center for Neuro-Behavioral Science; basically, a mental hospital. They weren't just going to send me home until they understood what was happening to me.

Later that evening, I threw up and had trouble digesting my food. I panicked again and couldn't seem to calm down.

Eventually, my dad's pains faded away. He returned to normal, feeling fine. My shakes seemed to disappear too, but my emotions were all over the place. At the end of our first full day in the hospital, they only released my dad. They kept me overnight because they knew I was having a mental health crisis, and they wanted to do something about it.

I wanted nothing more than to stay in my hospital room. The idea of staying stationary made my panic just a little easier to handle. But the doctor did not want me to be shut in. She encouraged me to play tennis with some other patients.

She asked her assistant to take me to the indoor tennis court. Reluctantly, I agreed. As she led me to the court, I saw rooms with bunk beds and patients wearing blue uniforms. They were already out of their rooms for a walk around an indoor stadium. They weren't allowed outside for safety reasons.

At the courts, the doctor introduced me to another player. He was old and mentally disabled. He had a childlike understanding of the world, but was kind, happy, and enjoyed playing tennis. It delighted him to get a partner. I didn't want to play, but I put on a brave face. I didn't want his feelings to be hurt.

I played tennis with him several times over the next few days, and actually enjoyed myself. The doctor cheered me on as she passed by. Each morning, the nurses would come in, check my vitals, and record the results in my chart.

After a few days, Dr. Ranny called me into her office. "Rick," she said after I took a seat, "sometimes, chemical imbalances inside a person's brain can cause mental health conditions much like those you're experiencing. Sometimes, these things are caused by genetics. Your parents told me about Karl, that he was sick too, but they didn't know what he had. Sometimes, other family members can influence our mental health, even if we aren't directly related to them like a mother or father or brother. However, using that information, doctors like me can sometimes pinpoint what illness a patient is suffering from and whether genetics or their environment caused it."

She was trying to gently tell me I could have a condition without working me up. But I didn't believe her. Even if she'd told me plainly that I had a mental illness, I probably wouldn't have accepted the truth. I wouldn't have taken it seriously.

Another day, she told me about a film, *A Beautiful Mind*.

I told her, "I saw part of that movie during high school in America." *A Beautiful Mind* was about a mathematician who had schizophrenia and battled it throughout his life. By the end, he understood his condition and recovered from it. The movie was good; I remembered seeing it in Mr. Murphy's history class.

She said, "Many people have had mental conditions before, but they overcame their mental condition because they didn't give up the fight. They are now leading normal lives. You can do that too."

During one of my last days at the hospital, Dr. Ranny again called me into her office. She said kindly, "Rick, you have to do something about your illness. If you don't, you might get trapped here in the dark place you're experiencing. You need to push yourself harder to get better."

I knew that part of what she was saying was true. Patients needed to take advantage of their good days by seeking counseling. If they didn't, their mental illness could worsen, making it harder for them to ever recover.

She continued, "After you get this sorted out, find a girl to marry!" She smiled widely at me.

I giggled. I still felt strongly about the vow I'd made when I was little—to never get married or have any romantic feelings about anyone. That was not on my list of things to do.

I eventually grew restless in the hospital. It felt like I was in prison. I tried to relax and sleep peacefully, but every time I tried to rest, Jith popped into my mind. I couldn't block him out.

My parents spent a lot of time visiting me, and they watched me try to get out of bed over and over. They tried to calm me down, but I couldn't be calmed. Eventually, fatigue caught up to me, and I finally got some sleep.

My dad told me that Jef was coming to India to see our grandparents. That led him into talking about Jef's marriage. I knew he wasn't trying to be rude; he was just trying to make conversation. I couldn't help but wonder, though, if he felt Jef was more important than my mental situation. That disappointed me. He was acting the same as always, like I didn't matter as much.

***

After two long weeks, the doctor said I was doing great and was ready to go home. Finally, I could get back to normal. Relief washed over me. It was about time.

I didn't know it then, but Dr. Ranny had officially diagnosed me with "unspecified non-organic psychosis." The American equivalent of unspecified non-organic psychosis is "psychosis NOS (not otherwise specified)." Psychosis occurs when a person loses some contact with reality. People with psychosis may experience hallucinations or delusions. I didn't hallucinate, but I had delusions, like my concerns about American and Indian spies watching me or people insulting and embarrassing me because I was not mature. I definitely lost touch with reality at those moments.

If a patient has some kind of confirmed psychosis but the doctor doesn't have the time to find the right name for it, they call it "unspecified non-organic psychosis" during initial documentation. This was my first official diagnosis. Dr. Ranny didn't know which psychosis I had. She needed more time for tests before she could call it something specific, like schizophrenia or bipolar disorder.

Upon my release, she turned over copies of my medical records to my parents but didn't show any of them to me. She only mentioned that I had a mental condition.

My parents didn't tell me about my diagnosis either.

Maybe they didn't want me to know in case I took it badly. I know they don't like to discuss mental health, mostly because they don't truly understand it. Perhaps they wanted me to move forward like a normal person. To be honest, I probably wasn't prepared to handle such information then. I couldn't even acknowledge it, although it would have been a prime opportunity to learn more about it. But I would have, at least, considered my actions before making dumb mistakes.

If only I hadn't been left in the dark for so long…

Before we left, I considered asking for an MRI to see if something was wrong. I'd always wondered. I told my parents about my idea, and they talked to Dr. Ranny.

Dr. Ranny warned me that MRIs were good at finding brain tumors and other physical brain injuries, but that it was hard to find psychological problems in a scan. She told me that if I had mental health issues, they were unlikely to show up on an MRI.

Still, she gave us the paperwork to get an MRI at a hospital in Koothattukulam. I was very anxious when the day of my MRI came. I'd never seen a machine like that in real life before, only in the movies.

The scan showed nothing, just as my parents had expected. Overall, that was good news. We left the hospital, and I drove us toward my mom's home in Kaduthuruthy. Soon, though, I felt nervous and panicked. I stopped on the side of the road and switched seats with my dad, letting him drive the rest of the way. This was unsettling, considering I'd just been released from the mental hospital.

A few days after my release, my dad and I saw Jith—the person I most dreaded to see on the face of the entire planet. My dad greeted him. Jith mentioned he was trying to become a guest lecturer at a local college. He could teach students, though not at the same level as actual professors. He had to take a difficult test first before he could do that.

That surprised me. He was once again trying to move up the ladder in the college world. His attitude and manipulative behavior would not fit in that setting. A long time before that, he'd tried to become a police officer, just like his father. He'd also tried to become a soldier. But those jobs didn't work out for him, likely because of his constant need to be the alpha male. However, he rarely displayed the same attitudes toward anyone who wasn't me. If he'd acted that way toward recruiters, he wouldn't have been able to join. His attempts to get into those fields told me he was always striving for higher status, no matter what.

Now he was trying to teach kids, just like my dad. I didn't think he could empower, inspire, and instill good qualities in his students while bullying others on the side. The whole idea behind Jith's push to become a professor was not to inspire but to claim power and social status. That way, he could get acceptance from people of high status or with high influence in society.

He knew life was moving on, and he just couldn't stay in one place. He had to rise up, or he wouldn't get what he wanted. He needed power...lots of power. He was a very ambitious person and had already joined the dark side. He always aimed higher to become successful. He would do anything and everything required. Power drove him.

He'd applied to several colleges, but they hadn't accepted him.

My dad said, "I can recommend you to Saint Stephen's College in Uzhavoor."

Jith tried not to appear too excited, but I could tell he was thrilled. I, on the other hand, was irritated beyond belief.

I'd told my dad about Jith's bullying behavior, yet here he was, offering to recommend him for a position that he wanted. Unbelievable.

This was becoming a dangerous situation for me. My bully was becoming more and more powerful day by day. I remembered when Jith had told me about finding a girl in America. If he became a professor or teacher, he had a higher chance of getting a marriage proposal from a like-minded woman in America. My dad could even recommend him to other family members, and those families might consider him as a candidate for marrying their daughters.

I was too scared to even imagine that scenario.

A couple of days after my release, Martha invited my family over to her house for dinner. I was heading right into Jith's house again, his territory. I dreaded it.

As we ate dinner, he lobbed a well-disguised insult at me. The insult was so poetic, artistic, and creative that even I couldn't repeat the sentence afterward. I'd never heard him speak like that before, much less say something so incredible that I wasn't able to repeat.

He hadn't just come up with that in the moment. He had prepared and waited for an opportunity to say it in front of everybody. He was undoubtedly proud of himself.

My family didn't notice, but Uncle V, Jith's uncle, did. His body language betrayed how uncomfortable he was. He knew Jith had aimed his insult at me. Uncle V wasn't aware of all the drama going on between us, but he could tell something was off.

Jith thrived on the fact that I came all the way to India and still failed my mission. He knew my dad had decided that we should go back to America, and he'd wanted to get in one last jab before I left, just like he had in 2013. He knew I wouldn't be coming back again, at least not with the goal of finding myself and my happiness.

From that moment on, my mental health continued to deteriorate; I got worse and worse. Jith had pressed heavily on the deep wounds running through my emotions. He'd done his best to be sure I was miserable. I couldn't eat or sleep. I had frequent panic attacks. Jith clouded my mind with fear.

Worst of all, my very concept of India was forever tainted by him. Things weren't better for me there; and now, they never could be. Going back to India was now one of my worst experiences, just like the bullying I'd endured in eighth grade had been.

I had no choice but to return to America, defeated. All my hard work over the past eleven years had been for nothing. My mission had failed miserably, and I still wasn't out of the deepest part of my personal Mariana Trench yet.

CHAPTER 25

THE LOWEST POINT

It is a long road
that has no turning.
—Irish proverb

When I came back to the US, I had nothing. I had been so sure I would find my way in India, but I only ended up failing. Depression overtook me. I felt empty, hopeless, and alone. Each day seemed more and more impossible as that foggy feeling that always seemed to linger grew darker and darker, forming a permanent black cloud in my brain.

Surprisingly, after our return I didn't fight with my family. I didn't get angry at them or insist on working on my mission. Instead, I just felt empty, unmotivated.

Maybe "emotionless" is a better way to describe it. I didn't feel like I was really alive; I was just going through the motions of things I *had* to do each day instead of truly living. The fire in my belly that had once kept me going had gone completely out. The coals were no longer even smoking. Whatever had driven me to move forward had vanished. I'd lost everything and vanished into a black hole of depression and anxiety.

For the next few months, I stayed inside my bedroom; there was no reason for me to come out. I didn't shower or change my clothes. Even simply brushing my teeth was too much effort. I had no peace. Instead, an endless loop of disbelief at my miserable failure played in my mind. I wondered how this had happened, despite everything I'd done to move forward. The depths of that feeling went far beyond anything I'd ever felt before. I felt like a cold, dead person with no soul, lost at the bottom of the ocean.

My family went on with their lives as though nothing had happened. It seemed they only cared about Jef's and Chris' futures, their marriages, but not me or my future.

I wasn't asking to be married, and it wasn't very realistic at that stage, anyway. The only thing I had ever asked was to get my life back. I'd only needed to be in India for six to twelve months. My family only needed to support me during that short time.

I'd never tried to get them to buy me toys, candy, or whatever was popular at the time when I was just a small kid. Getting better and fixing my life was the only thing I'd ever asked for. I would have done everything by myself if it had been possible, putting less strain on my dad. Yes, he'd taken me to India, but that's where his support stopped. He hadn't listened to me or shown me any respect. All he gave me was the bare minimum. It wasn't enough. I needed respect, and he couldn't give it to me.

None of it mattered now, though; all was lost. There was no recovery to be had. My spirit—that I had nurtured and struggled to maintain since I was in eighth grade—was no longer with me. It was dead.

I became quiet...very quiet. For the first time in a long time, our home was silent—not chaotic like it had been for the past few years. There was no more shouting, no more begging, and no more anger. No one caused a scene. The war between myself and my family members seemed officially over.

I sat alone in my room and asked myself, *Now, what the hell am I going to do? What is the next step for me?*

Even though I'd failed my mission, I was still desperate to move on somehow. I thought about how much precious time I'd lost, how much was still wasting away as I hid in my bedroom. I had to learn to keep my sanity in check and move forward to new and better things.

There had to be other ways to move on with my life. While I was in India, I'd seen so many people my age moving to new stages of their lives. They got married, had children, found steady jobs, and looked toward the future with hope. They accomplished things.

So what was I doing wrong? Where was I going? What did I want to accomplish with my life?

I had no answers but knew I had to find some. I had to take a step in the right direction. I decided to look for a job—something I'd never considered before.

My aunt Lucy worked at the airport five days a week. She thought I could get a job there too. I took a leap of faith. Getting a job would move me in the right direction, make me feel like I was accomplishing something.

My cousin Sophia, Aunt Lucy's daughter, helped me apply for a job at the airport. Two weeks later, I was hired. I was very proud of myself.

Lucy and I commuted to work together because we worked at the same facility. We even saw each other while we were doing our assigned tasks.

At first, everything was going well at my first day on the job. My boss was also a Malayali, and there were a few other Malayali coworkers as well. This put me at ease. My boss even paired me up with a Malayali trainer around my dad's age who told me how to do everything. I couldn't keep up with him completely, but I started picking up on the job and what I needed to do.

At least until doubts started creeping in and taking over.

I thought about school, about college, and about going to India and failing my mission. Everything I had tried to succeed at had backfired. Everything had led to misery. Wouldn't this job end the same way?

My confidence wavered. I believed I couldn't be successful. My mind got foggy again, and I couldn't maintain my focus.

My Malayali trainer told me that this job wasn't for young people like me. He wasn't trying to be rude, and it did not surprise me to hear him say that. People my age were supposed to have higher salary jobs. Most people believed I should aim higher and try to get a job within my skillset. If I stayed at the airport and didn't improve, I could end up employed there forever. I only got the job because I had no other options. I could move up the ladder eventually if I succeeded.

Throughout the day, my coworkers laughed and joked around. I couldn't interact or keep up with them because I still didn't know how to socialize. My body went into panic mode. I sweated and felt as though I were vibrating. I couldn't think straight. I felt sick and had an overwhelming urge to get out of there. I needed the comfort and isolation of my bedroom, not to be out in the world, trying to work. I wasn't cut out for this.

As the day ended, Sophia came to pick me up. "How was your first day?" she asked, smiling.

I hesitated. "It was fantastic," I lied. I just wanted to get home as quickly as possible.

Despite my reservations about my abilities, I went back for a second day. I accidentally dropped a food cart and broke a couple of plates. I panicked, assuming I would be in big trouble.

My partner told me it was okay. I didn't get into any trouble at all. I was relieved. But I couldn't calm my anxiety. By the end of the day, all I wanted to do was to crawl back into bed.

The pressure got to me. I wasn't focusing, and I didn't feel like I was doing a good job. The anxiety was too much to bear. So, the next day, I stayed home and called my boss. "I have to quit," I told him.

"Oh," he said, surprised. "Why are you leaving? Did you find a different job already?"

I didn't correct him. What was I supposed to say? I couldn't tell him I was too anxious, and I kept panicking at the thought of going back to work. "Yes. I'm sorry. I have to quit."

By the end of the day, I was second-guessing myself. I regretted quitting. I called my boss back to see if it was too late to keep the job. "If it's possible, could I come back to work tomorrow?"

"All right," he sighed. "I'll give you another shot."

I told myself that everything was going to be better, that I could control my anxieties and fears. I would get through the next day of work with no issues.

The next day, my boss asked me to come in to work earlier than usual. Within a couple of hours, my worries became so bad that I couldn't focus, and I kept panicking. I tried to control myself, but I knew my efforts were useless.

I went to my boss. "I'm sorry. I made a mistake in keeping this job. I can't work here anymore."

"Rick," he said gently, "you should not have come back to work then. I gave you a second chance, and you promised you wanted to continue." He was kind but clearly irritated at me, and he had a right to feel that way.

I was upset with myself. I felt like I had let him down. What choice did I have, though? I couldn't keep my fear from taking over. I gave him my ID, and he told me I would receive a check in the mail for the three days I had worked.

I called Sophia to see if she could come to pick me up. She couldn't, but her parents came to get me. I didn't know what to say to them. Finally, when we arrived at my house, I told the truth with a half-hearted smile. "Today was my last day of work. I quit my job."

The news shocked and concerned them, but I didn't tell them what had happened. I was embarrassed and a little ashamed. I really thought I could do it.

I completely ditched the idea of having a job. Still, I hoped that someday, I could overcome my mind and find a way to be successful and productive.

In the meantime, though, I began spiraling into the most intense depression I had ever experienced. I'd failed in my mission of going to India to get better. My dad's refusal to help, combined with my own fragility, had made sure of that. Now, I'd failed in America at my first job. My mental health had kept me from moving forward with my life.

This was one of the lowest periods of my life.

Each day, I grew more depressed, feeling like there was a huge pressure on my chest that kept me from breathing or moving. I couldn't eat. All I did was stay in my room and try to sleep each day away. I retreated from my life and from everyone around me.

CHAPTER 26

CRAZY IDEAS

When the head does not work,
the legs suffer.
—Romanian proverb

During this period, thoughts of suicide crept into my mind. I found myself thinking that I would do anything to take the pain away—that if I wasn't alive, I wouldn't have to face the pressures that were crushing me. I could be free.

At first, those ideas were fleeting: an image here, an idea there. Soon, though, they grew into full-fledged fantasies.

I could be free.

Even better, ending my life would make my family suffer. I was furious at them for not supporting me, for not helping me to heal, and for always expecting me to just "get over it." If I killed myself, they would feel pain and realize how serious I'd been about needing a change. The thought of revenge consumed me.

Three vivid suicidal fantasies formed in my mind.

In the first, I would convince my brothers to go with me to the shooting range. After we arrived, I'd pick up a handgun, hold it tightly, and peer down the barrel as I released several rounds into the field. Then, in a flash, I'd turn the gun to my head and pull the trigger. It would be quick and painless.

In another of my fantasies, I would go to the community pool or a nearby deep pond late at night. I'd step into the water and pull myself under. The water would fill my lungs until I passed out and drowned. My lifeless body would then float to the surface. But that fantasy was scary...it would not be a fast death.

In my final fantasy, I would slip into my kitchen and take a large knife. I'd bring it into the bathtub and cut my own wrists or throat. My blood would seep into the bathtub, and I'd die, leaving my body behind to horrify my family. However, that would be neither quick nor painless.

I kept these suicidal thoughts very private. My family couldn't see that I was harboring these ideas.

My suicidal urges were real, however. I honestly wanted to die. I wanted to find peace through what seemed like my only available outlet. I didn't want to stay trapped in this situation anymore.

In reality, I didn't have the guts to go through with any of my plans.

My mind started devising other ideas, other ways I could spread my pain to the world through publicity stunts, ways that I could die without being the one to do it.

I pictured myself bringing a small bag of fireworks and balloons into the cafeteria of my old middle school. I'd go in the morning when all the students gathered there before class. I would forcefully get inside the school while kids were exiting the school bus. I'd quickly move to the front of the crowd, then light the fireworks and throw them into any nearby open space. I would also pop balloons, so it would sound like gunshots.

The students would scream and run away as the firecrackers and balloons exploded. Everyone's attention would be on what I had done. I'd surrender myself right away. The school security officers would either shoot me, thinking I was a mass shooter, or arrest me and take me away from my life.

That fantasy soon morphed into one where I would be sure to die. I'd get an airsoft rifle and paint the orange tip black so it would look like a real rifle. Then, I'd dress up like a scary-but-cool-looking soldier in a camouflage outfit, complete with full military-style gear, and cover my face with a mask or wear a balaclava. I would get all these items from the website that sells airsoft products. Of course, I would only get blank-firing weapons, not real ones.

I'd take the airsoft rifle into a school and take some students hostage, forcing the security officer to shoot and kill me in order to save everyone else.

I knew I'd die in that scenario, but I'd die in style. Even better, I wouldn't have to be the one to do it. My pain would go away. I'd leave behind a suicide letter so that everyone would know my story.

Deep down, I knew I'd never do any of those things. They weren't me. I couldn't inflict emotional damage on innocent bystanders. Sometimes, I felt disgusted for even having these fantasies. I was just so lost and tired of my misery.

During these dark times, one idea did involuntarily come into my mind—an idea which I hadn't expected. This was even more evil than the suicidal thoughts or the school publicity stunts. This was the worst of the worst.

It was about my dad. In my mind, he needed to share at least part of the blame for how miserable I'd become. He'd let everything fall like dominoes. I was still furious at his betrayal. The way he spoke to me made me even angrier. His life was normal, and he enjoyed every bit of it. He didn't give a damn about me and refused to do anything to improve my life.

I burned with rage. My father was torturing me. I wanted to escape, to react to his strikes and get out from under his thumb.

I'm embarrassed that I ever thought of this, but I actually thought about hurting my dad, stabbing him with a kitchen knife. I didn't really want to *kill* him. I just wanted to show him he could no longer ignore me, wanted him to know that he'd hurt me deeply, that I was pissed off at him for ignoring and neglecting me all those years—and breaking his promise, which caused me to fail my mission. I thought that would finally make him come to his senses.

However, the idea of physically hurting my dad was hard to imagine. Even if I truly had wanted to stab him, I'm not sure I had the guts to even raise my hands to him, knife or no knife. I would likely chicken out, and someone would call the cops on me. My life and legacy would be over forever, but not the way I wanted it to be. I would become known as someone with serious mental problems, and my story would turn tragic. The perpetrators would be free from consequences forever while I spent my life paying for them.

Luckily, the idea of harming my dad came and went in a flash. I realized it wasn't good to keep those sorts of ideas cooped up inside my brain. I could get into deep, deep trouble later with law enforcement if I ever tried to act on them, and I could never come back from something like that.

So, I pushed the ideas out of my head for good.

These fantasies were wicked and did not reflect who I truly was. Back then, though, I was so low, so depressed that I couldn't stop them from forming. I never actually intended to follow through or hurt anyone, especially not myself or my family. But as I laid in bed, surrounded by a cloud of depression, unable to sleep, these ideas came to mind. They were my entertainment in a world where nothing brought me joy or comfort.

***

I was miserable, unable to contribute to society and unable to move forward with my life. I was getting desperate and needed to find a way to get my life up and running again.

I thought about my past, my childhood, my adolescence in America, and even my years of failure in India. One thing that I'd always loved was going to the movies. So many movies had shaped me, inspired me, and changed me. So, I started going to the theater again, searching for ways to improve myself. I went to the movies often with Chris.

Even though the theater was my place of joy, I often felt awkward and uncomfortable. Chris would ask if I wanted to see a movie. I would be excited about going, so I would agree. But then, during the movie, I would feel dark and depressed. I told myself that I wouldn't go to the movies again. But then, Chris would approach me again later, and I would agree once more.

I didn't understand why I was sometimes full of life and ready to enjoy myself, and sometimes felt so low. I knew nothing back then about *manic episodes* and *depressive episodes*. I was just lost, confused, and frustrated. I didn't understand how an activity I loved could make me feel so low at the same time.

Even my physical health was changing. For the first time, I gained a lot of weight. People who knew me noticed I was a few pounds heavier. My clothes didn't fit comfortably.

In mid-2017, my grandfather died at age eighty-seven. We returned to India for a month to lay him to rest and be with our family in Kaduthuruthy. A big part of me dreaded going back because of Jith.

I never knew when he was going to attack me, especially after I'd become his personal punching bag, liable to be attacked at every turn. Everything he said had a sharp dagger behind it, ready to pierce my heart and soul at a moment's notice.

I absolutely could not face any more of the mental torture he'd put me through, but this time I wanted to put a stop to his behavior the moment he tried to attack me with an insult. I wasn't sure where this new, tough exterior had come from, but I was ready to live inside it, excited to feel powerful after all this time spent as Jith's victim.

Soon after we arrived, Jith came into the room I shared with Chris to greet us. He said hi to me, then started chatting with Chris. There were no weird remarks, looks, or insults. I was relieved but still on guard.

After a little while, we went outside. Jith showed us his new car. "What do you think?" He grinned.

I wondered why he'd bought it. It was a small car, and he already had another one. But I didn't want to engage with him too much, and he left shortly after.

Surprisingly, Jith left me alone. I found out he had taken a job as a TA at a college, a step in his plan to become a professor. I was shocked. Being a teacher or professor was a highly respectable job. Average people would call them "sir." In America, it was common to be called "sir" most of the time. But in India, it was unusual. You had to have a respectable occupation to earn that title.

Most of the time, people in these positions had power, and Jith liked power and would do anything to gain it. I was worried about what his newfound power could mean for me, but his job kept him busy and distracted. At least, that kept me safe.

I refused to forgive him for his past mistakes and was planning to not let him get away with it, but I was also relieved that he was no longer targeting me. I'd lived five years in misery because of him and his manipulative mind games. I was careful not to let my relief let him somehow catch me off guard. I knew there was a possibility he might attack again.

A few days after my grandfather's funeral, we returned to our home in Kerala. I'd brought my gaming laptop, and I needed the extension cord again. The last time we had been in India, I had put it inside a locked steel cabinet after I had gotten it back from Jith's house.

When I went to look for it, it was missing again. Nobody had access to the steel cabinet except for Jith's dad, Jay. My dad had given him keys to the house, so he could keep an eye on our things. This time, I was even surer that Jith was responsible. I was already tired of his antics, and this was a repeat of a previous silly incident. He had to know he wasn't going to fool me this time.

Jith was busy with his new life, teaching and renovating his house. One day, Chris and I visited him, and he was excited to give us a tour and show everything off. Afterward, he told us he needed to take a shower because he had to go somewhere soon. I took that opportunity to search for my cord in his room. Sure enough, once again it was right there. I couldn't believe he had taken it again, but I was relieved to have it back. I took it without confronting him, leaving it at my mom's family home so that I didn't have to play his childish game again.

One evening, while sitting on our front porch, I told Chris about Jith. Chris didn't know about my negative experiences with him.

I said, "Hey, Chris. Jith is not a good guy. He is not a good friend. Don't hang out with him and be careful around him." I didn't want Chris to fall into one of Jith's traps, especially if the two of them had a confrontation. I knew Chris was tough, and Jith would know immediately since he was always watching out for people who could be potential adversaries or threats, always scanning his surroundings.

By warning Chris, I felt safer, and I wanted Chris to feel safe too. It slightly surprised him to hear what I said about Jith, and he noted my concern. He said, "Okay. Hmm..."

A few nights later, Jith came to our house. He actually chose to target Chris, which caught me by surprise. Jith blamed Chris for something insignificant that happened. The two of them had never had much of a relationship before, with very few interactions. I didn't know what Jith was really upset about or why he suddenly caused a scene. But as soon as Jith complained, Chris looked at him sharply and replied, "I don't know what you are talking about. Ask someone else to answer your question."

Jith quickly backed off and stopped talking to him, which was also surprising to me. He spoke aggressively and hadn't expected Chris' quick, equally aggressive reply. Jith knew Chris was not just a dog who barked; he could also bite hard if he chose. That was not the reaction Jith really wanted. He realized he would get hurt if he continued to push Chris, which could be embarrassing considering the people who could be watching. So, he quickly backed off without responding.

To me, Jith's behavior seemed almost cowardly. He would pick fights with and destroy those who couldn't or wouldn't fight back; yet, he wouldn't engage with an intelligent, tough person like Chris, who was sure to beat him at his game.

Realizing this left me feeling funny inside. In fact, I thought, *Oh…Poor Jith!*

That day, for the first time in a long time, I was very proud of Chris. I was proud that he'd handled the situation perfectly. Others would have been stunted by Jith's quick attack, but Chris didn't falter. It made me feel better for previously telling him about Jith's unfriendly behavior. I was proud of Chris for standing up to Jith. Chris was not weak, and I witnessed it firsthand. I felt good and happy. Finally, someone in my family stood up to Jith.

Jith once again came to my house during my last days in Kerala. He convinced me to go with him to a local shop near our home. Near our destination was another shop; one of the local men I'd known since I was a kid worked there, and he'd recently started to sell fish and fish-related products. He had always been poor and didn't have much cash. Whenever he got cash, he used it to buy beer.

Jith pulled some cash from his wallet and gave it to the man, who thanked him for the free money. I wondered why Jith would do that.

After we left, Jith put his hands on my shoulders and quietly said, "You know, Rick, sometimes, you have to give these low-level, stinky, dumb idiots some money so we can gain their loyalty and respect."

I was appalled. I thought, *Wow! This is how he views other people.*

Luckily, my last few days passed without any other incidents or interactions with Jith, and we returned to America. Upon our return, my energy rose from the depths of my soul, and I was ready to create a new life plan so I would never be at my lowest ever again.

CHAPTER 27

GETTING HELP

Help me during the flood,
and I will help you during the drought.
—Tanzanian proverb

I continued trying to get my life back on track. Even though I struggled, I found solace and positivity wherever I could. I took a hard look at myself and realized again, though it felt like a new revelation to me, that what I was battling was not of the outside world; it was a battle in my brain.

By the next year, I finally decided to seek professional help. It didn't matter whether the situations were my fault to begin with; I needed to get better, regardless of the cause. Based on a recommendation from Dr. Ranny two years prior, my parents found an Indian Malayali psychiatrist named Tobin. Together, we decided it was time that I sought answers and assistance. None of us wanted things to get worse.

I felt lucky to see the same psychiatrist she had recommended, though I wondered if Dr. Ranny had told Tobin about me. I hoped everything was going to be all right. This was really the only option I had to better myself, and I did my best to stay positive.

Still, I was very anxious to meet Tobin for the first time. Not only because new people gave me anxiety, but because this time, *I* had decided to visit a psychiatrist. I was the one who had told my dad to make an appointment. Nobody forced me to see him. My dad had been puzzled by my request, wondering why I'd finally made this decision. Maybe it was a miracle—something that needed to be done, even though I didn't feel completely confident in my decision.

Tobin worked in a small private clinic in Desoto, near where my mom worked, so we were familiar with the roads and that location. It didn't take us long to find his office.

There weren't any other patients at the clinic, which I liked. I didn't like to see or interact with other people in public. The building was quiet inside, with only a few faint sounds from the clinic's small radio.

I was very anxious, knee bouncing and palms sweating as I sat in the waiting room. Finally, Tobin called my name, and I followed him into his office. Since it was our first visit, my parents also came; I had no problem with that.

Tobin's office was nice, and we chatted for a bit, getting to know one another. He seemed nice, patient, wise, and trustworthy, willing to listen and guide me. He certainly made a good first impression.

It didn't take long for me to trust Tobin because one thought continued to swirl in my head: *You've got nothing to lose.*

For years, I'd felt that no good would come from seeing a mental health professional. Whatever had happened to me was my fault, and I wallowed in guilt. It also seemed that my parents had an agenda. They had tried to use mental health professionals to keep me from living in India, and while that hadn't worked, I'd been burned by their efforts. Ignoring help over the last few years had been a mistake though, and now I wanted to find peace. This was the only way I knew to find it.

Even as I began to think that I might have a mental problem, I was still unaware that a doctor had actually already diagnosed me with one. All I knew was that I had struggled and failed on my own, and it was time to lean on someone else for help. I was exhausted from the drama and the miserable feelings of the past few years. If talking didn't help, perhaps medication would.

After my first two visits, Tobin suggested I start a medication regimen. It would curb my emotional shortcomings and stabilize my mood so that I could focus. He was upfront in telling me, however, that it wouldn't solve all my problems. I had to work on myself too if I wanted to heal.

I was twenty-five years old. I didn't want to become a thirty-year-old, living in my parents' basement, doing nothing. I had a vision for myself, and that motivated me to work and do better.

After I started taking the pills, my parents and brothers remarked they were happy I was finally listening to them, seeing a psychiatrist, and taking medicine. Their remarks didn't encourage me, though. Instead, I felt a surge of anger at their remarks because I wasn't doing this to cater to their whims. I was in charge of my life. I was the one in control. I was making the choice to get better because I knew that there was a better version of me out there, and I wanted to become that. Their remarks forced me to hold on to part of my rage, because I refused to let them believe they had somehow helped me. They were the ones who had put me in that situation to begin with, so I displayed an angry attitude toward them.

I had an unusual amount of new energy, so I became very rebellious.

Tobin focused on getting me to see myself in a new way. He encouraged me to do something exciting, confident, and positive. He explained that it could distract me from my negative thoughts and help me get better. I wanted to get back to the person I'd been in 2005 when I first started being bullied. Therapy began to help me realize how deeply affected I had been—how the PTSD had continued to shape my life.

For the first time since my lowest moment, I decided to improve my life by doing something simple: changing my haircut. My style at the time was long, messy, and hard to control. I knew that my hair didn't make a good first impression on any new acquaintances.

So, I changed my appearance in an effort to get back to myself. I looked up a lot of Hollywood actors to see their hairstyles for inspiration—Tom Cruise, Matt Damon, Logan Lerman, Chris Pratt, and many others. Then, I looked at well-known Indian actors—Dulquer Salmaan, Sidharth Malhotra, Akshay Kumar, and Shahid Kapoor. Eventually, I found a few hairstyles that I liked.

Then I thought about Edward Snowden. I remembered his story had broken in 2013 when I was dealing with all Jith's drama and trying to spend time with Karl. I liked Snowden's hairstyle—the one he'd worn when he first appeared on the news—but my admiration for him went far beyond that. He had done so much for the world. He was the very reason every website had a privacy policy and privacy-related rights. Before his heroic efforts, lack of privacy on the internet was a serious problem. I valued privacy and knew that the online world owed him a great debt.

I watched every interview with Edward Snowden that I could find. I researched him online. His words and ideas intrigued me. I thought back to high school when I'd read the book *1984*. Although I'd never really been interested in reading, that book had stuck with me. Listening to Edward Snowden made me realize that our world was steadily becoming more and more like *1984*'s society. People were becoming dumber and dumber in front of a screen or a digital device while losing precious privacy-related rights. If this reality continued, the next generation would have no concept of digital privacy and may give up everything without a thought.

In my eyes, Edward Snowden was a superhero. Usually, superheroes only appeared in films and comics, battling evil forces. They did their best to follow the law and win, even though their job was incredibly difficult. There are few examples of true heroes in real life. Edward Snowden seemed like one—a good guy, a hero. I couldn't think of anyone else who had displayed that type of honest character before. He had good moral standards. He seemed very smart and used his intelligence to benefit people all over the world, not just citizens of the United States. That was something a hero would do.

The more I watched and learned about him, the more I appreciated him. I didn't think he was a bad guy, trying to harm the American people by betraying them. He was a role model for America and the entire world. He was a good guy.

When I cut my own hair, I didn't copy any actor's haircut specifically; I just used them as inspiration. I had to be careful. If I messed it up, I would have to avoid everyone until my hair grew back and didn't look silly anymore.

I honestly didn't care how my hair looked as long as it looked nice. My quest for a simple haircut and learning about Snowden made me a better person. Learning about him made me look at different perspectives and look at things in a proper way for the first time in my life. It made me realize I could think in a calm, professional way while dealing with life's hard situations. I learned a person could do good things for themselves and the world, even while losing their own comfortable way of life for the greater good, even if they faced backlash from powerful critics. They could still be cool and level-headed and remain focused when facing odds. Those traits were attractive; I wanted to learn them. Maybe that would help me on my journey to find peace.

Another part of changing myself to better my world involved finding a solution for the drama surrounding my relationship with Jith. My mind would often wander to him and put me in a negative place. I couldn't seem to move past it. I knew I needed to confront him somehow.

I decided to write down every nasty and off-putting incident that had happened with him. It would help me heal, and I would have it with me if I ever got the chance to confront him.

It was a very painful process. I dug up every unpleasant experience I'd ever had with him. I knew this was part of moving forward, so I had no other choice.

I wrote everything down on a piece of paper and took photos of it to store on my phone.

I realized I had been his personal punching bag. Like an inanimate object, when he hurt me, I did my best not to react. Jith had enjoyed every moment of the time spent picking on me. He didn't even need me to react. He knew that even if I looked unbothered, there was turmoil in my mind, and that brought him the greatest satisfaction.

After I made notes about Jith, I felt better for the first time in a long while. I'd taken the first step toward resolving the issues between us. Now, I had something to help me heal from all the psychological damage Jith had caused. If I could bring all his offenses to light someday, then I would feel as though I'd won the lottery.

I still didn't know how to confront him. It would be complicated. Jith wasn't just going to sit down and listen to my complaints. He would use them against me if he had the chance. Nevertheless, making these notes improved my mental health and would impact the way I faced mental hardships later. It made me feel a hell of a lot better.

I felt confident for the first time in a long time, perhaps even like I'd matured a bit.

CHAPTER 28

GONE TOO FAR

He who digs too deep for a fish
may come out with a snake.
—African proverb

After starting my medication regimen, I had a lot of energy to put toward moving forward with my life. But I wasn't used to all this liveliness, and I didn't know what to do with it. I was afraid that if I wasn't very active then I might go back to my past behavior where I would just stay in my bedroom all day feeling bored.

In the past, I had always relied on video games and movies when I got bored, but my mind was no longer only interested in entertainment. I needed to find something else to focus on, something to keep me going night and day. So, I concentrated on Tobin's suggestion that I find something positive and exciting to help me heal.

I thought a lot about the Second Amendment, the right to bear arms. I had first heard about the Second Amendment in history class when I was in eighth grade, during one of the first classes I took after I came to America. In the US Constitution, it says exactly this: "A well-regulated Militia, being necessary to the security of a free State, the right of the people to keep and bear Arms, shall not be infringed."

This was a strange concept to many countries outside of the US, and many people outside of America did not understand the importance of this right. The Constitution guaranteed American citizens the right to carry guns because if a tyrannical government took over, people would need the chance to fight back.

Around that time, several major school shootings made headlines, including the shootings at Sandy Hook and Marjory Stoneman Douglas High School. Many kids lost their lives. The loss of life was sad, and many people wanted to ban guns completely. Many others disagreed. More and more debates cropped up, pitting pro-gun groups against anti-gun groups. It was clear the nation was divided about the topic.

At first, I wanted to move on from the subject and find something else to focus on. Unfortunately, I didn't. People all around me were talking about school shootings, guns, the NRA (National Rifle Association), and the Second Amendment. I had never engaged with current issues before. There were people calling for a ban on rifles because of the tragic school shootings, and it became clear to me that they would not stop with that one demand. Their ultimate goal—which wasn't really a secret—was to erase the Second Amendment altogether. It wasn't really about the children who had died. I felt like part of the anti-gun crowd was using the dead children and taking advantage of tragic situations to further their agenda.

I didn't like the idea of law-abiding citizens not having the chance to defend themselves or the US Constitution from tyrannical governments. So, I was pumped to do something about it.

I dug up information about the Second Amendment. I wanted to know as much as possible before choosing a side, so I could understand why people were upset. School shootings were tragic, and losing young lives was devastating. But guns were an important protection and a guaranteed right. There was a valid reason they existed; without them, the worst parts of history could repeat themselves.

The more I read, the more I grew frustrated with anti-gun sentiments. The more I watched the major news networks, the more I became sucked into that world.

I particularly watched one highly sensational mainstream news media too much, which was very entertaining. I used to watch this news network when I first came to America when I was younger. This network tried to promote the viewpoint that guns are all bad and need to be controlled. I didn't agree with their reporting and their point of view on guns and rights.

I thought about it constantly, and quickly became obsessed with protecting my freedoms.

I knew I had some problems but didn't know I had a serious psychotic disorder. I was still left in the dark by my family and had no way of knowing that what I was about to do would negatively impact my mental health for long after it was over.

I decided to support the Second Amendment positively and openly. I bought an airsoft rifle to carry in public. Two days in a row, I went out in public, carrying my airsoft rifle. On the first day, I went to a Redbox to rent a movie. The next day, I returned the movie while carrying my airsoft rifle, recording everything on my GoPro camera.

I was prompted to open carry from YouTube videos of other gun rights supporters doing similar things. I learned from them how to interact with police officers in open carry situations. Looking back, it's hard to believe I actually went through with my open carry idea. But the idea seemed good at the time, and I went ahead with it, unaware of how it could go south.

Unsurprisingly, on both days, concerned citizens called the police. My exchanges with the police were interesting. They didn't seem to be interested in arresting or fining me. They just weren't very fond of what I was doing.

I'm sure I stood out to them as an unusual person. Maybe they even thought I had mental problems. But I remained respectful and cooperative, and they treated me in the same manner, advising me not to open carry in that way, especially after the recent school shootings. They told me that I was bound to attract the wrong sort of attention. Since I wasn't breaking any laws, though, I was free to go, and the police left.

During the interactions, I was only slightly nervous. I was somewhat prepared for whatever they might say or do, even if they took my airsoft and brought me to the station. While they talked to me, I felt normal. I never considered doing anything illegal or foolish. Because these situations were charged with adrenaline, I actually felt like a badass. I was ready to face any consequences from my actions.

When I arrived back home on the second day, one of my neighbors stared at me. I just laughed to myself and went inside.

My family considered what I had done as very controversial, especially my dad. I jokingly suggested my family join me in the open carry.

Jef laughed. "Not with a fake gun," he said sarcastically. "Maybe if we get some real ones."

I stood firmly by what I had done. But over the next few days, I gave a lot of thought to my interactions with the police. I came to regret my open carry decision, although I had no regrets about supporting the Second Amendment. But I started to look at my behavior in a new light. I carried a cheap airsoft rifle in the name of the Second Amendment. It was idiotic.

I also realized that I unintentionally insulted the entire pro-Second Amendment community. My misguided thinking led me to a poor decision. I didn't realize until it was too late that I was in way over my head.

The next day after my encounters with the police, there was a police SUV in front of my home. I felt that they were most likely monitoring me. I wondered if that was standard procedure, or if they were there to stop me from open carrying again.

The time I spent trying to support the Second Amendment was thrilling to me, almost as if I was in a dramatic movie scene. I didn't think it was the result of the meds Tobin had prescribed to me. I felt like I was a part of something, and I had never felt like this before. But I had the police called on me and had made a fool of myself. There could have been any number of far worse outcomes, had I made dumber decisions to resist cooperating with the police.

Even though I had chatted with them as requested, I had spoken to the police officers as if the incident was nothing. I wasn't at all nervous or worried about what they'd say. Never in my wildest dreams would I have expected anything like that. Cops were, of course, to be respected. However, I had acted almost carelessly.

Even I was beginning to regard my behavior as bizarre.

Looking at the situation from the perspective of the police, it was clear why they might be suspicious of me. I was a guy carrying a rifle in public, fake or not. Nothing could have completely prepared them for that. Were they nervous? I knew I would have been.

They worked in a high-risk job, and bad things could happen to them at a moment's notice. I understood why they didn't want me or anybody else to go walking around with a weapon like that in public. Everyone wants to feel safe. Nowadays when people see a gun, they seem to be very afraid of it, even if it's carried by a law-abiding citizen.

***

From that point, my thoughts again spiraled into fear and anxiety. I had made myself a part of something bigger, that I wasn't sure I wanted to be part of. The police were now watching me. They knew I was prone to erratic behavior. I tried to remind myself that I'd wanted to do something big to use up my newfound energy. In that respect, it had been successful. But at what cost?

My paranoia started getting the best of me. What if law enforcement never stopped watching me? They could track me anywhere I went and observe me from a distance. I even thought about that mysterious, golden Crown Victoria again, the one that I had seen several times while dropping my mom off at work and at the DFW airport a long time ago.

Every day, I grew more paranoid. I wondered if they were tracking my cell phone and internet history, looking for suspicious activity. My fear started affecting my sleep, and my mental health nose-dived again.

I questioned the wisdom of using a smartphone. The pros seemed to outweigh the cons because, in reality, there was no way to hide if the government decided to watch me. Things on the internet were not easily erased, and they already knew where I lived and everything I did on online.

I didn't want my cell phone around me all the time. Sometimes, I'd leave it in a different room. I even bought webcam covers to put on both of my smartphone cameras. I didn't like the feeling that someone could be constantly watching me. I felt like Big Brother or some kind of ministry from the novel *1984* was watching me inside and outside of my home all the time.

The government could easily have been recording everything without my knowledge using my cell phone cameras. They could watch anyone, but they didn't need to pay attention to most people. However, I was now on their radar; if they so decided, accessing my computer and watching my activity would be easy for them. They may even get notifications on their spy cellphone about me whenever I use digital devices.

I wasn't sure if that kind of surveillance was legal or not, but I was sure they could get away with it. The police probably practiced *predictive policing*—a mathematical, predictive, and analytical technique to identify potential criminal activity before it happened (which I learned about from Wikipedia). My situation reminded me of the movie *Minority Report.*

My open carry and run-in with the police was real, but because of my mental health condition, determining which, if any, of the resulting paranoid concerns was real proved difficult. My brain exaggerated things, making me wonder if I was actually living in reality. If I became depressed, the paranoia grew even worse.

My mind raced most of the time, over-dramatizing nearly every event. In those moments, I felt like a rogue secret agent in a movie, trying to escape from powerful forces.

I only told my immediate family about the open carry incident. I knew most people would react negatively, so I didn't advertise what I had done to friends or extended family.

Unfortunately, my family decided not to honor my wishes. Two of my aunts came to visit, and my parents told them what I had done. Of course, they confronted me, wanting to know more. I had no choice but to show my GoPro videos. I held my breath while they watched, anxious about their reactions, hoping to see some hint on their faces about their feelings and what they would say afterward. Surprisingly, neither of them judged me or reacted negatively. They encouraged me to stop, though.

A couple of months later, Zoey came to visit. When she asked what I had been up to, I mentioned that my friend Jones and I had gone to the Irving police department to get the 9-1-1 call records from my open carry complaints. I was curious about what was said and wanted to upload the recordings to YouTube along with the video footage from my GoPro.

Zoey was surprised and concerned to learn about my dealings with the police. I told her what had happened and assured her I hadn't been arrested. I showed her the videos.

Zoey was *not* supportive.

"Don't do that anymore," she said. "It's too dangerous. What if the police shot you?"

"I just wanted to support the Second Amendment. There are people out there trying to take away a citizen's right to bear arms. I wanted to demonstrate my support for those who stand on the other side."

We didn't see eye to eye. "I'm all for the Second Amendment, but doing what you did is dangerous," she said. "You don't know how badly you could have been hurt."

More of my relatives soon learned about what happened. When my Uncle Jenson and Aunt Marissa found out, I showed them my videos. They didn't say anything negative. However, they also told me to be very careful.

By that point, I was not proud of my actions. At first, I had just regretted that I had used an airsoft gun instead of a real rifle. But I eventually realized that I wasn't the right person to do patriotic acts of this sort.

I uploaded my videos to YouTube. There were a few likes and dislikes, and the comments were harsh but valid. People viewed what I had done as silly. They said that arming myself with a toy gun on the street in the name of the Second Amendment was stupid or weird. I agreed. Eventually, I took the videos down.

For my twenty-sixth birthday in May 2018, I went to a local indoor shooting range. My older cousin Josh had come to America from Ireland to visit us and his mother Marissa, as well as other family members. Jef planned to bring Josh to the shooting range, and I asked Jef if he would bring me as well. He agreed.

I was excited to go to the range; I had never fired a weapon before. I had never held or fired a handgun or an actual rifle. I had lived in America for most of the last thirteen years, but I never had the chance to shoot at paper targets.

An employee at the gun shop instructed us how to use the handguns, and we listened carefully. The three of us then went into the shooting range.

I saw a mother and her kid using the range. It surprised me to see a middle schooler there. The kid's mother gave him a handgun and told him how to shoot it. He listened and followed her directions exactly, hitting the target. I was embarrassed. A few months ago, I had been wielding an airsoft gun. Now, this much younger kid was using the real thing. I thought, *Wow! How did I become such an idiot? What the heck am I doing?* I was in my mid-twenties, and this kid who was barely a teenager seemed far more capable, intelligent, and mature than I was. What a joke I was!

I tried to push those thoughts aside and focus on having a good time. We had the chance to fire a few different handguns and an Israeli-made bullpup rifle. I was excited to see what they were all about.

Shooting firearms was a strange experience. I'm not sure if it was because that was my first time shooting a real firearm or because of the mental health issues I was experiencing. Either way, it was not what I'd imagined.

I never thought pistols had as much kick as rifles. In movies, it always seems that the shooter can hold their hands relatively still throughout the shot. I also had no concept of how loud each shot could be. Even though we had earplugs in, each shot that rang out was deafening. I was never as prepared as I thought I was, surprised by each one.

As I watched Jef and Josh shoot, I wondered if I would have the same experience at an outdoor range.

By the time we finished, I concluded that I didn't have the mental fortitude to be around guns and was afraid I might do something stupid, even by accident. I had loved the concept of guns since childhood, but now that I was experiencing mental health issues, it would be best to stay away from firearms.

I was glad for the chance to experience the range, though. That had been on my bucket list since I had moved to America. I was not disappointed at all and could mark it off the list!

CHAPTER 29
REVISIT WITH A LETTER

There comes a time when you have to choose between turning the page or just closing the book.
—Unknown

I was ready to move on to something more productive with my life. I decided to attend North Lake College the next school year.

I sat down with their little brochure in hand, going over the majors and class choices that North Lake offered. There were many things I skipped over immediately, including classes I'd never liked in high school. There was no way I was going to study English or writing, and I definitely didn't have an interest in pursuing a math career or becoming a teacher.

Surprisingly, I found myself drawn to nursing. Yes, my mom was a nurse, and many of my other family members were as well. It seemed like a profession where I could find a certain level of success. Honestly, the idea of becoming a nurse myself had always seemed far less exciting than a computer sciences degree. But as I looked over the classes and thought about being a nurse, something inside latched onto the idea. This idea actually came while I was staying in India for my grandfather's funeral back in 2017. Soon, I couldn't let it go.

I'd always struggled in school, and I hoped that if I tried hard, applied myself, and set high standards for myself, I could achieve anything I put my mind to. If I could get through this, everyone would be proud of me. Most importantly, I would be proud of myself. I knew I would have my work cut out for me, though. My mental health issues wouldn't go away just because I was in school.

I needed closure on my past. My middle school bullying experience still haunted me, affecting me so many years later.

As an adult, I realized that what happened to me never should have happened. The school hadn't been equipped to prevent issues like mine. I wanted to do something about it, not only for my own closure, but for all the kids who might face the same issues.

I sat down and wrote a two-page letter to the administration at Lamar Middle School. I told them about my torment on the bus, the pain it caused me, and how I'd carried that pain and anguish through my life. I described all of the obstacles that bullying created for me since the day I'd first been attacked.

I wanted them to understand my story and realize that bullying affects people, not just while in school, but in every step of life that followed. They needed to see that they had to step up and prevent these things from happening again. And I wanted an apology for my struggles that were partially due to their negligence.

It was very unlikely that I would receive the apology or even a written response. There was a 50-50 chance at best. But the request was justified, and I knew I had nothing to lose by asking for one.

I asked Jones to come with me to drop off the letter. So, one morning we drove to the school, and I delivered the letter by hand to the receptionist. I asked her to give it to the principal. I was aware that this principal was new and not the same person who was there when I was a kid.

She glanced down at my letter, started reading, and raised her eyes in surprise. "Of course, I'll give this to the principal," she said awkwardly. But the principal wasn't there. She instead gave it to a senior staff member at a nearby office.

She seemed to find it all very weird, which bothered me. There was nothing funny about what I had gone through. This wasn't a joke; it was my life. I was a victim of bullying, a fact that was clear from the beginning of the note. Though she didn't actually laugh at me, I saw her roll her eyes on her way into the office.

I can't really blame her for that reaction. Most people would find it odd that a young man in his mid-twenties would reach out to his middle school and ask for an apology for something that had happened several years prior.

Most people wanting to get back at a school that harmed them would show up with something far more dangerous than a piece of paper. They might even try to harm someone to make a point. Many people figured that's what the perpetrators of school shootings did. Luckily, despite having been through a lot since my eighth-grade bullying days, I didn't think like that.

I would not sue them if they didn't respond, either; I just hoped it might get their attention. I was nervous about whether they would take it the wrong way or laugh at me. My mind spun with the unknowns.

The receptionist emerged with her supervisor, who was very concerned. She could tell I had come prepared, and my intentions were genuine. She read the letter.

She was respectful, even though the moment was perhaps odd. We chatted for a minute, and I gave her my email address. I thanked her, and Jones and I left the school.

On our way to our vehicle, Jones joked, "Run! Run! Escape!"

His comments gave me a funny feeling in the pit of my stomach.

He continued, "Now, everybody is going to know you. Maybe the police will get involved too."

I replied, "Yes, I know. It's probably going to get interesting." I was full of adrenaline as I worried about what might happen.

After three days, I received a reply from Steven—the school resource officer. His tone in his email tone was professional but not warm or apologetic. He was happy to discuss my concerns. I realized that my chances of receiving an apology were slim, but I had to see this through.

Before I went back to the school, I prepared for the possibility that I might get arrested if something went wrong, though I didn't plan to cause any problems. Still, I did not know what to expect when I met with the resource officer.

I felt familiar jolts of excitement and energy bubble up inside me, just as I had during my open carry. I was thrilled, pumped full of adrenaline, and ready to talk and endure interrogation, just like someone in an epic movie scene.

I went to the school alone. A female officer met me. She waited for me to say something, so I told her that Steven was expecting me. She let me come inside the school and I met a school employee who told me to sit on a nearby bench to wait. After a few minutes, Steven came out to greet me and led me back to a small office.

He asked a lot of questions. "Why did you give the school a letter? Tell me about your experiences at our middle school. Tell me more about the bullying you experienced. What was that like?"

He knew about my encounter with the police and my open carrying incident. "I've seen video footage of your recent interactions with the police, telling them what you were doing and why. You were carrying around an airsoft, I believe. Can you tell me more about that?"

That made me laugh. I admitted to the incident and explained why I had done it. I hadn't fully come to regret my decision yet, and because of all the adrenaline pumping through my veins, I wasn't concerned about the implications my admission might have. My mind was all over the place, ping-ponging back and forth. My boldness was a direct result of my psychotic disorder. I even went so far as to give him my YouTube channel's name, inviting him to check out my videos.

"Rick, I want to let you know I'm recording you on a body cam as well."

I already knew that. We went through a few more rounds of questions.

"Tell me where you live and what you do." After my brief answers, he asked, "Do you love America or India, Rick?"

I told him, "I like America, but I like India too."

I realized then that I had been right to be a little paranoid. I was clearly a person of interest to the Irving police. They'd told Steven a lot about me.

After I answered all his questions, I wanted my own answers. "Do the buses and schools have cameras in them? Can you watch them to make sure everyone is safe?"

"Both the buses and school have cameras, but there's no one watching them all day. We use them to review incidents."

"What happens with a bullying issue?"

Steven told me the procedures. "If the bullying victim seeks help from adults, we have action plans in place to help the student feel safe again."

"What if the victim is too afraid to seek help? I was."

"We will know if something as severe as bullying takes place."

I concluded that if a victim didn't notify his friends, the staff, or any other adults, he was screwed. That didn't sit right with me. I knew firsthand the physical and psychological damage a victim would carry through his or her life. The school shouldn't allow this type of behavior to go on unchecked.

Steven said, "I highly recommend you visit someone at the family advocacy center here in Irving. It seems you were affected by what happened to you, and you could benefit from talking to someone about what you're feeling."

"No," I replied, shaking my head. "I'm good. No problem!"

Toward the end of the discussion, Steven said, "I can't offer you a formal apology letter, Rick. What I can do is tell you I'm sorry for what happened here. You were young and scared, and you didn't know that there was help available. We have no recordings from the school bus to use as proof of your situation, so we're not able to take formal action as an apology."

I was not surprised that they didn't offer an apology, but I continued to push for one. "I really think the school should apologize for how I was treated, how no one recognized what was happening and tried to intervene."

For a moment, he didn't reply. Then, he said, "I'll address it with the current principal, but I can't guarantee you'll receive one."

I knew I wouldn't receive an apology. I wanted to keep pushing, to say more, but I didn't know what else to add.

Just before I opened the office door to leave, Steven said, "I'll check out the YouTube videos you posted about your open carry."

"Great! I'm sure you'll like them. They're pretty epic." I paused. "Thanks for chatting with me." Then I left. The whole discussion had gone fine, and I hadn't gotten into any trouble. That was a plus.

My interaction with Steven had, overall, been good for me. He had explained things nicely and he genuinely sympathized with me. He was the first person to have apologized for what I'd gone through. He didn't have to do that, since it wasn't his fault. He hadn't even been there when I was being bullied. But I appreciated that he felt sorry for me. I didn't think it was fake.

The next day, I emailed him for the last time. I realized the word "apology" intimidated and troubled the school. That would require them to admit fault, and they didn't want to be held liable for what I'd gone through. Really, it wasn't an apology that I wanted as much as a response. I wanted some kind of official recognition that they understood what I had gone through and realize that this was a big thing and not a joke. I wanted them to realize they needed to prevent future bullies from harming students.

In the email, I said, "You don't have to reply to this email. Please, just consider what I'm saying for the good of current students at your school." I never received a response, which was expected. I just hoped that the message had gotten through to them, and they were taking some preventative steps.

I felt good about my decision to confront the school. It gave me a sense of closure. I still carried much pain from middle school, but I was on a journey toward healing myself and getting back on track after so many years.

***

Even though I had satisfied my desire to tell the school how they'd wronged me, my mental health took a turn for the worse. The severe amount of anxiety and fear that had been hiding beneath the surface was triggered by my adrenaline. I had confidence issues, often experiencing bouts of low self-esteem. Whenever I worried what someone would think of me or that I'd get into trouble for something, the downward spiral began again. It was often hard to drag myself back out of the depths.

This time, there was no escape. On top of the panic attacks that began in 2016, I developed symptoms of agoraphobia, a type of anxiety disorder in which the sufferer fears and avoids places or situations that might make them feel trapped or panicked, helpless or embarrassed.

This new anxiety led me to fear death. Since I thought about guns quite often, I had an irrational fear that I would meet my end at the barrel of a gun. I tried to stay completely away from anything that was gun-related online or on television. I didn't want to remember the details of my open carry mistakes, and each time I saw something about guns, I couldn't think about anything else.

My mind became a trap of never-ending fear, anxiety, and depression. Spikes of paranoia occurred around the same time, too. I obsessively checked to make sure that no one could spy on me, while simultaneously fearing police were already surveying my home.

Every night, my agoraphobia and paranoia kicked into overdrive. Most of the time, I sat on my bed, wrapped up, and wondered over and over again if I was being watched. I felt like I'd lost my privacy, that nothing I did was truly my own anymore.

I sweated all the time because of this tension, to the point of having foul body odor.

In order to counter my phobia, I closed the blinds very early, well before dark, and made sure no one could see through them. I also turned off all the lights inside my house and moved around as stealthily as I could in the blackness without making any sounds.

After it got dark, I wouldn't go downstairs, staying on the second floor in my bedroom because I feared people could come in at any second. I worried about having the wrong reaction if someone did show up. By hiding in my room, I gave myself just a little more time to react. I didn't want anyone to see me like that, scared and jumpy, stuck in an eternal labyrinth of petrifying thoughts. So, I just closed my bedroom door and tried to sleep.

I even marked the calendar in my bedroom with a large "X" whenever I went into panic mode or had a panic attack, mild or very serious. I wanted to track how many attacks occurred in quick succession. There were a lot of them per week.

Sometimes, while my paranoia and anger were out of control, I felt angry at my dad. He was the one who put me in this situation, blaming me for not having healed from my problems. I kept telling myself, "My dad is the reason for all of this. My dad is the reason I have psychological problems. He is the one who screwed up my life. Now, I am paying for it because of him."

Other things started affecting me too. I couldn't sleep in my bedroom by myself, and when I tried, I didn't sleep properly. Whenever I drifted off, I felt as though something bad was about to happen to me, snapping me awake again.

Not long before this, I watched the movie *A Quiet Place*, in which everyone has to be as silent as possible to avoid being attacked by sound-detecting creatures. The atmosphere of the whole movie was intense from the first moment to the last, and I felt as though my life had taken on that same intensity. While in my bed, I would look out of my room and feel like the sound-detecting creatures were coming up the staircase, ready to attack and kill anyone who made noise. I didn't want to make a sound, so I would just stay still, even though I knew those creatures didn't exist. I even thought I would see them at any moment to the point of hallucinating, although it never got that bad; I never saw those creatures.

I couldn't just remain paranoid forever; I needed to soothe my mind. I felt like a small, scared child—a baby. I needed to be around someone else at all times, and the only option was my family. My primitive instincts started to kick in.

To deter these vulnerable feelings, I started sleeping in my parents' room. I brought a small sheet and pillow and put those on the floor near my parents' bed. My actions puzzled them at first, but ultimately they were fine with me moving into their room.

I did my best not to distract, talk, or argue with them, even though my dad, a source of frustration and anger, was in the same room. The only thing I wanted was peace. I was deep in a dark abyss, surrendering to everything.

I often thought, *How can I recover from this? What can I do in order to get out of this never-ending trap? Who will help me?* I didn't have any answers.

I knew medicine wasn't going to help me, even though that was the only likely solution. I was convinced that my mental illness had nothing to do with genetics. To me, it was my environment that completely influenced my problems. If people didn't treat me right, my mind would turn upside down. Meds could only help so much; they couldn't fix everything. They were not magic pills.

I visited my psychologist every so often, and he still helped me. I showed him a copy of the letter that I gave to the school and used it as an opportunity to tell him about what had happened to me in eighth grade. He needed the info to understand me and my mental health better.

I also told him about my fear of death. He asked me to name what I was afraid of, but I couldn't tell him the root problem because I wasn't completely sure what it was. All I knew was that I was afraid of everything: gun-related deaths, injuries, and the scary, fictional, movie monsters. I told him I had agoraphobia and that is why I feared death, and this confused him.

I was too embarrassed to tell him about my open carry. I felt miserable and guilty over that situation, like I had humiliated the Second Amendment community. That had never been my intention, but because of everything that was going on inside my brain, I wasn't in the right place to process everything I was feeling.

I did express my interest in guns, though. I wanted him to understand my support of the Second Amendment, that I had a legitimate reason to be interested in guns and support gun rights. What had attracted me to the Second Amendment was not the guns themselves; it was the idea that people could take control, defend, and fight back against bad people if the need arose.

He asked whether I felt like I needed a gun now. I assured him that I didn't. I knew I still had a long way to go in my recovery. My mental health, my paranoia, my mood issues... those things weren't going away. Until I could get a handle on my mental health and find a way to a better place, I knew it was best to avoid guns. I wasn't blind to my issues, and I knew it would be irresponsible to own a gun then.

I could tell my doctor worried about me having a weapon, given my suicidal past. He didn't want me to do something horrible to myself or someone else, and I understood that.

PART FOUR:
MISSION REBORN

CHAPTER 30

LOVE IS IN THE AIR

"It's impossible," said pride.
"It's risky," said experience.
"It's pointless," said reason.
"Give it a try," whispered the heart.
—Unknown

As time went on, I continued to move forward in as many small ways as I could. I eventually came to accept that I would not get the closure I had been looking for, but I couldn't let that hold me back anymore. I had to move on, find a way out of the darkness, and heal.

My inability to socialize with people still haunted me. I remembered several instances where people tried to talk to me, only for me to freeze up and be unable to answer them—in particular, when my neighbor had said hi, and I panicked, then walked back into the house instead of responding. It still bothered me.

I decided to write a note to him to apologize and explain what I had gone through and why I had trouble interacting socially. I left the note on his front door.

The note was as much for me as it was for him. He hadn't let that incident bother him. We'd spoken once in passing since then and he appeared okay about what had happened without an explanation. Still, I didn't feel peace until I wrote that note.

I continued moving forward.

I loved to play a space-themed video game called *Elite Dangerous*. It was a fun game with spaceships and battles, and it helped me step away from my reality and relax for a while.

One night, I saw my online friend Cowboy07 in the game, and we were both standing at the same station. He was a skilled player, and I enjoyed interacting with him. I asked him if he was free to bounty hunt with me—one of the community goals in the game.

Cowboy07 told me he was busy working with three other commanders in a wing. The maximum number of players allowed on a team was four, but he said he would invite me to their side if one of them left. That was fine by me, and I worked on other community goals in the meantime—trading supplies and commodities between space stations in different solar systems.

I made a few trade runs and decided to log off. Just then, I got a message from him that a slot was opening up. I switched from my trading ship (called Type-7) to my fighter ship (Vulture), greeted him and the other players in the wing, and headed to their location.

I joined them in a supporting role, and we quickly eliminated several enemies. We soon found another enemy ship. Because I was closest to the enemy ship, it spotted me and attacked.

My spaceship wasn't taking any damage, but I lost my shield. I jousted the enemy several times, and soon, the canopy glass on my ship broke. I had twenty-four minutes of life support left before my character would suffocate and die, which was plenty of time for a retreat. I told the group what had happened and that I needed to return to my base.

While I was on my way to my base, Cowboy07 started talking indirectly about me in front of our other wing mates. "I don't understand why rookie players in advanced fighter ships don't fit their ships correctly," he said. He seemed to be making fun of what happened to me, and he sounded angry.

I didn't expect him to say that, especially not in front of others. I was embarrassed and upset, but I chose not to say anything.

I arrived at the station and repaired my broken canopy glass. Then it was time for me to log off for the night. I sent a message saying, "I have to go. Thanks!" I added another message. "I might need to read on the internet about some of this stuff."

One of Cowboy07's wing mates replied he could probably help me out.

Cowboy07 then asked, "What stuff?"

"The broken canopy glass," I answered.

Surprisingly, Cowboy07 stopped insulting me and started giving me advice about the broken canopy glass. He even gave me advice about the next spaceship I should buy.

I was surprised and relieved that he had calmed down and stopped being so harsh. But I was still hurt and confused. I couldn't understand why he would shame me in front of the other wing mates. I didn't mind that he had criticized me for a mistake, but the way that he had gone about it, humiliating me in front of the others, was uncalled for. I wasn't a great player, but I didn't think I deserved to be treated that way. I thought he was going to be nice to me since he had complimented me before.

I reflected on my online friend's behavior for a long time and finally remembered that he had already been in a bad mood before I'd joined him and his wing mates. After I had joined his team, he said something about another wing mate who had irritated him. It was obvious now that the other player must have put him in a bad mood, and I had joined right after that other player had left. Then, I'd made a mistake, and Cowboy07 had become even angrier. It relieved me that the source of his anger was actually someone else, not me.

However, this incident bothered me so much that I wanted to never return to the game. I stopped playing for a long time. It felt like having online friends was just as difficult as socializing in real life, and I didn't want to experience further letdowns.

Cowboy07 eventually unfriended me after I had stopped playing *Elite Dangerous*. He probably realized I was not coming back and that finding new friends would be best for both of us.

Despite negative experiences, I remained determined to move my life forward. Somewhere along the way, the paranoia had lessened a bit, and I found a small, positive energy within myself. I didn't want anything to screw it up like the last time, so I tried to ease forward, keeping my hope and positivity to myself.

***

As I continued to work on myself, I brought my weight back to where it had normally been. I could wear my old, clothes again, which added to my positivity. At the end of July, I decided to watch a movie—a risky thing to do because of my ever-changing mood. My psychotic disorder made it difficult to enjoy the things I'd always loved. I was now more sensitive to the story, and disturbing scenes bothered me far more than they had before. I felt the tension from the movie building within my body, and if there was no quick resolution, I would freak out and get wrapped up in my thoughts instead of focusing on the movie.

Whenever that happened, I remained in a bad mood for a while afterward. So, I tried to make a point of looking away during intense scenes, hoping to keep myself from spiraling.

With that in mind, I watched *Ready Player One*.

That movie spoke to me on many levels and reminded me of my own life. In the movie, the characters searched in a computer game for three keys to an Easter egg left behind by the game's creator.

I, too, felt like I needed to find three keys in my own life to unlock something important. Those keys represented three essential qualities that I needed to gain: confidence, healing, and social maturity. If I could overcome my obstacles and get all three, I could get my Easter egg—my original self, the one that I'd been trying to reclaim for years.

Ready Player One inspired me to continue my journey. I couldn't let anything stop me while I still had a goal to work toward. I felt like I was standing at the precipice of something new and exciting. More positivity grew within me.

Inspiration from the movie affected me in other ways, too. There had been a few cheesy, romantic parts that triggered strange thoughts. For the first time, I began to think about and become interested in girls.

I'd never had a girlfriend or even a desire to search for romance. A little whisper in my head made me wonder if I should even bother because I had promised myself I wouldn't. Malayalam films and real-life experiences had made me think twice about marriage. The Rick I wanted to find wouldn't look at girls. But I chose to bend the rules, at least for a short period. I would look for girls' images once, then never again. So, I proceeded, feeling adventurous and excited.

This was a new feeling. I decided to lean into my positivity and explore romance without looking back. I could now picture that part of my life. If I had a girlfriend, I wanted to know what she'd look like, and I didn't want to wait. It felt like new, fun homework.

First, I needed to find attractive girls. Never having thought about it before, my hormones were on high alert. Then I did something a little stereotypical and sexist. I went to Google, checking my surroundings to see if anyone was nearby. My computer was out in the open, and others had at least a partial view of my monitor and could see what I was doing. After checking to make sure that the coast was clear, I typed "hot girls" into the search bar. I went to the image tab and saw adult women of different races from all over the world. My heart pounded, and I could feel the blood flowing through my veins as I delved into that new world.

I decided to refine my search results and look only for Indian girls. So, I typed "cute Indian girls" and pressed enter. I was shocked and a little concerned. Most of the results were underage girls. I felt my heart rate quicken again, but for a different reason. What if the FBI was monitoring my online activities and could see that I had searched for this content? What if they thought I was a pervert or future sex offender? I knew agencies like the FBI monitored the internet to prevent child abuse, trafficking, and to find pedophiles before they attacked.

I quickly erased that search, knowing that the FBI would still know about it, and closed the browser.

I still wanted to look at more pictures, though, so I re-opened the browser and typed "hot Indian girls" this time. At least when the search results came up, there weren't any underage girls, so my heartbeat returned to normal.

Despite seeing many girls' images—some of them models—I somehow didn't feel satisfied. Then I realized why. These girls weren't Malayalis. If I was to have a girlfriend or wife, she would have to be a Malayali girl within the same Knanaya community.

The Knanaya are an ethnic group found in Kerala whose customs involve marrying within one's own tribe. Their community can be traced back to the area that is modern-day Syria. They moved to what is now known as Kerala in AD 345, following a merchant named Thomas of Cana. There were 72 families in all in the Knanaya community.

So, I narrowed my search to "Knanaya girls" and hit enter. A lot of images popped up. While I was looking through them, I checked for links to matrimony websites for further searching.

Many matrimonial websites for Knanaya women popped up, and I had a look for fun. This was to be my final search; I planned to just move on afterward. I had only one life, after all. I shouldn't waste it. I may not have another opportunity to do something like that.

When I first delved into that world, I wasn't that serious. I quickly changed my tune.

At first, it was hard to find anyone of interest. Most of the candidates' images on those sites were hidden for privacy purposes until you created an account. I wasn't sure if I wanted to register, so I tried to be content with what I could see.

That turned out to be very little, which proved so frustrating and disappointing that I was ready to stop searching. I scrolled down the screen one last time, ready to close the browser. There was one last website I hadn't visited yet. I clicked on the link.

Surprisingly, this site showed every candidate's image. Anyone could see the profiles for all the brides and grooms without making an account; it was free. I still felt disinterested and was about to leave the site when I scrolled to the bottom of the page. There, a smiling girl in a red dress caught my eye.

Curious, I clicked on her profile. Her image was still a small thumbnail, so I enlarged it to see her face better.

Her name was Yasmin and her picture blew my mind. Something clicked inside my brain, and I thought, *What did I just see? Wow!*

Yasmin was very beautiful and seemed interesting. She worked in the medical field and was my age. She lived only a short distance from where I'd grown up in Kerala. Seeing her made me excited, and her image burned into my brain; I could still see her smile each time I closed my eyes.

That night, I had a funny feeling in my chest. I couldn't believe that I had actually seen her! My body trembled, and my mind whirled with possibilities. Her picture stood out from all the others. I didn't know exactly why, but her beauty, her facial expression, and the emotion she'd shown in her photo amazed me. The picture might have been edited, but it didn't matter because I could see her soul from my computer monitor, halfway around the world.

My mind raced, and I was scared by how much she'd affected me. I eventually had a panic attack.

I hurried to my room before others could see my face, unwilling to give away anything in front of my family. If someone had asked, I would have acted suspiciously, so I rested under the blowing ceiling fan in my bedroom with the door closed. All I could see in my mind was her profile image.

I didn't know what the heck to do to move forward after my discovery. The longer I thought about her, the more my confidence issues and doubts grew. Should I proceed to learn more about her or just leave well enough alone? Despite my panic at being discovered, deep down I was thrilled. I had finally discovered something that could make my life better.

It's now or never, I told myself. *Either I need to learn more about her or completely ditch the idea forever. If I proceed, I may be embarrassed if others learn about this.* Mockery was far from my comfort zone, yet I still felt compelled by Yasmin. Either way, I had a big decision to make.

While I laid on the bed, seriously thinking about my future, I did something unbelievable, something I'm not sure the real Rick would have done. I told myself, *Screw it! I'm going ahead. Whatever comes next, I will face it head on, and I will be ready to deal with any potential consequences. I don't care if I get embarrassed by this. My life is screwed up anyway. Who cares? I am going ahead!*

From then on, it was officially out of my control; there was no turning back. I completely left my old way of thinking about romance behind and embarked on a new journey that I had never gone on before. I entered a new realm in my life, and oh boy, it felt good!

The next day, after Chris went to work early, I made sure nobody was around and again looked up the site with her profile again. I wanted to know more about Yasmin! But in order to see more than just the one photo and her basic information, I needed to register and upload documentation from my church, proving that I was a Knanaya.

That was a big disappointment but understandable. People on that site didn't want just anyone to know about them. Registering was the only way to see more information and photos. I knew registering on the website would be nearly impossible to keep from my family, but I didn't entirely ditch the idea. I wanted to get the certificate later without my family knowing. I decided to try that path later.

The more I searched for information about Yasmin, the more I felt my life changing once again. I didn't know whether this was a positive or a negative feeling: love. I'd felt nothing like it before.

I was officially hooked on Yasmin. I never expected to see a girl like her. I was in a wonderland that had been previously locked away. I was in a great mood, my spirits high. I forgot all about how badly other things were going in my life. All that mattered was Yasmin. I was awestruck!

I began to have crazy ideas. I took photos of myself to upload to the matrimony website in the future, just in case I made a profile. I took a lot of photos in different poses with my slim Canon camera. To avoid my family catching me, I took them in the middle of night while everybody was sleeping.

Finally, I got one photo of myself that completely amazed me. I actually looked happy in it. Very happy. There was nothing fake about the photo. The emotion on my face and my facial expression were genuine. I was very relaxed and open, appearing very comfortable in my pose. Usually, my photos didn't look good, and I believed myself not to be very good-looking. This one, however, was very different. Despite my bad haircut, it was a good picture of me. I hadn't seen myself this happy in a photo since eighth grade.

I tried taking several more, but I couldn't replicate the same emotion. That one picture was a once-in-a-lifetime unique photo.

My crush grew deeper as the days flew by. I couldn't sleep properly; I kept waking up in the middle of the night, thinking about Yasmin. Throughout the day, my thoughts wandered to her. The agoraphobia I'd been experiencing the last four months almost completely vanished after finding Yasmin's photo. Silent chemical changes were happening in my brain.

A new era of my life had officially begun, and I was finally feeling alive. I didn't want to look back.

CHAPTER 31

THE GROWING AFFECTION

*Love has produced some heroes
but even more idiots.*
—Swedish proverb

I couldn't keep my new discovery entirely to myself. I constantly felt like I was going to explode, and the only person I could comfortably about Yasmin was Jones. So, one day, I opened up about my interest in her, that I couldn't even sleep at night because I kept thinking about her. He urged me to confide in Chris, but I wasn't ready to share those feelings with him yet. Chris and I could talk about other things, but not this. It was out of my comfort zone. I begged Jones not to say anything to Chris or anybody else until I was ready.

He did, however, convince me that we should tell *someone* in my family. I agreed he could tell Scott. Even though Scott and I had a rough past, I never hated him. He was still like an older brother to me.

The following day, Scott called. Jones had mentioned my feelings for Yasmin, and Scott invited me over to talk about it.

I went, nervous to discuss the feelings. I wasn't sure what to expect or what he would say. We settled on the couch in the living room, neither of us saying anything. I looked at Scott, and he watched me carefully.

"Do you want to get married?" he finally asked.

His question confused me. I was seriously interested in Yasmin but hadn't thought much about marriage, at least not yet.

"I'm not sure," I answered honestly. "This is my first time having these kinds of feelings." I paused, considering his question a bit more. "I don't really think I'm ready to get married, but I'm definitely interested in Yasmin."

Scott searched for her on Facebook, but he couldn't find her. We googled her name instead and finally found a picture. After looking at it for a moment, he asked, "Are you ready to deal with romantic feelings?"

I shook my head.

"Do you even go outside?" he asked.

I didn't. I was scared to go outside or be in large crowds. It gave me anxiety that I couldn't overcome. "I know I have struggles and issues," I said. "But if a girl like Yasmin was interested in me, I could do things I didn't think were possible. Just seeing her has already mostly cured something I've been struggling with, and I know I would want to overcome more obstacles for her."

After a moment, Scott spoke. "I once knew this Malayali guy. He was in his late twenties, early thirties, married, and had several kids. They had a nice house and everything they wanted. The problem was that he didn't contribute to his household. His wife worked all the time, made all their money. He didn't do anything. It wasn't that he couldn't find a job. He just didn't want to. So, he did absolutely nothing. Do you want to end up like that?"

I knew what Scott was trying to do. He was trying to warn me that if I married Yasmin, I might become a freeloader. But I wasn't like that guy. I wasn't planning to marry, have a wife and kids, and just sit at home all day. I was willing to do anything and everything for my new love, including work, study, and whatever was needed to make a relationship work. I wasn't a freeloader, an opportunist, or lazy. And I would never use her as my sexual object. Never! That wasn't my motive. My feelings for her were real. I wasn't like that guy at all.

It was true that I didn't currently have a job, a degree, or even basic common sense at times. Maybe what Scott was saying was true: if I tried to have a relationship with Yasmin without first bettering my position in life, I would be looked down upon. People might say all kinds of bad things about me. I certainly didn't want that to happen.

After Scott told the story about that man, I seriously thought about my situation. I didn't want to be seen as a freeloader. But I wasn't like my two successful brothers. They knew how to live in the real world, and they could marry if they wanted; I didn't have that capability yet.

I felt that Scott was trying to talk me out of pursuing Yasmin. He didn't think I was smart enough or successful enough to handle a relationship. He didn't want me to be trapped in a relationship I wasn't ready for, even though I felt ready, despite not really understanding what I was getting myself into.

But I had to face the facts; he was right. I couldn't live on my own yet. I still struggled in many ways and needed to work on myself. It hurt slightly that he didn't support me, though. I remembered when he had tried to keep me from going to India. How could I be sure he was truly on my side?

After about half an hour and a bit more idle chatter, I left his house and headed home.

I knew romance was a pipe dream. I wasn't smart, and I didn't have a nice job. I couldn't take care of a wife or a family yet, and I wasn't handsome enough to attract someone as beautiful as Yasmin. Most importantly, I wasn't mentally ready for a relationship.

Knowing something and accepting something are two different stories, though. I knew the facts, yet I wanted to believe that Yasmin and I could find love together. I was trying to change, trying to find my way back to normal. I wanted to be successful. I wanted to go to college, get a degree, and find a good job. If I was able to do that, I would be ready for marriage. Or for a relationship, at least.

But I wasn't there. My dad had kept me from my goals, kept me from healing and getting better. He'd wasted five years of my life, allowing others to take advantage of my mental health issues. He'd stood in my way, keeping me from getting better.

So, of course, I couldn't pursue Yasmin. Part of me wanted to contact her parents and tell her that I was interested in her. But I knew everybody would be against that idea, and it wouldn't be viewed as a "normal" thing to do. I was in no position to talk to her parents. What did I have to offer? Even if they accepted me, I had nothing to give her. I didn't want to destroy her life.

But I wasn't ready to give up entirely.

I created four Indian matrimony accounts to keep looking for other Knanaya girls. In America, young people usually find their potential partners by themselves rather than having their parents look for a suitable mate. They go on a few dates, become boyfriend and girlfriend, try living together, and marry at a later date when everything worked out. But in our Malayali community, parents looked for a mate for their children through matrimony websites. It was less likely for parents to do this for children born in America.

Signing up for a matrimony account was risky. Anyone who knew me could be on the sites, and they might find me while they were surfing. The surname Pallattumadom would certainly stick out. If anyone who knew me discovered my profile, they would definitely notify my parents.

That would be the end of my fun.

Normally, the fear of being discovered and humiliated would be too much for me to even consider signing up. But I was hyper-focused on Yasmin and moving forward with romantic ideals. I couldn't forget her face, nor did I want to. I wasn't thinking straight.

I decided not to subscribe to the paid versions of the matrimony websites even though they had more features. The free versions would work to start with.

Early the next morning, while everybody was sleeping, a man from Kerala called me. He was an agent from one of the matrimony websites where I'd registered. When I'd created the account, I'd filled out every detail on the form, including my email, cell phone number, location, and other personal information. One site had even required me to provide my parents' phone number, and I'd given them that information as well, thinking, "Okay. No problem."

Even still, I hadn't expected anyone to call.

I spoke quietly with the agent for a moment, hiding under the blanket on my bed because I didn't want my family members to hear me. He tried to pressure me into getting the paid version of that matrimony website. I avoided his requests, worried that my parents would find out what I was doing since I would have to use their credit card. I didn't want them to know, so I couldn't give in to his demands.

I told him I would subscribe to the paid version later and that I was busy at the moment. I ended the call and hoped they would leave me alone after that.

Later that day, I deactivated and closed my accounts. Having ventured out of my comfort zone made me feel reckless and on edge, and I no longer believed being on the sites was a wise choice. I promised myself that I'd reopen the accounts after I started college. I didn't deserve to be unhappy because of what the bullies had done to me.

I was feeling more aggressive than usual, acting crazy and wild, like an animal in the wilderness preparing to fight for a female during mating season. I acted harsh and spoke abruptly. I didn't remember ever feeling this way before; it made me feel like I was out of control, spiraling.

The more I thought about my situation, the angrier I became at my family. They had no interest in helping me. They just wanted me to see my psychologist, so they didn't have to deal with my problems anymore, not because they wanted me to heal and become the best version of myself.

During one of these moments of frustration, I texted Scott. I told him that the purpose of seeing my psychologist wasn't to benefit him, my dad, or anyone else. I wasn't a social experiment and didn't want to become someone I wasn't to make everyone else happy. I wanted to restore my original self and become the happy kid I'd been before I was bullied.

Scott had been a major factor in my dad's resistance to returning to India in 2013. It was Scott who'd shown my dad that he could keep me from doing what needed to be done. If my dad had supported me, then Scott would have supported me, too. However, he took my dad's hesitation as a doorway to getting on his good side.

A voice in my head told me that Scott didn't hate me. I knew that. Perhaps he even regretted what he had done. But I knew I couldn't let everyone else control my life. I needed to restore who I really was, and I had to let Scott know he would not stop me this time. I would find the key to my happiness.

The first step was going to college, which I had wanted to do for a long time. I was finally ready to move in the right direction and hoped this was proof that I would do whatever it took for a chance with Yasmin, for that dream. Even if that dream was nothing more than sticks, ready to crumble at any second, I was committed.

I really needed to have a job before pursuing Yasmin, and before that, I needed to study for that job. I didn't have time for messing around with a major I might not love, and my interests in computers and technology appealed to me more than nursing. I'd loved computers since I was in the fourth grade. So, computer information technology was a natural choice. Nursing just wasn't my dream job.

The IT field offered plenty of possibilities. I could become a computer support specialist, a computer technician, or any other IT-related individual. Those choices all sounded interesting, and I was ready to move forward.

I tried to make a new college e-connect student account on the college's website. I was excited when I pressed "Submit." However, the website said, "Error." My heart dropped.

Then I remembered that I couldn't make a new account because I already had one under my name. I had a student ID number, only I couldn't remember my password. So, I reset it and successfully logged into my old account.

The only thing I needed to do was to see an advisor to discuss my career path. The college had put me on academic probation since I hadn't finished school in 2012. That would be easy to fix though, and I'd be back on track with my education.

Focusing on school was a welcome distraction from my heartache of knowing I wasn't ready to pursue my dream girl. I couldn't forget Yasmin completely. Honestly, I didn't *want* to forget her. She'd inspired me in a way nobody else ever had. Because of her, I could see a future for myself that I never thought I'd find the will to pursue again.

I saved Yasmin's photo and put it next to the amazing, happy photo I'd taken of myself. I looked at it while listening to romantic songs. I was just daydreaming, but these fantasies were an important step for me. They made my brain feel good, better than it had for a long time. My body was releasing feel-good chemicals, and I was reaping the benefits. I felt like my brain was healing, so I kept daydreaming. I did this day and night.

These fantasies never had anything to do with sexual acts; they were all innocent. I imagined us dancing to romantic songs together on a sunny day, some place with a lot of flowers. Sometimes, there was even a hint of fog in the background. I imagined her smiling at me while we sang together, with that same smile from her photo. We held hands, and she put her head on my chest while I wrapped my arms around her. It was a beautiful scenario. Thinking back on it now, those moments may have been cheesy, but back then they were exactly what I needed.

My fantasies reminded me of love scenes in many Malayalam films. Whenever two people realized they were in love, a song would play in the next scene and they would dance to the song, sometimes alone and sometimes with backup dancers. There were no sexual scenes, just pure, romantic moments.

In my fantasies, Yasmin and I were always perfectly compatible. I hadn't been interested in girls before, but if I'd had a normal life—if I'd never been bullied or had been able to heal properly—I could have had a girlfriend by now. She would have increased my quality of life. Maybe now I finally had a chance at that reality. I just needed to fix things first.

Almost every day I listened to all kinds of songs, especially romantic ones. The music would pour out through my headphones or computer speakers, making me feel better. The songs kept me distracted from any negative thoughts and bad feelings about my life. Yasmin was the only person on my mind.

CHAPTER 32

LAST CHANCE

Better an hour of thought
than a year of regret.
—Slovakian proverb

Shortly after I discovered Yasmin, my family made plans to visit India for my cousin May's wedding at the end of the year. That made me think about how my chance to return and stay in India had been taken away from me by my family and my mental health issues. My quest had been thwarted by factors outside my control. I thought about my crush and current heartache. I thought about school. While I wanted to attend college, my mental health had to come first. I couldn't just give in to what my family wanted, pretending everything was fine.

This time, I wanted to take control of my own life and stay in India.

I was determined to get back to my mission once again. Now was my opportunity. To prepare, I banished all negative thoughts. I promised myself that I wouldn't fight with my dad, my brothers, or Scott, even if they tried to ignore my concerns. I was going to move forward and reclaim the person I once had been. My renewed fervor for my mission was because of Yasmin—and for her, too.

This time, because I had hope, I would succeed. I would find the key to my happiness and finally heal. I wanted to achieve this by or before I turned thirty years old. I vowed that this would be my last and final deadline. No more deadlines after this. I needed to make this count at all costs.

Scott said that he also planned to go to India to attend his cousin's wedding. That meant I could finally confront Jith in front of Scott. Until then, I could prepare for the final showdown. That got me excited, even though I still didn't know how to confront Jith. I didn't lose hope.

Without delay, I made plans to go to India as early as I could. I was going to ask my dad to let me stay; this time would be the last, however. I didn't think he would say no this time.

I started attending church again. I used to go to church regularly and participated in church functions and activities. But after all the struggles I'd faced, I had lost a tremendous amount of faith in God and stopped going.

It had been a while, and I wanted that connection again. I asked Jones to go with me. He agreed and told me that my younger cousin Ken wanted to go too. We made plans to go the next Sunday. I decided to attend church with a new look. I gave myself a haircut.

However, while trying to trim the sides and back of my hair, I accidentally cut too much off. It did not look good. I tried to fix it by cutting it shorter, but that didn't work out either. Eventually, I had to buzz my whole head. The thought of having people see me like that at church was mortifying. I told Jones and Ken that I couldn't go.

A day or two after that, I got a WhatsApp message from my cousin Leo in Kerala, India. I hadn't talked to Leo since

I'd come to America, but we saw each other whenever our family visited India.

We started talking a lot. He was looking after my grandmother Madelyn. I told him about my hair incident and sent him pictures. I also told him about a terrifying dream I'd had that day.

"Maybe that's because you don't have any girls to love!" he joked.

It surprised me that he brought up girls. What a coincidence! If I hadn't been interested in Yasmin, I would have probably skipped that subject completely and acted like I didn't hear him. But my mind was fixated on romantic things, so I didn't mind him bringing it up.

I told Leo that I was trying to find Knanaya girls online. He told me about a website with a lot of them. I didn't tell him about my crush on Yasmin from the matrimony website. I did tell him that I was thinking about coming to live in India at the end of the year, and about my dad, Scott, and my frustrations.

I discussed importing a motorcycle from America to India and wondered if I should buy a bike or a car there instead.

Leo sent me two pictures. The first was of a smiling young man with a motorcycle. The second was the same guy after he had crashed his bike. He'd lost his leg. I was already hesitant about buying a bike, but the pictures turned me off the idea completely.

Leo probably thought it was risky for me to drive a motorcycle in India. He would rather I drove a car because it was safer. Safety came first! It would be a shame if something happened to me in India.

I turned my attention to buying a new car, but later ditched that idea too. My godfather Paul would probably be willing to lend me his when I got to India. I didn't need to spend that much money.

After a few weeks had gone by, Leo sent me a picture of a girl with his family.

"Do you know this girl?" he asked.

"No," I wrote back. "Why?"

"Her family is trying to marry her to a close friend of mine here in India. She's from America and lives in Texas."

This was confusing to me. I wasn't sure why an Indian American family would want their daughter, born in America, to marry a man who lived in India instead of someone who lived in the US. They could be incompatible because of cultural differences, and the relationship might not work out.

Leo's friend asked him to go with him to meet this girl. When I told Leo he should go with his friend, he asked, "Are you interested in her?"

A few days later, after he went with his friend to meet the girl, he sent me a couple of pictures.

The photos were of a different girl, not the one he'd shown me earlier. He texted, "Rick, the girl I showed you earlier was not the same girl my friend and I went to see. This is the girl. She is the one who is trying to marry my friend."

This new girl's name was Starla. She was very pretty. It turned out that she didn't live in America; she lived in India. She lived near Uzhavoor, where my dad had been a professor. Leo said she was a very active and a socially engaging person. She was smart and enthusiastic but had failed her degree for some reason. Starla and I were almost the same age. Suddenly, Starla also had my attention along with Yasmin.

Leo's friend didn't have any plans to marry her, which was welcome news to me. I was happy and excited. However, much like with Yasmin, I didn't have the capability of communicating with Starla either. But I didn't want to look at everything negatively. I wanted to make the impossible into the possible.

It didn't matter to me if Starla had failed her degree. If I could sort out my mental health problems, then I could get a job and support a family. In that case, she wouldn't even have to work if she didn't want to.

Leo then told me, "Someone from the US or the UK recently married a girl from around here. You can too." That made me chuckle. "Rick, if you like her, ask your cousin Scott about her. He can hook you up by contacting her family."

Leo probably had no idea that I wasn't really capable of marrying anybody, that I wasn't mentally ready to embark on that journey. Nevertheless, he recommended her to me. He told me, "Don't wait for your older brother. Her family is actively looking for a new partner for her, and if you wait, you'll be too late."

I asked, "Do you want to be involved in this? Do you want to talk about me to Starla and her family?"

"Uh, no, Rick. It wouldn't be a good idea if I was present. They already know me because I was there with my friend. I don't want to risk seeming uninterested or damage anything."

So, Leo wanted me to marry her! I was happy.

This brief interaction made me want to go to India even more. If I could just sort out my life, the world was full of possibilities for me. A wife, a family—those things I was never sure I could ever have—were now within the realm of possibility. I just needed to work my issues out.

Leo thought I should start a Facebook account so I could be in closer contact with everyone. I had never been interested before, but after hearing him talk about it, I figured I had nothing to lose. I signed up and uploaded a couple of photos.

I didn't tell anyone about my Facebook page except for Leo. I didn't know how much I would use the account, and I wasn't planning to send any friend requests. Little did I know that the People You May Know feature would lead many people to my page; I ended up with ninety-one friends in just a couple of weeks!

I used to be sure I would never use Facebook because of concerns about my privacy. I'd learned somewhere early on that they didn't have privacy-related settings. I'd thought, *Why do I need Facebook, anyway?* I had even promised myself when I was in high school that I would never create a Facebook account. But now, I changed my mind.

Facebook opened up a new level of understanding about the world. Before using their app, it was like living under the rock. I didn't know what was going on around the world or what people did in their spare time.

I used Facebook every day, browsing through my newsfeed, and learned a lot about how people I knew lived. I saw their family pictures, and got to know them, remembering their faces just by looking through their profile photos. Since I didn't interact with others often, I wasn't familiar with anyone. Suddenly, I could learn new things about their lives just by using the app. My knowledge grew every day.

Talking with Leo also opened my eyes to a whole new world of possibilities. I could see a life for myself—an image of who I could be, who I might have been if I had never been bullied or if my family had supported me and helped me. That realization was only possible because of Leo and Facebook.

On another random day, while browsing through my Facebook newsfeed, I saw that my older cousin Sarah shared a post about a kid who took his own life at just thirteen years old because he couldn't bear the bullying he was facing.

It was a sad story. I knew how much pain he must have been in, how he must have thought suicide was the only way to relieve that pain. I remembered thinking that myself when I was going through my own bullying experiences.

I recalled a dream I had while deeply sleeping. I was thirty years old, and my life had not gone as planned. Dejected, I let myself go the same way my uncle Karl had—by not doing anything. My dad wouldn't let this happen and brought me to a psychiatrist and two men with syringes to subdue me. Terrified, I tried to run away from them. But they cornered me and held me down. Right as they were about to inject me, I woke up.

That dream shook me. It reflected my fears about my dad controlling me and my life never being my own. My dad was lucky; he'd never faced bullying. That hadn't been enough for him to want to help me find myself in India. I'd lost motivation and many years trying to find the stamina to improve my life on my own. My mental health had put me in a place of trying to choose between whether or not I should keep living, and it seemed as though my family had paid very little attention to me.

That dream further strengthened my resolve; I needed to go back to Kerala. I needed to be happy.

CHAPTER 33

BEGINNING OF THE END

*The path is made
by walking.*
—South African proverb

Tobin noticed something on my neck one day as we conversed. "Is there a lump there, Rick?" he asked. "Have you ever had that checked out?"

I hadn't.

He wondered if I might have thyroid problems. "Thyroid issues can affect your mood and cause depression," he said. He told my parents that I should see a doctor to get it checked out.

I wasn't really sure I had a lump. If I did, it had to be small because it didn't bother me. But thinking about that lump had me worried. What if it was something dangerous or life-threatening?

In the end, I decided not to have my neck checked since I could barely see the lump.

When I later visited Tobin, I asked him directly if I had mental problems. "If I do, what do you call the illness I have?"

He didn't answer. He quickly changed the subject and talked about something else.

I wondered why he wouldn't tell me the name of my ill-ness. Usually, American doctors were very transparent about their patient's health. Even if it was bad news, they had to give a patient information if they asked for it. But Tobin didn't fill me in. Perhaps he thought it would be best if I didn't know. Perhaps he meant to fill me in later.

He must have written about my illness on the form he filled out every time I visited him. I hoped he had good rea-sons for not telling me; if I learned about a mental disor-der that I had, maybe he thought I would get upset or think too much about it. I might take it too seriously and further damage my mental health. Worried about all the unknowns, I didn't bother to ask about it again.

Life was going well, and I was keeping myself busy with other things. I thought often about Yasmin. I looked her up on Facebook; maybe she'd made an account since Scott and I had looked.

She had.

When I found her page, I was even more amazed. I had only seen one photo of her on the matrimony site. But she had plenty of other photos on her Facebook account. I looked at every single one. I compiled whatever information I could gather about her to determine what kind of person she was. She appeared to be very honest and innocent, exactly what I'd thought the first time I'd seen her.

I will be the first to admit that it would seem creepy if a stranger went through every photo on my social media ac-count. That seems like the definition of the term "stalking." I never considered myself that type, but it seemed like that was what I'd just done to Yasmin.

I visited Tobin with my parents again later that month. While we talked, he realized I was acting differently and became suspicious. He asked me about it—but how could I tell him about Yasmin and Starla in front of my parents? I was trying to keep my crushes a secret.

When I didn't answer, he said, "Rick, you may need to see a counselor. I will refer you to someone. It seems there is a lot going on with you, and it might be good for you to have someone else to speak with."

I quickly replied, "No, Doctor. That won't be necessary. I'm okay. No problem."

I wanted to tell him about the girls. They made me feel motivated and excited to better myself...but I couldn't do it in front of my parents. I always had my sessions with Tobin in front of them to prove I had nothing to hide. This, though, was a secret I definitely *did* want to hide. Nothing good would come of them finding out I had a harmless crush.

When I next viewed Yasmin's account, I learned that she was in a relationship with a man from Florida. I was both disappointed and relieved at the same time.

I was disappointed because if I had been in a better mental state, if my dad hadn't stood in the way of my healing, I would have reached out to her when I first saw her profile on the matrimonial website. Who knew what could have happened then?

I was relieved because I was happy for Yasmin. Even though I had never interacted with her, she had been a big factor in my life. I wanted her to have a pleasant future.

I found the picture of her I'd saved on my phone and deleted it.

Even though I wanted to be happy for her, the missed opportunity still crushed me. I'd never know what might have happened if I had been encouraged and supported. If I'd had the chance to find my original self, I might have connected with her.

I felt angry and cheated.

Time continued to pass, and our trip to India grew closer. I would have a big decision to make. I did all I could to prepare.

In October, Scott's third child had his baptism. I was nervous to go because of all the people. Crowds had been a big factor in keeping me away from church for five years. But I knew I had to attend. I went with my brothers and Ken to Scott's house and posed for photos with his son.

The entire time, I felt tense and anxious, but tried to put on a "happy" face for the pictures. I didn't want to act awkward or upset anybody.

When we got to church. I discovered that there weren't as many people there as I'd feared. What a relief!

After the baptism, we gathered in the church hall to celebrate. The crowd was significantly larger there, occupying all the available space. I worried because many people were going to see me; I would probably stick out after not having been to church in five years.

Vodka, brandy, and other alcoholic beverages were served at the party, which surprised me. The priest must have allowed it. My brother gave me a plastic cup full of brandy, and I drank the entire thing. The drink was more potent than I'd thought, and I felt wobbly. I found a chair to sit in, but I couldn't focus. My world still swirled.

Luckily, my anxiety faded away. I floated, weightless and unbothered.

Before we left, Scott spoke to me in private. He thanked me for attending his son's baptism. He probably thought I would never have come, given our past and the fact that I usually stayed home. He may have also felt bad about what he'd done after I attended his father's funeral, but I was never certain about that. I appreciated him telling me that. Maybe, deep down, he thought of me as a little brother.

The next time I saw Tobin, I told him about the baptism and getting tipsy. He laughed and wondered aloud, "What denomination are you?"

"Knanaya Catholic," I answered.

He smiled. "That explains it. That sort of thing only happens in the Knanaya community." He paused briefly, then cautioned me against drinking in the future. He said it wouldn't be good for me because of the medication I was on.

I assured him that it was a rare occurrence, and I was not usually a drinker.

I told him that my visit was a farewell for a while since we would soon leave on our trip to India. What I didn't tell him was that I planned to stay, it could be several years before I would see him again. I didn't know how long exactly because I didn't know for sure how long I wanted to stay in India.

I asked him if he would like to be my Facebook friend.

He looked at me with a sad smile and said, "I can't. I'm not allowed to interact that way with my clients."

"I understand."

I had a strange feeling as I left his office that day that I would probably never visit him again. I wasn't sure how long I'd be staying in India and by the time I got back, Tobin may have moved on with his life or even retired. He was a good psychiatrist.

I had a flashback to a joke he'd made during a past visit. He'd told my parents and me, "People who are born in May are very stubborn." He'd smiled.

I'd paused for a few seconds. I hadn't understood why he'd said that at first. Then, he'd continued, "I was also born in May."

It was meant as a harmless joke. Looking back, I realized that I appeared a little stubborn. He had probably not understood my relationship with my father. I had spent much of my time trying not to surrender to my dad's will, no matter what.

I said goodbye to Tobin and left the clinic.

After a couple of weeks, I checked Yasmin's Facebook profile to see whether she was engaged. I could immediately tell that she and the guy from Florida had broken up. I was flooded with happiness once again.

A slight glimmer of hope shot through my mind like a falling star, but it was gone just as quickly. Romance was still not an option for me in my current situation. I had nothing yet to offer a potential spouse.

Still, I felt my excitement return. When I looked for Yasmin on the matrimony website, I couldn't find her profile page. I wondered why. While Yasmin remained on my mind, I also let my thoughts wonder to Starla, the girl that Leo had shown me.

The days brought us even closer to our trip to India. I felt the anxiety and stress of the trip weighing heavily on me. Some days, I just wanted to lie in bed in peace and not have to face the day. That would not push me toward my goal, however.

The day before we left, I wanted to get new jeans. I felt like my old ones were out of fashion, so Chris and I went shopping. He bought two pairs of jeans and two new shirts for me.

As we were wrapping up, I started to feel sick. I had a slight fever, and my nose was running. I didn't feel well, and my face was pale. Were people staring at me? I couldn't figure out what was wrong. I panicked. We went home, and I prayed that I would be well enough to travel to India the next day.

I struggled throughout the day, but by the next morning, I felt a lot better. I was ready to grab the opportunity by the horns to change my life and succeed. This time, I wouldn't be deterred. My mission would come first.

Chris dropped us off at the airport. We made it quickly through customs and boarded the plane. On my way down the narrow aisle, I accidentally hit a woman with my laptop bag. I quickly apologized, but inside, I panicked. Would she yell at me? Curse at me? Make me feel bad for hitting her when it had just been an accident? That would be a horrible way to start off my new adventure. Luckily, she didn't say anything or seem bothered.

We arrived in Abu Dhabi in the United Arab Emirates and then flew to Kerala, India. I had forgotten what a long, drawn-out process flying to India was; but at least the flights were uneventful, which I was thankful for.

We departed the plane and went to grab our bags. When I leaned forward to pick mine up, I heard two men giggling behind me.

I was confused, but then realized that they could see the top of my boxers over my jeans. I hadn't worn a belt because I didn't want to deal with taking it off when I went through airport security. In America, this would have been no big deal; many young people intentionally wore their pants like that as a fashion statement. In India, it's a more sensitive thing and is considered inappropriate for a female to see such a sight. I was embarrassed and regretted not wearing my belt.

Aside from that, everything at the Kerala airport went smoothly. We arranged for a taxi to take us to Kaduthuruthy to visit my mom's family. My godfather Paul had arrived from the UK the day before to prepare for his daughter's wedding.

We only planned to stay at my uncle's house for a couple of days, but he insisted we stay for our entire visit. I worried that this would disrupt his plans, but he waved off our concerns. He was delighted to spend more time with us, so we agreed to stay.

Over the next few days, we visited my grandmother Madelyn and other family members. Madelyn sometimes had memory issues due to aging and other medical ailments, so she usually forgot most things she was told.

Leo and his family were there, too, so we visited them. It was nice to be reunited. They all noticed that I had lost weight, and my body looked healthy again. That night, we went back to my uncle's.

The next day, Leo came to Kaduthuruthy to see us, and brought along his friend. We planned an outdoor trip, my first one since 2013. I was both excited and nervous.

We went to a lake. While we waited for a ferry, Leo and I took some photos. I took out my new Canon camera that I'd bought in the US.

While I was turning it on, Leo gave me a funny look. "Why are you shaking?" he asked me, pointing at my hands.

I glanced down. "Um, I guess my nerves are…I'm just tense because of all the excitement of being out today."

I wound up having a lot of fun on the ferry. Afterward, we went to the theater to see a Malayalam film. I was enjoying being back in India, seeing family, and picturing my mission going successfully. It was doing a lot of good for the new, positive outlook I was trying to cultivate.

CHAPTER 34

MORE TROUBLE

Where there is a sea,
there are pirates.
—Singaporean/Malay proverb

Over the next couple of days, my uncle, my dad, and I visited some of Paul's relatives to invite them to May's wedding. The first person we visited was Joji, my mom's distant cousin, who appeared to be in his late fifties. This was the first time I'd ever met him. Uncle Paul asked him to come with us so it would be easier to find the other homes we needed to visit.

We delivered the other wedding invitations to many homes. Whenever we were outside, Joji smoked cigarettes. He couldn't help but smoke. By the time we got to the last house, it was late in the evening, so we stayed and ate dinner with Joji and the family.

Over supper, my dad asked, "Joji, were you smoking outside?"

Joji didn't like that question and answered gruffly. "So what? Do you have a problem with that?"

My dad said nothing. He hadn't asked to upset him. He had simply been trying to make conversation. Joji was not open to discussion on that topic. The sudden tension put me on high alert mode. Something told me that my dad's innocent question was going to lead to a big outburst.

It didn't take long for Joji to turn his attention to me. "Where do you get your money? Do you work? Or do you just get free money from your dad?" he snarled.

I wasn't sure what to say. Something was definitely going on. I glanced at my dad, hoping he would help me out of that awkward situation. I could feel Joji's eyes burning a hole in me. I worried that if I responded, I would offend him. I was stuck somewhere between fight and flight mode. I almost said something, and I could have. I was unprepared and afraid that whatever I said would come out disrespectfully and cause a bad scene. I didn't want to look even worse in front of others.

Joji wasn't even targeting me with his question. He was actually trying to shame my dad, but my dad was not the type of person to care. It didn't affect him.

Finally, my dad changed the subject—though my mind remained stuck on Joji's malicious question, so I missed the rest of their conversation. I was doing my best to push back the negativity and worry that was threatening my brain. I was being so careful to avoid conflict in Kerala, and I didn't want to let it bother me now.

Later, I learned Joji was under the influence before we arrived at the last house for supper. He was drunk and the alcohol had inspired him to speak so rudely. Still, he knew exactly what he was doing.

Despite my best efforts to repress the feelings, I became angry and upset. Joji thought I appeared weak. If my brothers had been there instead, they both would have had a witty comeback. Their body language might have warned Joji not to say anything. But because I was still on my road to healing, he'd kicked me while I was down.

We dropped Joji back off at his house later and returned to where we were staying, I was furious with my dad and let him know it. "You should never have let Joji speak to me like that in the first place," I told him.

"He was just joking," my dad replied, trying to brush it off. He always downplayed situations like this.

I disagreed, but I stayed silent. I wouldn't achieve anything by arguing with him.

A few days later, May's cousin Amalu came to my uncle's home. She was several years younger than me and when she wasn't giving me odd looks, she ignored me.

I was surprised that she didn't make any efforts with me. I tried to overlook it, but the next time Amalu came by she deliberately ignored me again. Perhaps I didn't talk to her like normal people because of my lack of social skills. I was afraid, and it made visits awkward and uncomfortable. I tried my best to ignore her.

May's wedding approached quickly, bringing more of our family to India. On December 26th, my mom and Chris arrived. Jef didn't come because he had just gotten a new job and wanted to stay in his employer's good graces. It would not have been smart to ask for time off so early in his employ.

Besides the wedding, we had another family event to celebrate as well: Leo's firstborn child's baptism. All our family attended. After the holy mass, we gathered in a nearby hall to celebrate.

Amalu was there. She looked unhappy the second she saw me. I could see her whispering to people, including May. I had the distinct feeling that she was talking about me.

I heard the word *maturity* in English, which made me even more sure she was whispering about me. I knew only too well that I struggled with that.

The more I watched, the more the situation got to me. My chest felt tight, and it was hard to breathe. I forced myself to exhale slowly, trying to keep my cool.

What really stung was May seemed to be participating in the gossip. I wasn't sure, and I forced myself to look away. I did not want to believe that.

I was overwhelmed and upset. I'd never done anything to this girl, and she had no reason to have this attitude toward me. Once again, I was inexplicably involved in some kind of drama I couldn't seem to avoid. Everybody seemed to love to pick on me. How many more people would I have to deal with like this in India?

My social awkwardness made me stand out from the crowd. If you can't socialize well with others, people will pick on you. I was only trying to finish my previously stalled mission, but because of these new attacks, I thought I might never get myself back on track. All my efforts would once again be for naught.

Since May appeared to be participating in the drama, I decided I was not going to her wedding. On the way back home, I told Chris that I wasn't going. I also told my parents. I was angry, and it manifested in anger toward them. They didn't know about Amalu and May's whispering, and I didn't tell them. The whole situation upset me. I just wanted something to go smoothly for once, and I went on the defensive, once again blaming my family for not listening to me in 2013. My brain told me that if they'd paid attention, I wouldn't be dealing with drama now.

I stayed in bed late the next day and didn't go with my family to one of May's parties.

The next day, May called me. She wanted to know if I had a problem with her. I wondered if Chris had told her what was going on.

We talked about it. She insisted she would never talk about me or be mean, and she still apologized. I didn't entirely believe her, but she seemed friendlier now. She told me that she really wanted me to come to her upcoming events: *Othukalyanam* and *Mylanchi Ideel*.

I didn't know if her invitation made me feel better, but it didn't feel bad either. I tried not to look at her negatively. She was my cousin, and I didn't want to screw up our relationship. Somehow, I had to see things positively. I didn't want to upset her, especially now as she was getting married and preparing for a new life.

I reluctantly agreed to come. I attended her wedding and the other activities without problem. Everything turned out fine, and I was glad that I'd decided to go. It was nice to see May happy and enjoying life, even if I was still stuck in my past and trying desperately to find a way out of it.

The day that my mom and Chris returned to America, Leo invited me to see a random movie. I agreed. It would be a nice change of pace.

We sat down in the theater in front of two young women and one young man. After a few minutes, I heard them talking.

The guy said to the girls, "That guy in front of us looks like a foreigner. Watch out! He might befriend and marry you, take you out of the country!"

The girls laughed.

I felt weird. Were they talking about me? I wasn't sure if I should take what the stranger had said as an insult or a compliment. Why did they think I looked like a foreigner? Maybe it was because of my haircut?

It was more proof to me that I stood out from the crowd. Coupled with all my recent experiences in India, the good mood I'd been in since arrival slipped away. The affection that I harbored for both Yasmin and Starla—the affection that had brought me so much joy—faded into the background as the fog of unease and distrust settled over me. I didn't want to slip back into that dark place that had been my home so often in the past, but I didn't know how to avoid falling down that hole either.

CHAPTER 35

KEEP GOING

Fall seven times,
stand up eight.
—Japanese proverb

While I was hanging out with Leo and spending time with family in India, I couldn't get my mind off Yasmin. My thoughts drifted to her throughout the day and night; she was my bright spot.

Time was my enemy. I knew that. She might find someone else. I needed to fix my issues and prepare myself. Only then could I contact her. If I could just finish my studies, I'd have something to offer.

But I still wasn't in the right place mentally. I was slowly drifting back into the darkness. There were good days and bad, but I still was far from accomplishing my mission.

I couldn't escape my past. Each time I tried to put myself into a new situation, I felt as though my brain was going to explode. Still, I was moving forward in small ways. I knew that some of the best things I'd ever done in the past were writing apologies and seeking forgiveness from people I'd wronged. My attempt at an open carry still bothered me, so I sought healing by writing a letter to the Irving police department that I would hand-deliver when I went back to the US.

Day to day, I continued to struggle. My dad wanted us to visit one of my aunts in Ernakulam and take in a few tourist sites. Off we went, with Leo joining us.

We got to my aunt's house in the evening, too late to visit any of the tourist sites. After we freshened up, we headed to the mall so I could buy a speaker system for my gaming computer, which I had brought from the US.

I had an uneasy feeling but tried to push it aside. I wanted the speaker and to have a good time with my family. But as we shopped, the tension grew. I panicked again, worried that people were watching me, judging me. I kept looking around, trying to catch anyone staring. My anxiety grew more intense. I tried to stay focused, and eventually we found the speaker and bought it. Miraculously, I made it back to my aunt's house while avoiding a breakdown. I knew I should be fine after I slept.

The room where I would sleep had no curtain, however. Even as I tried to relax and fall asleep, I became hyper-focused on the lack of curtains. Anybody could see me, could look at me. I grew agitated.

My dad saw my frustration and found some curtains in a cupboard. He and Leo put them up. That simple act softened my heart toward him a bit. Though he tended to ignore my emotions, he always did his best to help when I was panicking or visibly upset. He wasn't evil, just careless at times. He wanted to help.

He just didn't know how to deal with my emotions. He was capable but clueless in that area. He only knew how to deal with battles of the body. Battles of the mind were not his forte.

After they put the curtains in place, I finally found some peace and fell asleep.

The next morning, we went to a tourist spot called Marine Drive in the waterfront district. The wind blew, there was a salty scent in the air, and everything was beautiful. It felt good to be there. We took some photos and time seemed to stand still.

I had been to the tourist area before when I was little. Well before I traveled to the US for the first time, my family and I sometimes came here whenever we visited my aunt. This was my favorite place to hang out. I could see boats and ships passing by. It was a long way from my home, so when we visited there, we made those moments count, made them worthwhile.

Leo and I sat on a bench, watching the backwaters and tourist boats. We were quiet and relaxed.

Out of nowhere, an older lady approached, watching me in particular. "Can I see your hand?" she asked. "I can tell you your future."

It felt a little uncomfortable, but Leo and I didn't really mind. I'd never had a fortune teller telling me about my life before. So, I thought, *Why not?*

"I'll need payment first." She opened her book and showed me her payment plans. I was hesitant but intrigued. I thought to pay her 500 rupees, but Leo suggested her cheapest plan for 200 instead.

"Give me your hand," she said after pocketing her money. I opened my hand.

She started talking about my past, present, and future. "I can see that you aren't that bright." She looked to see my reaction. "I'm not saying this to be mean. I'm only doing my job."

Her words surprised me. I thought she would say nice things. I wondered if I'd made the right decision. Still, she was right. I still wasn't as mature as I should have been.

"Let's see," she continued. "You are living in your third home, yes?"

I nodded.

"And you are financially stable. You are looking for love, and you've already found someone. But it is not working out. Eventually, it will, one day soon. Not all is lost."

Images of Yasmin and Starla flashed through my mind.

She smiled up at me. "You have lovely eyes. I can tell you are very innocent and cannot consciously trick others. You have a good heart, but you are not yet mature."

I felt like I was in a movie. She was speaking truths about me that I hadn't told her, that she couldn't have possibly known. She was probably very experienced in reading other people's personalities and body language since she'd been doing this for ages.

She offered to read Leo's palm, but he declined.

I felt both a little weird yet still happy about what she told me. The results were not exactly as I'd expected, but I was satisfied. It felt good to know I still had a chance with Yasmin and Starla. Overall, I felt positive about my life and my future because of that fortune teller. I was glad she'd offered to read my palm.

We spent the rest of the day at Marine Drive before heading back to my aunt's house. Then, the next day, we went home.

***

As the days went by, my morale got lower, and my moods constantly fluctuated, unable to find a balance. I continued questioning myself and my situation. What business did I have, wanting to pursue a girl? I wasn't in the right place to focus on them, and I wouldn't be able to reach out to either of them. It just wasn't in the cards for me with either Yasmin or Starla.

My mental health was still a mess, and I was no closer to completing my studies or pursuing a job. I had no experience in the real world. Nothing had really changed for me since I'd discovered them, and I knew I needed to let go for my mental stability.

Despite the fortune teller's predictions at the beginning of February, I made a tough decision about Yasmin and Starla. I deleted all their photos from my phone. Thinking about them was just too hard.

Later that month, my childhood best friend Lucas visited. He was currently living and working in Oman as a chef. Leo and I got together to hang out and enjoy one another's company.

Around that time, I got a text message from Jamal, my distant cousin and Jones' older brother. He lived near me in the US and was one year younger than me. He said, "Hey, Rick. I am coming to India for a few weeks to attend my grandmother's funeral. I'm going to visit you while I'm there. I want to see Scott's home, too." Scott's wife was Jamal's cousin, so Jamal and Scott had a close relationship.

Jamal had never been to my place before, so I happily replied, "Yeah! Sure! You can come. I am ready to pick you up whenever you're ready." Jef and he were very close because they'd worked with each other at their jobs. I could use this as an opportunity to improve my relationship with him. He'd been the first one to greet me when I'd arrived in America in 2013, and we'd slowly grown closer since.

In the days following his grandmother's funeral, Jamal messaged me to pick him up at a bus stop in a nearby town.

Lucas went with me, excited to meet him for the first time. When we met up, Lucas and Jamal introduced themselves and quickly and naturally became friends. Everything was going smoothly, which made me happy.

Back at my home, Jamal met my dad and the rest of my family. We then went to visit Scott and Jith. Thankfully, Jith was in Oman when we stopped by. The trip was filled with food and drink as we went out to a local bar and restaurant, then came back to my house with beer and even more food.

While we talked, I accidentally revealed the reason I had come back to India: I had come to fix my life after being bullied. This was the first time Jamal and Lucas had heard the story. I honestly felt relieved after I told them. We casually discussed it, and I even told them about my problems with Jith.

The next day, Lucas and I dropped Jamal off at a local bus stop and said our goodbyes. I heard nothing more from Jamal until after he'd arrived home. We chatted back and forth as we always had. My confession about my bullying hadn't changed the way he saw me. I felt I could trust him, that he was someone in whom I was comfortable confiding my personal concerns.

So, I told him one more crucial detail.

The *real* reason I'd come back to India wasn't just to fix myself. It was because of my crushes. This news amazed Jamal. He had looked at the same matrimony site where I found Yasmin. He always checked a candidate's social media accounts and contacted them whenever he could. He wasn't trying to marry anyone, though; he was doing it for fun.

Jamal was a flirter, a womanizer like Mason, yet more laid-back. He just wanted to chat with the girls, and I wondered if that was actually a good idea.

He told me a story that made me believe it was not.

One girl he chatted with on Facebook liked Jamal very much. She told everyone in her family about him, intending to marry him. She wanted to go to the US. When her family talked with Jamal and found out he had no intention of marrying her, he got into trouble. In fact, his entire family was upset for a while once they found out.

When he learned I was interested in a few girls, he suggested I look them up on Facebook and message them directly. The idea excited me. Maybe I *could* reach out to them after all!

Days later, Chris told me that he saw an advisor at an IT school in Dallas because I had wanted to find information about IT classes in America. Chris had become an IT professional a few years before. He explained how to choose a program and then complete different certifications. For example, if I wanted to do the computer user support specialist program, I needed to complete four mini-courses, such as CompTIA A+ and CompTIA security. If I passed those courses, I would get one certificate each week. The total time needed to take classes was only about four or five weeks.

This sounded perfect. There weren't any specific start dates for the classes, and I would go from 8:00 a.m. to 5:00 p.m., just like a job. I liked that idea. The only downside was it would cost a lot of money to enroll. But in truth, money wasn't a problem. Courage, on the other hand, was. I was still afraid to move forward.

After I talked to Chris, I wondered whether I could find a similar program in Kerala. That way, I wouldn't have to return to America, and I could continue to work on myself as I studied.

The course work would be doable for me. I already knew a bit about the hardware-related computer aspects. I knew how to build a computer from scratch—I'd taught myself by watching online tutorials. Sadly, I could have learned all of that before becoming an adult.

I thought about seeking a computer course and the future possibilities it could produce: a proper education in a field I liked and, eventually, a good job. The concept of solid employment let my mind drift back to the idea of romance. If I could get on the right track, find myself, and pursue a career, then why couldn't I have a relationship eventually?

I looked at the Knanaya website again to see if there were new girls. Of the girls I had originally seen a couple of times and become interested in, only a few were still on the site. The rest had moved on. I swiftly had their pictures downloaded again.

I thought about what Jamal had told me about contacting girls through Facebook. I didn't want to let this opportunity pass me by. It was almost Valentine's Day. What better time to reach out and give this a shot?

On the 14th, I messaged one girl through Facebook Messenger. I waited, but after two days, she still hadn't replied. I had probably said too much in my message; I should have just said hi and started a conversation.

I sent her a friend request, but after another two days she still hadn't accepted. I was disappointed and started doubting myself. I withdrew the request. I accepted that I'd messed up. I didn't know what I was doing. Because I lacked social skills and maturity, I was no better off now than before I'd sent the message. Perhaps that tactic was good for people like Jamal, but I wasn't that kind of guy. I shouldn't have sent the message or friend request in the first place.

Later that month, I visited the website again. While I was looking through the pages, I checked for and found Yasmin's profile again. I got excited once more.

Starla's profile, the one Leo had shown me, was no longer on the site. I had no way of knowing if she had found someone else and moved on or not. She had no other social media accounts that I could find...so Yasmin became my sole focus again. Despite having deleted it only recently, I re-downloaded her picture.

CHAPTER 36

CONFRONTING THE BULLY

Until the snake is dead,
do not drop the stick.

—Ivory Coast proverb

In March, the worst person ever to enter my life came back. When I heard Jith was coming to India to attend his cousin's wedding, I was not happy. He'd made my life miserable for *years*, pushing me away from my goal. I didn't want to see him or deal with his games again.

One day, Scott, my dad, and I sat on the front porch together and the subject of Jith came up. Scott had returned to Kerala temporarily to attend his younger cousin's wedding. My dad knew all about the drama between me and Jith and briefly updated Scott. I elaborated as he continued, explaining what Jith had put me through. My dad wanted our problems resolved and our fighting ended once and for all, making his life a lot easier in the long run. Scott suggested he arrange a meeting with Jith.

Jith respected Scott, never doubting or questioning him. They were close, like brothers. Scott was the reason Jith was successful. He'd taught Jith how to live in the real world before he went to America. He had taken him under his wing and showed him the ropes.

Jith became a very intelligent bully over time. He knew when to hit and when to withdraw. He could hide his true self from the people who were on top of the social ladder. His specialty was fooling other intelligent people, especially the influential ones. He knew they were the key to his own success, and he would do anything to get what he wanted. His skills always amazed me.

In reality, he had never gotten over his own bullying experience. He'd just buried his problems. That's why he got angry and projected that anger onto others whenever he had the chance. It made him feel good inside.

The only way to deal with Jith was to meet him face to face. I knew that, yet part of me dodged the idea, wanting to avoid him at all costs. Despite all that, I couldn't avoid the inevitable; our paths were bound to cross eventually and resolving our differences would make any future meeting more tolerable.

I decided I was ready to end this dog and pony show once and for all!

I had serious doubts that a conversation with him would help, though. Jith wasn't the type of person who had regrets. Instead, he calculated every move, designing them for optimum gain. If no one held him accountable, his behavior would continue. He was very clever. I needed to drop a bunker-busting bomb on him.

I remembered the notes I had made about his bullying the year prior, including photos I took of those notes on my cell phone so I could confront him in the future. Finally, I could put those notes to good use.

I agreed to Scott setting up a meeting.

After Scott and Jith's cousin's wedding was over, Scott brought Jith over to my house. I was nervous. This would be my first time to confront him and dredge up our ugly past.

But Scott was there. I was glad there was a third party. In front of Jith, I explained to Scott how Jith had treated me and that he held a long-standing grudge against me.

Jith, of course, denied it. "That isn't true," he said. "Why would I have a grudge against you?" He didn't seem bothered by my accusations, but I could see the worry evident on his face.

I wasn't about to back down. I opened my phone to the list of everything he'd done to me, ready to bring it all to light.

Being a master manipulator, Jith realized that I had come prepared and was not backing down. This could make him look bad, so he needed to quickly adapt in front of Scott.

So he didn't try to defend himself. Instead, he tried playing the nice guy. With every new instance I listed, he insisted I had misunderstood him. He'd never felt a grudge toward me and was never upset that I hadn't introduced him to my family members.

It was complete bull crap. He was trying to catch me off guard and make me doubt myself. But after all this time, after all I had been through, I wasn't about to let that happen. I stood firm and stuck to the truth.

At one point, he stood up to leave. He didn't say anything, just headed for the door as if he was done with our conversation.

That was a very unusual tactic for him. He rarely retreated from a fight, but perhaps he realized that this time there was no way to talk himself out it. He chose to leave rather than fight for his honor as a final attempt to control the situation.

That was totally unexpected. I was so confused at his new behavior that it took a moment before I finally realized that I got him by the balls for the very first time!

But Scott got up too. He asked Jith to sit down and listen to everything I had to say. Jith realized he was really and truly stuck. If he left now, he would look weak in front of Scott. He'd look like a coward in front of a mentor. He couldn't let that happen.

With no other real choice, Jith sat down again. Maybe he thought he could recover if he feigned confidence. Regardless, he stayed, hoping to get it over with as quickly as possible. I wondered what kind of game he would play in front of Scott. I was worried; Jith was very clever.

I read through all the incidents I'd written down. At first, Jith again denied any wrongdoing. But as I went through my list one by one, he changed his tune. The only way Jith could end this was to *admit guilt.* So that's what he did. But his admissions were completely phony. I could tell by the look on his face that he was faking it. He was very good at faking his emotions and thought Scott would likely fall for it.

I pointed out, "You intentionally screwed up my life!"

Jith went on the defensive, his emotions leaking through in his response. "What now?"

Obviously, he wanted to intimidate me, to make me think twice before I said something else. He was literally challenging me in front of Scott. He was skilled in that way, and we both knew it.

Scott didn't say anything, and just kept watching us in silence. I thought he would react, but I don't think he wanted to distract the two of us from our talk.

I could feel myself becoming emotional, but I couldn't afford to let anyone know that was how I felt. That reaction was exactly what Jith wanted from me; if I responded by getting emotional, it would be that much easier for him to control and manipulate me. I continued with my litany, not wanting to lose focus.

Every time I mentioned an incident, Jith said he was guilty. But when I asked him what he was guilty of, he wouldn't say anything. He would only stare at me awkwardly. I had seen through his act. Scott fell for it, however. He cut him some slack, which irritated me even though I'd expected it.

Jith had no regrets whatsoever, which made me even more emotional. My focus waned. I was angry. He was lying in front of Scott to preserve his status. I fought against all those emotions welling up inside me, threatening to pull me back into the dark cloud of depression and anxiety. If I let myself lose control, Jith would have all the power once again.

Eventually, Scott concluded Jith had tried repeatedly to embarrass me and had bullied me.

Jith just nodded his head as if he agreed but showed no signs of shame or remorse for what he had done.

I asked him, point blank, if he regretted his behavior. "If you do, why did you never reach out to me or ask my forgiveness?"

"I did," he said. "I tried to send you messages through WhatsApp, but you didn't reply."

Unfortunately for me, that was true, although it had only happened once. If Jith had really been sorry, he would have tried again, sending a text or a voicemail to apologize. But he didn't. Not that it even mattered, because he would have been straight up lying anyway. That's why I had never responded; I couldn't trust him. He was just trying to trick me, just as he had done before.

After I said my piece, Jith tried to shake my hand. He was trying to play me. If I shook his hand, he could say that everything was forgiven and forgotten.

But it wasn't. So I refused.

"The only way I'll forgive Jith is if he takes a lie detector test," I told Scott. "It's hard for most people to see past Jith's lies, and that's why I'll only trust a lie detector." Of course, I knew you couldn't just go out and get a lie detector test. Even if we could, Jith wouldn't be willing.

Finally, Scott realized that I had said everything I needed to say. So, they both rose to leave. But before they did, I read a list I had made of Jith's good and bad qualities. That list was the cherry on top of the sundae. Jith just smiled. I could see that he would never be sorry for what he had done.

We were both victims of bullying, but the difference between us was that he had sold his soul to the devil at the price of becoming successful; I hadn't. He'd lost his goodness and innocence, what made him who he was, and he hadn't cared to try to get it back.

He'd been a nice guy when I had first met him. I'd expected him to be kind and willing to help me when I first came back for my mission of self-recovery. His maturity and intelligence could have helped to make my life better.

Instead, he'd taken the opportunity to be hostile, and start a war with me that lasted for years over a simple misunderstanding.

I couldn't believe that young, innocent Jith became a career bully, that he could abandon his values and positive traits to become someone rude and unrecognizable. Despite knowing what I'd been through and recalling what it had been like for him to go through the same thing, Jith had chosen to bully me. It was a conscious decision, and I couldn't ignore that.

I'd given him a lot of chances, and I'd tried to forgive him. But he had never expressed any genuine regret for the way he had treated me and probably never would. Any forgiveness I might have for him had expired.

All Jith ever did was act, never showing people who he really was. Each time he went out, his mantra became, "Lights. Camera. Action." I knew this; there would be no reconciliation with my cousin.

I wanted to teach him a lesson badly to make him pay for what he had done. But I felt bad for his parents and sister. I didn't want to hurt them by hurting him.

There was no hope for him, and I didn't need him any longer. He had made his choice. I would not fall for his manipulative and toxic behaviors any longer. I had a life, and I wouldn't give him the opportunity to screw that up again. I needed to cut off all contact with him.

This time, I was going to do it permanently! *No more toxic relationship!*

A few days later, Jith came to my house with his mom and grandmother. I heard the car pulling up and saw them outside the window. Before he could make it inside, I went to my room and locked the door. He came up and called for me, but I didn't answer. I wanted nothing more to do with him. He wasn't sorry for anything he'd done to me and was only there to play more mind games with me. I didn't want any confrontation; I just wanted to be left alone. That's all I had ever wanted from him, to be left alone. Jith would leave India for work in Oman soon enough. I only had to avoid him until then.

While I waited for Jith to leave, I thought about my father. I still blamed him for many of my issues with Jith. He'd caused our initial conflict against my wishes, he'd never had my back, and he'd made excuses time and time again.

The anger I had so long held for my father bubbled to the surface as I stared at the ceiling. I hadn't gained peace, even after my talk with Jith. We were still technically at war as he had shown no signs of remorse. Between the rage I felt for my father and my worst enemy, my mind clouded again. My behavior changed in that instant, and I began to act out.

When my dad came home that evening, I told him I was going to make him proud by becoming a *penupidian*. Penupidians are males who enjoy having sex with many girls, whether they are married or not. I was going to make a Tinder account and find women. I felt a little wild at that moment.

My dad didn't react at all. There was only a hint of surprise in his eyes.

Deep down, I hadn't meant that. I didn't want to be a penupidian. I just wanted to get in my dad's head a little, making him think I was going to do something irrational.

I followed that up by telling my parents never to bring Jith to our home again. I said he was dangerous, and I believed he would show up again, despite my wishes, since bullies sometimes never let go of their victims. I told my parents that if he did show up again, I might do something stupid, and things could get ugly!

They seemed to take me seriously for the first time. They told Jith not to come to the house anymore.

I didn't see Jith for quite some time after that. I did my best to put him out of my thoughts. Then, one evening I received an international call from a number I didn't recognize. I answered. When I heard the voice, my stomach dropped.

It was Jith.

I hung up immediately. He tried calling me two or three more times, but I ignored him. I was determined to heal and didn't need to deal with him.

My mental and physical health was wavering. Maybe it was because of Jith and the old pain being dredged up. Maybe it was because of my constant struggles to get back to my original self. Maybe it was the lurking realization that I wasn't ready for a relationship. Whatever it was, I was falling again into a bad place.

My uncle asked me why I looked very skinny. I hadn't noticed any weight loss yet, but that was certainly what was happening. In fact, since February, I had been steadily shedding pounds. I didn't know why; I was still eating as I always had, yet I was growing thinner and thinner.

When I looked in the mirror, I was as skinny as I'd been in 2016 when I'd refused to eat in front of my parents as a protest.

I also experienced strange stomach problems, which I suspected was related to my extreme weight loss. My mom was worried, so she went to see my old doctor, Dr. Ranny, and asked for her advice. Dr. Ranny told my mom I was too stressed, causing my stomach to produce more acid. More stomach acid would cause an ill feeling. She prescribed a few meds to reduce the acid and sent my mom on her way back home.

When my mom told me Dr. Ranny's suspicions, it all made sense. My time in India was quite difficult, despite my determination. It was affecting my body, not just my mind.

I was pushing myself to my limits, and my entire being was suffering.

I didn't know what to do besides take the meds. For the first time in a long while, I considered going back to America. I remembered the lump on my neck and suspected that it might be some kind of thyroid problem, which can cause extreme weight gain or weight loss. I considered getting my thyroid checked, but I decided to let it go and resist the temptation to go back to America.

I needed to meet whatever fate was waiting for me in India face to face.

CHAPTER 37

THE TIME HAS COME

It is useless to shake the branch
that bears no fruit.
—Samoan proverb

At the beginning of March, I actually thought about creating a Tinder account. Even though I'd told my dad that to upset him, it ultimately didn't seem like a bad idea. Marriage was off the table for me; I certainly didn't think I was going to marry Yasmin. She would probably marry before she turned thirty, like any other girl in the Knanaya community. She would find someone else soon. I was not even close to ready. By the time I finished college, she would be gone forever.

There felt like no point in even trying. I would not complete my mission in time to have a relationship and marry someone, especially not Yasmin. But I didn't want to lose all hope, so I kept a few photos of girls that I had liked. They represented a future that I couldn't have then but might attain someday. That idea gave me a reason to keep going.

After a lot of thought and consideration, I decided not to go through with the Tinder plan. I didn't have a credit or debit card to subscribe to the paid version, and I didn't want to deal with any messages from robots or people looking for things I wasn't interested in.

I decided I would put off the Tinder idea until I got a job.

Panic attacks still snuck up on me from nowhere, brought on by small and seemingly insignificant things. One night, I drove my childhood friend Srijesh and his friend to a movie in a nearby town. When I returned home, a sinking, panicky feeling overtook me. I didn't know where it came from, but it enveloped me quickly.

My brain felt like it was short-circuiting, jumping from one thing to another. I had suicidal thoughts again for the first in a long while. Was the world ending? I felt trapped inside my brain.

Luckily, I had a backup plan in case something like this ever happened. I went to my room and relaxed in a chair under a blowing fan. I looked at that best picture of myself that I had kept with Yasmin's photo. When I looked at her, it didn't seem weird. She was gorgeous and seemed kind. That made me feel better. Eventually, the panicked feeling faded away.

I was learning how to deal with my panic attacks, learning how to distract myself enough for them to pass without incident, even if I couldn't completely prevent them from happening.

After a while, I started thinking about the other pictures of girls I had saved. I wasn't keeping them for nefarious reasons. They were a light, a beacon of hope for me. They were an inspiration to move forward.

But I realized that if anyone else found out about them, I might look a stalker. That made me feel too uneasy, thinking that others would consider me as strange or creepy. So, I deleted all the pictures, except for Yasmin's. Hers was hard for me to let go of.

But when my mind drifted back to her, I felt like I would never have anything to offer her, that I would never even have the chance to meet her, let alone date her. I didn't want to be someone who was lazy or completely dependent on his wife. That would look bad and be embarrassing for us both.

On the matrimony sites, women were looking for men who brought money and skills to the table. I didn't think anyone wanted to marry a person who was immature and incapable. I needed to have a proper education and a good job. I should have had those things by now since I'd lived in America for the last fourteen years. Who would find me attractive, knowing I was unstable? Those women wanted a good partner they could count on. With me, a relationship would fail. I just wasn't ready, and marriage was no joke.

I started to think that I probably had no choice but to become a *penupidian* if I wanted a relationship. But that's not the person I am. I didn't want to rid myself of the innocence I'd fought to keep all those years. That was all I had left on Earth.

Thinking about girls and relationships really wasn't getting me to a place of healing, though, so I switched focus.

I sent a Facebook message to Joji, the relative who had targeted me in December. That incident had been hanging over my head, and it was time to move on.

So, I wrote him a message, telling him that my mom had said he was a comedian. "If you were a real comedian, you wouldn't have tried to embarrass me to upset my dad. If you try to pull that kind of thing again, I will prove that two can play that game." I sent the message, which left me slightly worried because it felt too aggressive for my own taste.

He never replied. He wasn't tech savvy with smartphones and likely didn't know how to type out a reply on his phone. I tried to look up his Facebook profile a while later, but it was nowhere to be found. Maybe he blocked me. If so, I was glad.

I could now consider the incident closed and move on. That chapter was over.

I thought more and more that I again needed to delete Yasmin's picture. I'd held onto that fantasy for too long. It wasn't attainable, and I couldn't be sure it was helping me to move forward as I'd hoped.

Once I'd made that decision, I finally felt free, much freer than I had for a long time. I didn't cry but was sad. My fantasy had come to an end, and I let Yasmin go. She had been on my mind much of the time over the past nine months.

I saluted her as a gesture of thanks and deleted her picture. *Goodbye, Yasmin...Goodbye.*

The sad truth was that her picture had kept me going better than any of my family ever had. Her photo had turned my drab world colorful again, with splashes of hope and renewed energy. Without ever knowing me, she had helped heal my agoraphobia for good. My life would have been drastically different if I hadn't indulged myself with her picture over the last eight months. She didn't know how much of an impact she'd had on my life and likely never would. Now it was time for me to let go of her and focus on me.

Freeing myself from Yasmin gave me a new perspective. After having lived in India for six months, it became obvious that living there was bad for my mental health. I wasn't making progress. Going out and seeing other people my age only made me painfully aware that I wasn't mature. Jith and the bullying I'd experienced years before prevented me from living the life I wanted to live.

I'd always thought I would achieve my mission in Kerala, but that hadn't happened. Too much time had passed; I had wasted too many opportunities. Kerala wasn't my sanctuary any longer. My mission had failed.

I still wanted to find myself and my happiness, both for myself and for my family. I didn't want to just survive; I wanted to get my life back. I wanted to live. But it was finally clear to me that it was not going to happen in Kerala.

I was too old for this, too tired. My father and I didn't agree most of the time, and we were arguing about my failing mission. I wanted to be done with my father like I'd been with Jith. With him, survival was the only option, and I wanted a better alternative.

So, I came back to America in July 2019. On my last night in India, I said goodbye to Leo, who was staying at my house. I left for America with both my parents, not knowing whether I would ever return to India again.

I weighed only 140 pounds and was six feet tall. Somehow, I needed to survive and heal, both physically and mentally, for my sake.

PART FIVE:
THE INEVITABLE BIG BANG

CHAPTER 38

A RUDE AWAKENING

*Desperate times call for
desperate measures.*

—Unknown

For a year and a half after I left India to return to America, almost nothing noteworthy happened, although I did manage to regain most of the weight I'd lost.

After everything I'd gone through, everything I'd failed to do, everything I'd tried to complete, I thought my life's story had ended. Maybe I'd learned what I needed to learn and I could, eventually, have a bright and happy future. During those eighteen months, I finally felt more at peace than I ever had, successfully holding back the darkness most of the time.

Little did I know that the peace and calm I felt was nothing more than a bandage, a temporary fix to a problem that was bound to explode sooner or later.

In June 2020, my parents finally told me that I had been diagnosed with a mental health condition. I had wanted to know what was really going on with me. My issues had hung over my head for a very long time, and I wanted to understand them. So, I asked my parents for my Indian and American medical records. That way, I would know everything once and for all! With that knowledge, I could move on with my life.

I was not overly upset to learn that something was actually wrong with me. In fact, that knowledge filled me with relief. Now, I had an explanation for the darkness that constantly invaded my brain and the fogginess that made me act uncontrollably.

But on December 26, 2020, the day after Christmas, I snapped.

I'd had minor arguments with my family for the past year and a half, but was careful not to escalate our arguments to a full-flamed war that would never end. Despite our arguments, nothing got out of hand. We were speaking safely, doing our best to be civil. Someone would always back down if something was about to go wrong. That was how everything remained under control.

But on this particular day, December 26th, things got wildly *out* of control.

Maybe there was something about the year 2020 that caused me to reach my breaking point. It wasn't a great year for the entire world because of the COVID-19 pandemic. Perhaps the stress of the virus, coupled with all the changes we all had to make throughout the year played a part in pushing me too far. I can't say for sure.

However, I can't blame everything that happened on the pandemic. There was another reason why I was so unstable right before I exploded.

Sometime in the middle of 2020, I received a mysterious voice message from Scott's mom via WhatsApp. I automatically opened the message without thinking because I was using the app. That was a big mistake.

The first thing I heard was a sound that I never wanted to hear: Jith's voice. He somehow had managed to sneak his message through my aunt's account, knowing I was more likely to see it that way. If I had seen the message was from him directly, I never would have opened it.

When I heard his vile voice, I was sucked in. I couldn't escape.

In his message, he "apologized" to me. His apology was phony and full of holes. He was clearly trying to intimidate me without others noticing, which pissed me off. He wanted the "last word" before he completely ignored me and moved on with his life. He wanted to prove to Scott and my dad that he was willing to take responsibility for his actions.

The longer I listened, the angrier became, almost to the point of a mental breakdown.

After I listened to the message, I told my dad about it. I explained how Jith was trying to make me look like an idiot and get away with the problems he had caused without consequence.

My dad said that I should forgive him and move on. "Jith said he was sorry. You should accept the apology and not question his intentions." This response made the rage bubble inside me.

I didn't know how to react to my dad. My emotions were all over the place, and I felt ridiculous. "How can someone intelligent like you think that Jith's fake apology was genuine after what he's done to me?" I asked. "Jith tries to take advantage of everyone!"

With an exasperated look, my dad said, "You will never accept an apology from anybody. That's your problem."

I had no words. I couldn't believe his stance. Jith was getting away with his crappy behavior again, which further pissed me off.

My head was overwhelmed with anger and depression, feelings which lasted for months, causing me to destabilize even more.

I still felt that way in December, and Jith's mocking phony apology weighed heavily on me the day I snapped.

The initial spark came from a minor argument that my family and I had started to have regularly. I was experiencing very low morale. My mood wasn't great, and I was depressed. I couldn't put my finger on why, but something told me that the minor arguments were to blame. They'd seemed like no big deal at the time, but the pain of each one built up, pushing me closer and closer toward my fault line.

It happened in the afternoon.

We had been talking, and the conversation went from pleasant to out of control in a heartbeat. Both of my brothers and my parents said some things which quickly shoved me past my limit. I felt like they ganged up on me. My brain overloaded quickly, receding into the foggy darkness I had thought was getting better.

Arguments like this had become rare. Although they still happened occasionally, I always backed down unless they somehow backed down first. I was afraid the police might get involved if things escalated, or that one of my family members would talk about the problem with someone. I didn't want what happened in our house to affect anyone else. Whenever it had, it never ended well for me.

In a flash, I decided I'd had enough. This time their words quickly convinced me that my life was going nowhere. A loud, angry voice in my head told me, *React! Do something they won't expect! You can't just do nothing!*

I paced all through our two-story home, upstairs and down. My body thrummed with adrenaline, and a need to retaliate brewed deep within my belly.

Suddenly, I had an idea. I grabbed my cell phone from the charger in my bedroom and headed downstairs where my parents and brothers were. Jef was ready to go to work, dressed in his work uniform. They watched me with wide eyes, waiting to see what I'd do next.

I opened my cell phone and dialed 9-1-1. As it rang, I stared at my family. I knew they would hear everything I said. The worry was clear on their faces, and a few of them hissed, "What are you doing, Rick?" I was undeterred.

When the 9-1-1 operator picked up, I said, "I'm going to kill my father!"

The gasps from my family were likely audible to the operator, but I didn't care. I paused for only a moment, making sure the message had gotten through. When the operator tried to say something to me, I ended the call.

My actions appalled my entire family. They had read the signs, knew I was struggling with symptoms of my mental disorder, but they didn't realize it would convince me to do something like that.

To their credit, they remained calm, never yelling at me. Instead, they just looked on in horror, asking, "What have you done? This isn't a joke!"

I felt like I was on a mind-altering drug. My body seemed foreign to me, wild and out of control. I felt completely weird.

I had no intention of actually harming my dad. I was bluffing, doing it in order to get attention from the police. I wanted to force my parents and brothers to deal with them. It seemed like fitting payback after the way they'd treated me that morning and, honestly, all the years since I'd first been bullied in eighth grade.

Unfortunately, I would have to deal with the police too. They took threats like mine seriously. I didn't want to deal with them, but my rash decision-making didn't lend itself to what I wanted. It would have to be done.

It was likely that my life would take a turn for the worse in the very near future.

My dad leapt into action shortly after I hung up the phone. He told my mom, "I have to find Rick's old medical records. They prove that he's got a mental health condition. The police will want to see that, so they understand why Rick's acting the way he is." He headed to his bedroom where he kept our important papers, trying to track down the records from my hospital stay in India in 2016 and the records Tobin had given him while I was under his care in 2018.

As my dad headed for his room, my head spun with other ideas, ideas that were scarier than bluffing to the police. I wanted to do something truly dangerous and unpredictable, something so off-the-cuff that everyone in our neighborhood would hear what I'd done once I'd undoubtedly go to jail for it.

By this time, everybody had gathered around me, wanting to make sure I was okay. Breaking free from them, I went to the kitchen and picked up a large knife from one of the kitchen drawers. Then I began pacing around the room once more.

Again, everyone asked, "What are you doing with the knife, Rick? Put the knife back into the drawer!" They were still worried about me, suddenly much more aware of my movements now that I was wielding a knife.

I went to my dad's room to see how his search was coming. I joked, "Hey, Dad, what are you doing? Come on. Let's stay in this room and chit-chat before the police come." My dad gave me a funny look, and I followed up with, "The SWAT team is going to come soon. I've never seen a SWAT team before."

I was coming across as pure evil. The joke I made to my dad made me feel like the murderous villain in a horror movie. I was playacting, pretending to be someone I wasn't for the sake of creating drama.

My dad tried to leave the room, but I held him back. I grabbed his right hand with my left, the knife firmly in my right hand. When I couldn't get a grip, I grabbed hold of his collar, pinning him in a sort of awkward headlock. I demanded that he stay there with me in a voice that almost didn't sound like it belonged to me. I spoke like I normally would, in my normal tone of voice. I didn't scream, raise my voice, or even sound angry.

I had no intention of harming my father with the knife. I couldn't bring myself to do that, no matter how upset I might be with him. In my head, everything I did resembled something they would do on a reality series: all for show, no one getting hurt.

Even though I had no plan to do harm, if truth be told I wanted my family to be afraid. I wanted them worried about what I'd do next.

I kept the knife away from my dad, pointed away from his body. I was careful not to touch him; I truly wanted everyone to stay safe. No one else knew that was my number-one concern, and my mother and brothers reacted out of fear when they saw me grab the back of my dad's shirt.

Chris jumped in, worried that I might try to harm my father. He thought I was unstable, so he acted on instinct. He didn't want to wait until it was too late. So, while I was talking with my dad, Chris tried to remove my left hand from my dad's collar while wrestling the knife from my right hand at the same time.

A small struggle ensued.

Eventually, I let go of my dad, and he hurried away from me. Chris let go of me too, after he'd made sure my dad was standing a safe distance away from me. Then, everything calmed down again. I backed away from all of them, keeping my distance.

My family went outside through the garage. I followed them at a safe distance.

Chris stayed between me and my dad, just in case I tried something else. He grabbed a long stick from the front yard for protection in case I attacked again, ready to ward off my advances if I moved toward them. He was going to protect my dad at all costs. He knew I was not likely to attack anyone else, as I'd made it very clear that my problem was only with my dad, not anyone else.

We stood in the yard for a while, staring at one another. I wished there was a way for me to tell my family that I hadn't planned to hurt anyone. I'd only tried to scare them as payback for all the things they'd said to me, but there was no way they'd trust anything coming out of my mouth.

What they could never understand was that I felt like no one ever listened to me. I had to do something outlandish to get their attention, to make them see what I felt like on the inside. This had been my chance to show them who I was, but now that I'd involved the police, I was sure that more things were going to change than I'd intended.

I wondered how long I would be in jail for my infraction. I felt like my life would be over forever. The police would take me away from my family for what I'd done, and I assumed they would put me away for a long time.

I realized that I only had a few minutes left before the police showed up. I wondered whether they would blow through the front door or come in through the garage door. I wondered if they would try to find me the moment they arrived or if they would wait.

All I knew for sure was they would be there soon. So, I carried out a destructive idea that would cost a lot of money.

CHAPTER 39

NOTHING LASTS FOREVER

A bad beginning,
a bad ending.
—Romanian proverb

I went back inside and up the stairs. I had the overwhelming feeling my life was over because of what I'd done. So, I went to my room, picked up my expensive gaming desktop, and dropped it to the lower level, letting it crash to the floor near the front door. The desktop *shattered*, landing on a big, round red rug. Despite being dampened by the rug, the sound was deafening.

I thought about stopping there and resting on the couch until the police came. However, I remembered it had been Chris who had sent me over the edge that morning. Something he'd said had made me angry, and I wanted revenge. An idea popped into my head for something else to destroy, and I headed off to get it.

In Chris' room, I picked up my old gaming desktop that I had given to him so he could play video games, and dropped that down the stairs. Then I picked up the internet router that he'd purchased and dropped it as well.

Finally, I pushed our small TV down the staircase. It slid down the stairs easily, making a satisfying crunch as it hit the bottom.

I calmed down a lot after that and sat down on the upstairs sofa.

Then I made another rash decision. I opened the Facebook app and made two separate posts. The first post said, "I'm going to kill my father." The second one said, "Happy Christmas."

Within a minute, my phone was ringing. It was Jamal. His first instinct had been to make sure I was alright. I was tempted to answer, but I didn't want to be on the phone when the police came.

So, I ignored him.

I stayed upstairs on the sofa, positioned neatly in the middle of the wide, open space at the top of the stairs. Anyone who came up could see me right away.

It took a few minutes and a few deep breaths, but my brain started to quiet down. There was no more drama, no more chaos. The fuzzy clouds in my head were still there, but I no longer felt violent or out of control. I felt like I was done, my payback finished.

All I had to do now was wait for the police. I was ready to face the consequences for what I had done. I was going to get arrested, and likely taken to jail.

I finally could hear noise out front and realized the police were already there, talking with my parents on the front lawn. My dad was probably giving the police the information about my mental illness so they would know how to proceed, how to talk to me, and how get me to comply with their demands.

I heard a voice over a loudspeaker call my name, asking me to come outside with my hands up. I didn't obey. I didn't want to go outside. I assumed that if I didn't come out quickly, they'd come in, looking for me, so I waited. That way I could rest as long as possible.

I still had the knife in my hand. It would be best not to be holding it when the police came inside, so I rose and laid it down at the top of the stairs. They would be sure to see it there and know I was unarmed. That would reduce the chances of me getting shot accidentally, which I was understandably worried about. It would be a shame after all of this if I got hurt or died. I hoped they'd see I was trying to cooperate; I didn't want to make things complicated.

Before the police came in, I went into my room and put on my new blue shirt, a fresh pair of socks, and new shoes. I made sure to put my cell into my shorts pocket too. I knew the first thing they would do was ask me to put my hands up. To be funny, I rehearsed putting my hands up several times.

I waited anxiously for them, calmly thinking about my future, wondering what would happen to me over the next few days. *Jail first,* I thought. *Then, probably a mental hospital to help me get a little more stable. After that, maybe court?*

It grew darker outside as I waited. I still didn't want to go outside because I needed to rest before I had to deal with the police.

A door opened somewhere near the kitchen. Whoever entered had come through the open garage. A moment later, I heard a few voices speaking Malayalam, not English.

It wasn't the police but members of my family: Aunt Ellie, Aunt Ruth, and Cousin Zoey. They called my name, looking for me. I was relieved it was them and called back so they could find me.

As they came up the stairs, I thought about each one of them, about how they knew what I'd done. I couldn't rewind time or erase their memories of the events. I felt bad as bits and pieces of my past with each of them flashed through my brain.

Aunt Ellie was the reason I'd had the chance to come to America. I'd always appreciated that, even though my life had not always been great after we left India. Coming to America was a dream for many, a chance others would have jumped on if offered to them. Sure, I'd been bullied—the catalyst for many of the bad things that had happened to me. Without that, my life in America would have been fantastic and awesome, just like it was for so many other Pallattumadom family members. Aunt Ellie had offered me all of that, and now she had to see what I had done to my house and my family.

Aunt Ruth was my dad's youngest sister. She had known me longer than almost anybody else. She had come to the hospital in Kerala shortly after I was born. Aunt Ruth had been the first Pallattumadom family member to carry me when I was just a newborn. Now, I was in my late twenties. I was sad and embarrassed that she had to see all the destruction and drama the sweet baby she'd held had grown up to cause.

My cousin Zoey had been a little rough to me during my first year in America and for years after that. But once I'd told her about my school bullying experiences, we had been fine. We had an understanding. I thought she might understand what was going on with me on this particular day too.

As they came up, they saw the knife lying at the top of the stairs. Zoey carefully picked it up and went back to the kitchen to put it away. Then, they all came up to me.

One asked, "Rick, what happened? What's going on?"

I just smiled back. I didn't know how to react. They were worried and saddened by what had happened, concerned by the destroyed computer equipment on the floor of the main level.

We talked. My voice broke from nervousness, but I tried not to show it. Despite having calmed down since my outburst, I was still trembling in my mind, scared about what was coming next.

I was surprised that my aunts and cousin were first to come in and find me, rather than the police or the SWAT team. "Where are the police officers?" I asked. "Aren't they coming in? I've been waiting for them all this time. That's why I'm sitting up here, not coming out. Why aren't they coming in?" I was appalled. Did the police not care about what I'd done?

I told them I'd made two Facebook posts.

Ruth asked me, "Why did you do that? What did you write?"

"One post said, 'I'm going to kill my father.' The other one said, 'Happy Christmas.'"

She was shocked. "Rick, you should delete those posts. Everyone will see them, and that will be embarrassing." Worry was clearly written on her face.

After I thought about it for a few seconds, I decided that deleting them would be for the best. I hadn't considered who might see them when I'd posted them. It was clear the negative impact those posts could have on me and my future. Deleting them was the best idea.

While we talked, Zoey said, "Rick, one of Chris' hands is bleeding. The cut on his hand came from your knife. You knew you had cut him, right? He's wearing a small cloth around his hand to stop further bleeding."

I was shocked, and I paused for a minute in disbelief. *How had Chris been cut?* I hadn't expected that. I felt bad for

Chris. He was my younger brother. I was supposed to look out for him and keep him from getting hurt. I had been careful with the knife, even while I was holding on to my dad. I worried the police might charge me with even more crimes if they saw Chris hurt.

I said, "Wait. What? Was it his hand or fingers that were cut? Is it a minor cut or a serious one?"

I didn't remember seeing any blood on the knife when I'd laid it down by the stairs. When could I have cut him? A moment's consideration let me remember Chris trying to grab the knife from my hand. He hadn't been trying to take it away from me, simply keep it away from my body while I had my dad pinned by his collar. There had been a small struggle. The lower edge of the blade must have sliced his hand.

That had been an accident, but it probably wouldn't matter; I would likely still get into trouble for the cut. I would never have hurt his hand intentionally, even if I was out of control. I felt like I'd crossed the line before, and now that feeling was magnified tenfold. Chris should never have been cut.

Zoey texted someone, sending information about me to someone in my family so they could relay it to the police. It was important for them to know whether or not I was calm and ready to talk.

The police were still outside. I felt much calmer, but I still had consequences to deal with for my actions. Anxiety about those consequences made my stomach churn. I strongly felt that the police would arrest me. They wouldn't leave without me in custody. At the very least, they would want to talk about my actions.

I took a deep breath. Time to face the music.

I asked Ruth about the police, wondering why they hadn't come in. She told me there had been a lot of officers and SUVs outside at first, but now most of the vehicles had gone. There were only a few left.

Zoey told me that the police officers wanted to talk to me. "That's the next step. Are you ready, Rick?"

"Yes. I'm ready to talk with them. Are they going to come in, or do I have to go outside?"

"I'll check," she said. She shot off a text to whomever she'd been communicating with since coming inside. A moment later, she nodded, and looked back up at me. "You'll have to go outside," she said quietly. "The police aren't coming in."

I took a few deep breaths and prepared myself so that I could concentrate and interact respectfully with them.

There was little daylight left, as it was somewhere between five and seven in the evening.

I went outside through the front door, all the while thinking, *This is it.* I knew I would not be coming back home for a long time while I paid my debts.

CHAPTER 40

ARE YOU A MALAYALI?

When we least expect it,
the hare darts out of the ditch.
—Dutch proverb

As I pushed out the front door, I saw three police officers standing a few feet away. I approached them, careful to keep my hands out of my pockets where they could see them. I normally preferred to shove my hands into my pants pockets when I was nervous about public interactions. That night, I didn't want to give them the impression that I still had a concealed weapon of any kind.

I glanced around to see whether there were any other officers, vehicles, or nosy neighbors outside, watching me from a distance. I couldn't see any, which was a good thing. I knew it was a possibility that neighbors watched me through the windows from inside their homes. I had caused a commotion in the neighborhood, and I couldn't conceal what I had done. I had no room to complain.

I hadn't seen my parents outside. I wondered if the police had told them to stay out of sight. Maybe they were hanging back for safety reasons in case I tried to go after my dad again. I understood, even though that knowledge broke my heart.

Chris and my friend Jones stood a short distance behind the officers, watching me as I came out of the house. I could see Jones recording me or taking a few photos on his cell phone. I couldn't complain about that either, but I wondered what he would do with the footage. Maybe he wanted to show it to me later, after I had come back from wherever the officers were about to take me. He wouldn't share the video with others, so I didn't have to worry. Jones had proven himself to be an honorable and good friend. Perhaps it was a good thing that he recorded these moments in case I ever wanted to see that footage when I came back, to keep myself from ever repeating my actions.

As I approached, the officers greeted me. I did the same, staying calm but alert. I still wasn't well-practiced at speaking English, and I didn't want to accidentally misunderstand whatever they said to me. It took me a few minutes to understand what they were trying to say.

We didn't chat for long. They quickly got to the point, saying they were not going to arrest me, but were going to take me to a local mental hospital—not to jail. They also said I would not be criminally charged with anything.

For the first time all evening, I felt relief. I wasn't going straight to a local jail, getting a mugshot, then being thrown me into a holding cell until they could decide what to do with me. Instead, going to the hospital was all that would happen. My body sagged a little as the weight of the fear I'd been carrying all afternoon lifted.

Two of the officers filled me in on what they were going to do. The third officer came up behind me and asked me to put my hands behind my back. I complied, and he slid handcuffs securely around my wrists. I had never been handcuffed before. There really is a first time for everything!

I expected one of the officers to read my rights like you see in the movies and television shows. "You have the right to remain silent. Anything you say can and will be used against you in a court of law…" None of them did, however. Since I wasn't being taken to jail or charged with a crime, they had no reason to read me my rights. I was simply going to the mental hospital to rest and recover.

I wondered how long I would be away from my family. Despite what I had done, I really didn't want to be separated from them. I had never done anything illegal before, and I'd never imagined I would. Now, I would pay for it with my time spent in the hospital.

The officer told me I wasn't being charged, but maybe they would uncover a reason to after further investigation. Would they still charge me for something later? I wasn't sure. I didn't understand how the legal system worked or punishment for crimes, but still felt there was a strong possibility I would be charged.

Regardless, my life was changing drastically and forever.

One officer put me into his SUV and we went straight to a local hospital. By the time I got there, it was completely dark outside, as black as midnight.

I didn't know how long I would stay in that hospital or what would happen to me. But I listened and followed directions as best I could. I ended up on twenty-four-hour observation.

I wasn't the only patient there. Many others were in the same room with me, all of us sitting in comfortable chairs.

Hours passed. I lost track of the time. Eventually, an Indian doctor called me into a nearby room. His face seemed kind of familiar. Had I seen him before in a photo? I wasn't sure.

The doctor seemed to recognize me too. After I came in and got comfortable, he spoke to me in English.

"Hi, Rick. My name is Michael. I'm a doctor here at this hospital. Are you a Malayali?"

"Yes!"

"Do you speak Malayalam?"

"Yes," I said again.

He probably recognized my last name—Pallattumadom. I felt relief at that but was still worried. If he spoke Malayalam and was from Kerala, did he know other members of my family?

He switched from English to Malayalam, and I immediately relaxed. I didn't have to worry about putting my thoughts and feelings into English. Malayalam was obviously easier for me to speak, especially during intense situations.

He continued with his questions. "Are you a Knanaya Catholic?"

"Yes."

"Where's your church? Is it near here at Farmers Branch?"

"Yes." *He must have attended that church before,* I thought. I wondered if he was a regular member or had been visiting one Sunday when I'd attended with my family.

The more questions he asked, the weirder I felt. I hadn't expected to chat with anyone familiar in the hospital, and the idea that I was speaking with someone who might know me struck me as odd and funny all at once. I laughed on the inside.

"Do you know...Sebastian Pallattumadom?" he asked.

I thought for a few seconds. Of course, I recognized my last name. But did I know someone named Sebastian? After I'd thought for a moment or two, I suddenly had an "Oh, crap!" moment.

"Uh, yes, I know Sebastian. He is one of my dad's cousins." Sebastian had come to America a long time ago. He was a medical professional. He went to our church too. Michael and Sebastian must have known one other since they were both Malayali medical professionals. Maybe they were friends!

After the getting-to-know-you questions, we talked about what happened earlier. He wanted to know the details about how I'd felt and why I might have done what I did. When we finished, Michael ended with a final question. "Are you taking medication, Rick? Would you take some if we give it to you?" I wondered how much he knew about my background and my psychotic diagnosis.

I nodded. "I'll take medication. I have no problem with that."

"Okay. Good." He smiled at me, opening the door so I could leave the room.

I sat in one of the comfortable reclining chairs, going over our conversation in my head. I wondered how Michael knew my family and church. I worried he might call Sebastian and tell him about what I'd done. I didn't want him to. *Would he tell more than just Sebastian?* I tried to ease my worries by reminding myself that Michael was a doctor. He couldn't just go around telling people about his patients. He had rules to follow that kept me safe and my info private.

That thought helped to lessen my nerves but didn't eradicate the tiny voice in the back of my head worrying that he might still spread the info around. Was I really in a position to complain after calling 9-1-1 with a threat against my dad?

CHAPTER 41

EXPECTATION VS. REALITY

You don't really see the world
if you only look through your own window.
—Ukrainian proverb

Eventually, that hospital transferred me by ambulance to a different facility several miles away. I arrived at the new hospital late at night. As I climbed out of the ambulance, I had a strange feeling that I had seen those hospital doors before.

In a flash, I realized why they seemed so familiar.

I was in Desoto, at the same hospital where my mom had once worked a long time ago. I used to drop her off here many times. That had been during my paranoia period. Since I'd rarely gone out of the house, this place stuck out in my head. I would recognize those doors anywhere.

I stayed at the Desoto mental hospital for the next nine days. There were at least ten other patients there for various mental health reasons. We all did group therapy and other activities together. Our therapists educated us about the causes of our mental illnesses and showed us techniques to help us get better. They called it "behavioral education." They handed out papers that detailed these subjects. Many other patients tossed their pages into the trash after each session, but I collected all of mine.

A psychiatrist saw me every few days. We didn't talk to each other very much. Mostly, they asked questions and inquired about how I was feeling. They started me on medication a few days after I'd arrived. I hoped to see an improvement in my mental health.

The longer I was there, the more excited I became looking forward to discharge day. All I had to do was get along with the nurses, doctors, and other patients and follow my care plan—attending and participating in group therapies and other activities.

During my stay, I spent a lot of time people-watching. I observed not only the other patients at the facility, but also the staff members. I learned something unexpected: each member of the staff—nurses, technicians, therapists, and psychiatrists—worked in shifts. Not everyone came into the building each day or at the same time.

I also witnessed at least six staff members—all of them techs—become very angry, though they weren't engaged with the patients who caused their outbursts. Their reactions surprised me because most of the instigating issues were normal encounters, not overly dramatic or demanding situations. I wondered if they were prepared or equipped to deal with mentally disturbed patients.

For example, one tech got mad because an older woman, Kayla—a former teacher—touched his arm while talking to him. This was just part of her nature; she sometimes did that while talking to other patients, including me. It was a harmless touch—although technically no one was to touch anyone else because of COVID-19 protocols, overall safety, and personal space reasons.

Kayla touching his arm infuriated the tech. He became so angry that when checking other patient's vital signs, he always asked whether they were going to touch him too. He didn't mention Kayla directly, but I knew who he meant.

The hospital seemed to have some kind of "no confrontation" policy with patients, especially those most unbalanced and unpredictable. The rule was in place for the safety of the staff as patients might react poorly or lash out. The only way for the tech to express his frustration was to talk to other staff members and patients.

He asked me, "You aren't going to touch people, are you?"

I tried to make our interaction go smoothly, since he was obviously in a bad mood and just letting off steam. I immediately told him, "No. I don't touch people." He seemed to relax briefly. Crisis averted.

The hospital tech didn't need to overreact to this incident. This part of the hospital was only for mental patients. Many had behavioral problems and other issues. Staff could react if a patient was a danger to everybody, but this was a harmless touch. He should have taken a few seconds to cool down. Then, he could have told Kayla politely that she was not allowed to touch anybody. She would have listened as she was always cooperative and friendly. Instead, he became angry—a rather unprofessional move.

Perhaps he was having a bad day, but that was no excuse.

Another example: a tech became pissed off while we were eating in the cafeteria. I didn't see exactly what set him off, but all of a sudden, he walked very quickly to a nearby door and pushed on the door, but it didn't open. He had forgotten to swipe his ID. He angrily used his employee ID on the card reader beside the door, which opened, and he stomped out of my line of sight.

When he came back, he still seemed mad. I thought, *What just happened?*

This was a scary moment because I worried he was angry at me. I panicked. He didn't make eye contact with me, but I still thought he kept looking at me. I was dealing with paranoia around that time, so I didn't know if this was true or not. I just didn't want to offend anybody while I was there.

After we got back to our unit, he kept pacing back and forth in the hallway. I wasn't sure why he was pacing. Was it because of me? Sometimes, I accidentally ignored others if I didn't know how to react to the situation.

Wanting to end the excruciating doubt, I decided to confront him. "Hi," I said.

He greeted me. "What's up?"

My question was laced with worry. "Hey, uh…Did I offend you in any way?"

He replied, "What made you think something like that?"

Unsure, I asked him, "Did I ignore you in the cafeteria? I have schizophrenia, and sometimes I don't know how to socialize with others. So, I may make mistakes."

He said, "No. You didn't do anything. Everything's good. Don't worry about it."

I paused, giving him a confused look.

He asked, "You good?" I paused again, and he raised his hand to fist-bump me.

My worry gratefully subsided. I fist-bumped him back. Okay, then. No problem.

Something similar happened with a lady tech. I got paranoid after she got mad and expressed her anger out loud while we were all in the cafeteria. Since I had talked to her that morning, I wasn't sure whether her anger was directed at me or not.

Most likely not, since she never confronted me nor mentioned me by name. But I couldn't keep from thinking about it.

I witnessed dozens of such interactions while I was at the hospital.

There were other employees who hung out with patients. I didn't know their job titles. They didn't check vital signs. They just sat and talked with us to pass the time, although they were also there to help break up potential fights. Typically, there were two people in the L-shaped hallway with us and two nurses in the reception area.

One day, one of the employees told a patient, "If somebody steps on my shoes, I'm going to whoop his ass."

Another said to a patient, "If someone disrespects me, I'm going to beat him up."

I wasn't sure how to feel about those comments. They might have just been parts of fun, casual conversations, but they all sounded serious. What if they actually followed through if someone treated them poorly? Those things shouldn't be said around emotionally disturbed patients in a mental hospital. These patients might apply these philosophies in their own lives instead of the guidance and advice of their therapists. Their bosses would never approve of their language. No therapist would talk like that. They have professional standards to keep.

These incidents and my observations completely changed my perception of mental health facilities and their employees. Maybe these things only happen in that facility, but I questioned whether I could feel comfortable and open around them, whether I could count on them without fear.

By the time I'd observed all these things, I was only halfway through my required time at the hospital.

On December 31st, a little before midnight, I was in my room, feeling sad. I felt like I was missing something or had forgotten something very important. I only realized a few hours earlier that it was about to become January 1, 2021. Other countries around the world were already celebrating their first day of 2021 with fireworks, and I had watched a few of them on television earlier in the evening.

I would spend some time on New Year's Day away from my family. Would I even get the chance to say, "Happy New Year!" to them? The cutoff for when we were allowed to make calls was 9:30 p.m., but I felt so desperate that I asked if I could phone my mom just long enough to wish her a good start to 2021.

I was a little afraid to ask the nurse since calls this late were against hospital rules. Eventually, I worked up the courage to ask her. I tiptoed out to the desk where she was sitting and gave her my best smile. "Hi. Can I call my mom to say Happy New Year to my family?" I asked kindly.

She paused, so I quickly added, "I only need thirty seconds. That's all!" I didn't want to give her the impression that I would talk for long.

I didn't need to be worried. The nurse gave me a nod and said, "Okay. You go ahead."

I was thrilled when she handed me the receiver. Then, I tapped in my mom's number, held the phone up to my ear, and waited with a pounding heart while it rang.

My mom picked up after only a few rings. I said, "Hey, Mom. I don't have any news, but just wanted to say Happy New Year. Will you tell Chris, Jef, and Dad this as well, tell them I said Happy New Year?"

My mom was surprised that I called her so late. We had also talked earlier that day, but I hadn't remembered then that it was New Year's Eve.

She sounded happy to hear from me again. "Of course, Rick. I'll pass the message on to the rest of the family."

"I know I'm not supposed to call you this late, but I was missing all of you and wanted you to know that I was thinking about you all tonight." I paused for a moment in case my mom said anything. When she didn't, I said, "Well, I'd better go back to bed. I'll call you tomorrow."

I ended the call and gave the phone back to the nurse. "Thanks!" I told her.

"You're welcome, sweetie. Happy New Year."

"Thank you. You too."

I hurried back to my room, feeling very happy and emotional. I stood beside the window and looked out. It was dark, and I took my glasses off, letting the tears building in the corners of my eyes roll down my cheeks. I didn't want anyone to see me crying. I hated getting emotional, and it was embarrassing when someone found out. After a few minutes, I wiped the tears away with the backs of my hands.

When I was sure I'd dried my face, I went to my bed, feeling glad, blessed, and mostly happy that I had done something good. I had wished my family Happy New Year just before midnight and the dawn of 2021. That was a good omen, a good way to start the new year.

I would have regretted it for a very long time if I hadn't done that. This was the first time I'd been separated from my family for New Year's, and it was all because of my behavior.

I missed them like crazy, but I hoped that my time spent in the mental hospital in Desoto would be worth it and finally help me heal.

CHAPTER 42

AN EYE FOR AN EYE

Revenge is a confession of pain.
—Latin proverb

After celebrating New Year's on my own, I spent my remaining four days in the hospital growing more excited for discharge day. The hospital staff had moved many more troubled and difficult patients to other locations near my unit. So, there were eight people total in our unit, rooming in pairs.

Of the eight patients, only two were males: myself and another guy around my age. We were both quiet like the rest of our unit members.

I anticipated having good days for the remainder of my stay, just like I'd had the first five days. I began having weird experiences, though. Something changed in our unit.

After spending a few days in the hospital together, a patient learned about everybody else: their strengths and weakness and capabilities. That was how I knew something weird was brewing. Some of the patients were getting a little cocky and exhibited risky behavior. There was a chance a problem might occur.

I kept my guard up, stayed alert, and watched every move of the other patients. I didn't want to be caught off guard if something unexpected happened. I feared a well-executed verbal attack and other unkind actions. I didn't want any confrontations. All I wanted was to spend my time in the hospital and to be discharged as soon as possible.

One night, almost everybody was asleep in their rooms except for me and another patient, Tania. We were accompanied by a tech. I was pacing up and down the L-shaped hallway like usual, a symptom of restlessness. I was wearing socks with flip-flops, the only comfortable shoes I had, since the laces from my regular shoes had been removed for safety. I was slipping a little as the sock seemed to be affecting my foot, but other than being a bit wobbly, everything seemed normal to me.

The tech and Tania were talking to each other. Tania seemed to be the most intelligent person in our group. She always engaged with others, joking or even discretely intimidating others. I was keeping an eye on her too, because of her behavior. As she and the tech talked, they looked at me from time to time.

Suddenly, the tech got up from his seat and began to walk like me, obviously mocking me. He and Tania laughed wickedly.

I was shocked, unable to believe my eyes and ears. I was very surprised that it was an employee making fun of me. Tania's part in this was unsurprising, however.

I was struck by two giant revelations: The tech—whom I had no previous problems with since we hadn't had many interactions—was supposed to take care of us and was, instead, mocking me. Second, Tania—who had been friendly to me before—was making fun of me intentionally.

I searched my memory, trying to remember any event where I might have offended or ignored the tech. I couldn't remember anything like that. I typically minded my own business and walked back and forth in the hallway to pass the time. I hadn't done anything else.

Or had I? I suddenly wasn't sure. Something must have happened. Otherwise, he wouldn't be mocking me where I could see him. This bothered me deeply and almost immediately I could feel a severe depression setting in.

Then, the tech abruptly left.

I began to pace again. What should I do? What could I do?

Another tech came in soon after and saw something was off with me. He asked, "Hey, Rick. You okay? Everything's good?"

For the first time, I shook my head no. I signaled for him to talk with me in the hallway, away from Tania.

"Your other tech just embarrassed me," I told him.

"Hmm…What did he do?"

"Uh…He made fun of me by walking very wobbly in front of me. I don't know why. I don't remember offending him. I truly don't understand why he would make fun of me!"

The tech couldn't believe it. "He did that? I'll ask him about it."

I wanted to say more to him, but the stress made it difficult to verbalize my thoughts and feelings. So, I asked him for a paper and pen. He gave me a paper and a red crayon because sharp objects weren't allowed.

I went into the bathroom and started to write. While I was in there, I could hear the first tech come back into the hallway and talk to the second tech.

The other tech asked him about his mocking behavior. "Why did you do that?"

The first tech loudly replied, "He always walks like that!"

I heard him from the bathroom. They talked more, but I couldn't hear the rest of what they said.

I gave the second tech the letter I'd written. I don't exactly remember what I wrote, but the gist was that I needed to be at peace and didn't want to deal with any drama.

He asked, "Would you like to talk to the other tech?"

"No. I'm good." I didn't want to interact with him. I just wanted to go to bed and sleep since it was getting late.

That was the last time I saw the rude tech.

I hoped the worst was over. Although everything was solved between me and the rude tech, I had unfinished business with Tania. I prepared to ask her why she laughed at me. I knew she would be discharged soon. If I didn't confront her, she would get away with it, and I couldn't let that happen!

The next day, we all gathered for another group therapy session. During our session, Tania became upset with Kayla. They had a standing feud. Kayla once told a therapist that she felt threatened by Tania's behavior. As usual, Tania wanted to assert her dominance around other patients, and made sure everyone knew who was boss.

I didn't like her bullish attitude and wanted to put an end to it. Even if she didn't change her ways, she needed to know that nobody was going to be her vassal.

Upset by Kayla's comments, Tania said she was leaving the room. I knew this was my last chance to express my displeasure. Other high-risk patients were there too, and they posed a potential threat to the peace I was seeking. I didn't want them to hurt me either. I needed to make my desires clear.

I gathered up my strength. Everyone would hear whatever I said. I was the quiet person in the group, and they would definitely notice me speaking up. I answered one of the questions the therapist had given to us previously. She'd asked us for three personal goals to set for the future. I hadn't had a hard time finding three.

With Tania still right outside the room, I said loudly, "These are my three goals: Avoid drama at all costs. Don't fight or argue with people with malicious intent. Don't repeat the behavior which led me to this hospital."

The therapist nodded okay, watching as one of the high-risk patients stormed out of the room, just like Tania. I didn't realize my three goals would cause that much commotion.

The therapist ended the session. Everybody left. A few stayed in the hallway, but most of them went to their rooms. I walked outside the group therapy room, adrenaline pumping, but Tania was nowhere in sight.

Later, I learned that my declarations had caused Tania's blood pressure to change dangerously, so she had to rest in her room. She was already angry toward Kayla and hadn't expected my response. She knew I was talking about her, that she'd embarrassed me the previous day. She never thought a quiet and passive guy like me would go after her at that very moment.

I admit, I almost felt like a bully, but I had no other choice. I didn't enjoy it, especially after learning about her blood pressure. But that was the only way to handle her bad behavior. She was dangerous, and if I didn't respond, she wouldn't get the message. Worse things could happen, and surely would have if I kept her bad behavior in my mind forever. I needed to close our chapter and move on before being released from the hospital.

Tania reminded me of Jith. She was smart and knew exactly what she did to others. I knew she was unlikely to change her ways, but my response was justified. She needed someone to stand up to her, to let her know she wouldn't be rewarded for her bullying behavior.

These incidents further informed my perceptions of mental health facilities, their employees, and fellow patients. I thought hospitals were supposed to be safe for patients like me. The hospital should have been a place to heal and solve problems. That is why there was group therapy and other activities. Instead of healing, there was only drama.

It may seem hard to believe, but I called 9-1-1 to get help from society since my family had failed so many times. After I got to the hospital, instead of relaxing and solving my problems with a psychiatrist or therapists, I lived in constant fear.

Group therapy had its purpose, and I learned a bit about different behavioral subjects. However, I just couldn't focus on healing. I worried about dealing with other patients' wicked personalities. I didn't expect to hang out with narcissistic people when I was trying to escape them. Everybody was in the same boat, and we knew difficult situations could arise. My hospital stay wasn't comfortable like I'd expected and became just another pure survival situation, like I'd faced in the past.

Before my last day, a social worker came to get my paperwork ready. She needed my help to fill out certain forms. One was the discharge goal. She asked me, "What goal or promise will you make to yourself before leaving the hospital?"

I quickly found one. "Don't do any dumb stuff."

She wrote that down, and that was it.

Since I had cooperated during my hospital stay, they were ready to release me. I had done my part and was excited to leave. I'd changed with all the drama I'd endured in the hospital, though I didn't know how I'd survived.

All I did know for sure was that I didn't want to be admitted to the mental hospital ever again! I thought, *It is in my best interest to just live at home without causing any trouble.*

CHAPTER 43

NO MORE SECOND CHANCES

Control your emotion
or it will control you.
—Samurai proverb

I spent my first day of 2021 in Desoto.

I was released from hospital care on January 5, 2021, around noon. The year 2020 hadn't been great for me with both personal issues and the pandemic, but now it was 2021. I didn't want to do any dumb stuff, didn't want to repeat what had happened ten days earlier. I was extremely lucky and very thankful that I hadn't ended up in jail after everything I'd done.

As I got ready to leave the hospital, I felt like a new car, complete with that new car smell. My departure represented a new start for me, a life full of adventures and new things to explore. I was so joyful to be going home as I headed to the lobby. I couldn't wait to be reunited with my family.

Chris and my mom were already waiting for me near the front door. We chatted for a moment, then we left the building together, heading out to find our car.

Our SUV was already waiting near the front entrance. I'd assumed Mom and Chris had come alone, but as we approached, I realized someone else was waiting inside, sitting in the driver's seat. Our tinted SUV windows made it hard to see. At first, I thought it might be Jef, but it was my father, patiently waiting for me.

For a moment, I thought having my dad there would be awkward. The last time I'd seen him was ten days ago, when I threatened him with a knife. I wondered why he chose to come and get me. He could have stayed at home; Chris and my mom would have been enough. I wasn't sure, but I was glad he was there. It was easier for me to see him in this SUV first rather than to see him at home.

I tended to get emotional during situations like this, and my dad never handled that well. I typically tried to avoid highly emotional situations, but there wasn't much I could do about it this time.

No one said a word about what had happened a few weeks before as we rode home; no one commented on what I'd done to cause me to miss out on time with my family. We spoke casually just to pass the time.

I looked outside through the tinted glass, watching other cars and people traveling on the road. They were all going to their own places and minding their own business. They weren't breaking laws or causing a scene. They were all moving on with their lives. It felt like a completely different world compared to what I had in my mind, a world I had never been to before.

When we finally parked in the garage at home, I pulled my hoodie over my head and went inside immediately; I didn't want to be seen by any of our neighbors. Nobody had been outside as we drove up, but I didn't want to risk it.

Inside, everything looked normal. It was quiet and clean as usual. The last time I'd seen this place, I had left it in chaos.

The floor had been littered with destruction. All of that had been removed; everything was cleaned up now.

Upstairs, I thought about how much had changed over the past ten days. I heard Jef call out something to me from another part of the house. I had been excited to come home, but now I felt emotional and wanted to be left alone. I tried to reply, but my voice broke; it didn't sound steady. I didn't want Jef to see how sad I was. How would he react? So, I hollered back that I was going to take a shower, just so that I could have a few minutes to collect my thoughts.

I turned on the switch for the small exhaust fan in the bathroom. The quiet disappeared, replaced by the steady whirring of the fan. Just like that, I began to cry. *My way of life has almost ended.* It was a quick cry, not unusual for me. Feeling a bit better, I turned the hot water on and took one of the longest showers I had ever taken. The warm water felt good flowing over my body. I needed to get my emotions in check before I saw my family again.

I needed to take some time to feel refreshed.

So I stood in the steamy spray, telling myself not to repeat what I had done ten days ago. All I wanted was peace. I didn't need to react out of violence or anger to show my family that I meant business.

The shower wasn't only cleaning my body. It was sweeping out my mind too, clearing out all the dark thoughts and emotions left over from my incident. I felt better with each passing moment. I could feel the peace settle into my bones.

I thought back to when I was only thirteen. I had taken an oath to go back to Kerala—a courageous choice designed to get my life back on track. That hadn't worked out in the end, but I had tried my best. Ten days ago, I'd almost lost everything, feeling lower than I ever had.

Never again.

As I finished up in the shower, I made a new oath. It was a simple oath, but still one that could challenge me. I wanted this oath to guarantee me success. No more screwups. No more second chances!

So, I vowed to myself that I would *never* cause any incident like that ever again, especially not one that could be detrimental to my family and my own existence.

That vow led me down a new line of thinking. I had to do something about my father. Nothing was ever finished without him. So, I made a decision. I still believed he was the reason I'd been subjected to bullying in middle school, the reason Jith had bullied me, and the reason I couldn't heal and resume my life. I had been weak and was set up for failure.

My father had known I wasn't like my brothers. I was terrible at socializing. I didn't know what to do in social settings. He knew all those things. He could have helped me, yet he chose not to assist. He was the problem.

I needed to move past what he had done without putting myself in another dark place. My dad wasn't a bad guy; he just never truly understood my situation. I had hope, though, that he had learned something from my latest incident.

I decided to leave my dad out of my future as much as possible. He would never understand, so I had to do my best to move on without him. If I didn't, issues like we'd had two weeks before could build up again and again. The final part of my oath swore I would never let problems like that escalate again. I would avoid them if possible.

I didn't resent my dad, but I didn't need his drama in my life anymore. If I could avoid that, there would be no more problems. Only peace.

I turned off the hot water and stepped out of my bathroom, feeling fresh. It was a new year, and I needed to move forward by thinking positively, holding my head high, and looking out for myself. I needed to do what was best for me, no matter what anyone else thought. There could be no more second chances for anyone who wanted to breed drama and issues into my life.

CHAPTER 44

A FINAL NAIL IN THE COFFIN

*Better to prevent
than regret.*
—Salvadorian proverb

In the weeks that followed, I felt my story had ended. I thought that by thinking positively, I could somehow write myself a "happily ever after" ending and close my book.

But fate wouldn't let me leave without one more thought-provoking message. I'm tempted to call it a grim warning, even. It was a surreal experience that left me with a realization I couldn't ignore.

Two months after I left the hospital, I had an unusual number of vivid dreams. I didn't know whether my medication caused them or the recent crazy events. Many were random and easily forgotten. Others were related to my real life. These dreams had patterns. Most were about things I viewed as threats, while others centered around what could happen in the future. Uncertainty was a big theme in my dreams, and one dream pounded a final nail into my coffin. It forced me to let go of certain hurts related to my family and gave me strength, pushing me further into healing.

When I woke from the dream, I tapped out a short description on my cell phone. "Two people from the future with futuristic tech saved me in the middle of the night from mysterious, ant-like creature swarms in my bedroom, and I woke up in the distant future."

I didn't want to forget any extra details. So, to the best of my memory, this is what happened:

I woke up in the middle of the night because of a big swarm of small, mysterious, black, ant-like creatures. I was sitting on my bed. The creatures came into my room through the floor, like sand. I tried to move away from them but didn't have enough space. They covered nearly every inch of the room. I was quickly cornered with nowhere to escape. They enveloped me, using some kind of magnetic field to grab me. I was totally helpless. I was pulled forward slowly into the swarm.

Two men suddenly came from out of nowhere and snatched me. One of them successfully detached the magnetic field and pulled me from the clutches of the swarm. They both used some kind of future tech equipment and weapons that I didn't recognize. The swarm quickly dissipated.

The other man asked, "Are you okay? The creatures are gone. You're safe now."

I panicked, unable to get any words out. It suddenly struck me how tired I was, and I fell asleep once more.

Later, I woke again, still in the dream. A woman, a companion of the two men from earlier, asked, "Are you okay?"

"What's going on?" I wanted to know.

She ignored me. "Get some rest. Once you've slept enough, you can leave your room." Then she left.

I didn't go back to sleep, though. I waited a moment before I got out of the bed and walked out into the dimly lit hallway. It seemed to deteriorate before my very eyes, much like the rest of the house. I wondered where I was and why I was there. I soon found one of the men who rescued me and asked, "Where am I?"

He showed me an orange hologram of the building and its surroundings. Everything I saw, all the technology, seemed far more advanced than anything I'd known. I was in some kind of underground facility beneath where my house had been—a man out of time.

I asked, "How am I alive? And what is going on around here? What's happening? Why did you save me? Where is my family?" I was worried, panicking because I was so confused by what was happening around me.

The man handed me a few letters, a video camera, and an old calendar. I wanted to ask him about them, but he didn't seem like he would welcome questions.

It didn't take long for me to discover that these items were from my family. There were some pictures with writing on the back and notes addressed to me. These items seemed to be very old. Was my family no longer around? How old would my family members be if they were, by some small chance, still living? I felt sick to my stomach. I was about to get some horrible news.

I feared that my family was dead, and I had gone on living as a young man. The world had gone through an apocalypse. I had awakened in the distant future, and I didn't know what year it was or anything that had happened since I'd fallen asleep. The longer I waited to hear the news, the more certain I became that my family was no longer living.

I looked through the items again. The photos and videos were of my parents and brothers. While they looked happy, I could see the sadness in their eyes, the pain they felt at facing the new world without me. They missed me. Looking at the calendar, I saw that someone had highlighted certain dates, but I had no idea what they meant. The only thing I could gather was that when the apocalypse had struck, I was in a coma.

I recognized my father's handwriting on the backs of the photos. Each note said something similar. "Rick, we love you forever. No matter what happens to us, we want you to know that. It's possible we might never see you again. You're in a coma, and our world is unstable. But we love you forever. Dad."

I fell to my knees, helpless, sobbing like a baby. My family had their chance to say goodbye to me, but I hadn't gotten a chance to do the same. That realization slammed into my chest like a freight train. How would I ever find peace when I missed my family so severely? I couldn't bring them back. All the good things and experiences we'd shared were gone forever.

By this time, both men and the woman had gathered around me, trying to calm me down. They did their best to sympathize, but they really didn't know what to do. They looked at each other and shrugged, confused. How could they help someone learning the worst news of their life for the first time? I cried for what felt like hours, wondering how I would ever survive alone now that everyone I loved had passed away.

That was as far as the dream went.

At 4:45 a.m., I awakened to my real life, soaked in sweat, and breathing heavily as my heart pounded. I didn't know why I had these realistic dreams. But I had somehow escaped from them because I couldn't bear any more sadness and emptiness. Those feelings hadn't subsided now that I was awake, either.

Thoughts of my family came back, and soon I was crying quietly. I had been so immersed in the dream that part of me wondered if I was still there, not quite back to the real world yet. It seemed more like a memory than a dream. I felt compelled to check that everyone was alive, and I breathed a heavy sigh of relief when I discovered everyone still there, safe, asleep in their rooms.

The dream itself seemed like a warning, a wake-up call, one I didn't want to experience again. It was very hard to ignore and seemed to set everything straight.

The one thing I always feared the most was losing something precious to me. In this case, my family. I couldn't imagine a world without them. They may have done things to me I didn't like, but I didn't want to feel anger and resentment toward them anymore, eager to punish them or seek revenge. I just wanted to go back to a time when things were okay. I didn't want my family to disappear. If they left, I would be alone, depressed and lost without them.

I had to let all my negativity go. Family was everything to me, and I didn't want to lose them. Ever.

I also didn't want to regret anything that had happened in my past. The only thing I wanted in my life now was peace, the same peace I'd lost when I was bullied. That was all that mattered to me. If I wanted to secure my inner peace, the only way to do that was to avoid drama, avoid people with malicious intentions, and think about my actions long before I did them to avoid foolish choices. All I had left was my legacy.

December's incident had been a close call, and that dream was a wake-up call—one that I never wanted to repeat. I had to take the opportunity I was given to create a new, stable life for myself. If I didn't get control of myself or come to my senses, something worse could happen that could end my life; I needed to prepare myself for the future. I didn't want to leave this world having accomplished nothing—having become somebody I was not. That was not the legacy I wanted to leave behind.

There would be no more chances. The person who I had cherished since I was a kid would be lost if I allowed one more screwup. I didn't want to be the villain in my own story. I couldn't be that guy. A bullying victim didn't deserve an ending like that.

CHAPTER 45

CONCLUSION

I'm now confident that this part of my story is well and truly over. I've come to realize that sometimes you have to let go of the hurt and pain of your past because it will take you nowhere and make your life worse, no matter who caused the problem.

I had to let go of the hurt and forgive my family, especially my dad.

These are the things that I have learned over time.

First, for those responsible individuals who are supposed to care for bullied victims, being a good and credible person is fine; but it's not good enough if you don't consider their mental well-being, ensuring that you're doing enough for their mind and their body. If something bad happens, especially to a loved one, doing nothing will not solve the problem. That person needs healing from their trauma, and genuine help in a timely manner, to make everything better. Untreated wounds can fester and become contagious, infecting one's mind completely, screwing up their entire life while you look the other way.

Living in a positive and prosperous environment with people who genuinely support and care about you is key. A person, whether a victim or not, must do their best to avoid bad influences as well, even if that person masquerades as intelligent and successful. No one wants to be surrounded by wolves in sheep's clothing, pretending to be good and helpful people during a time of healing and recovery when they're actually destroying any progress. It's a recipe for disaster and can be catastrophic for vulnerable individuals, especially those already emotionally damaged by bullying or other hardships.

Even someone who is a member of your family can be detrimental to your mental health, and no one is obligated to keep a person in their life who treats them poorly. Anyone who doesn't want what's best for you can ruin your chances of healing from your trauma, even if you're on the right path.

That said, the power of true and genuine love cannot be understated. Love can heal all wounds, even those hidden in your mind. It may even give you a chance to come back from utter destruction. The feeling of love can empower you and make you a one-of-a-kind superhero. You'll feel you can do anything, overcome anything, and be who you want to be. You can use that power to make your life better.

The next thing I learned: love can make you a better person.

If you lose all hope—if you feel broken, lost, and alone—true love can reignite your spark for life. It can pull you out of that hopelessness and give you the gumption to get back up, and accomplish things that seemed wholly out of your reach before. With love, you can achieve the unachievable, and make the impossible possible.

Regardless of what happens in your life, the one thing you must remember above all else is never let go of the good parts of yourself. You know who you are and who you want to be, and you must never lose sight of that, no matter how dark your life may seem. It's easy to give up on yourself when faced with insurmountable pressure, but you must never give in.

Never.

You must hold on to yourself and believe that at some point you will get to work back toward that person, that identity. *You can save you.* The world can be ruthless, but you have to hold on to the hope that love and goodness can always triumph over hate and evil. You can and will prevail. Just hold on to yourself and never surrender.

Last, if you do forget who you once were and become someone unrecognizable and scary—someone you don't wish to be, for any reason—go back to your childhood. Remember that sweet, innocent person you were, and try to bring pieces of that person back into your life. That's what kept me going all those years when I felt like I'd completely lost my identity.

Those pieces of your childhood are laced with goodness and purity, worth more than most precious metals on Earth. You can return to those traits and bring them with you into adulthood. Value yourself more than you value what happened to you. Understand that you're important, your background is important, and who you are inside is important. Reset yourself. Go back to the values and traits you loved about yourself before life became so difficult.

There is nothing to lose in trying. When the whole world is against you, it's easy to become a monster. Don't let yourself fall into that trap. Go back to who you are, who you were meant to be. No one deserves to become someone they never wanted to be permanently.

With all of that said, I still struggle with my past, *but it no longer consumes me.* Accepting what happened in the past doesn't mean accepting where I am now as the only possible outcome. The future is up to me and me alone.

I am who I am now, a product of my experiences and thoughts, bred from what I've lived through. My life could have been different if others around me had seen my distress and extended a helping hand. But I am also a man who knows that it's too late to change the past and accepts that the only way to navigate life is forward, not backward. What's done is done. I am the only person who can heal me, who can decide to seek help or medication if I need it.

It's easy to blame others, even if I have reasons, but I've moved past that. I've accepted the faults of those who surround me, I've forgiven them, and I'm ready to seek a brighter future.

Despite everything, I still care deeply for my dad and my family. My dad pushed me and gave me some hard times that caused me to experience some terrible situations, even if it was unintentional. But I still like and respect him. After all, he is my father—the only one I'll ever have.

This is the hand life dealt me, and I refuse to give any more of my time to those who have taken so much away.

I'm still working every day to meld who I was in the past with who I want to be in the future.

I have *schizophrenia*. I now know that this disorder is linked to PTSD from childhood trauma, bullying, and neglect. I understand so much more about who I am, why I am the way I am, and the obstacles that I will continue to face as I move forward.

I could have avoided my mental illness if I'd chosen to become somebody that I wasn't, but that was never a viable choice. I would rather have inherited an incurable mental illness than to have become a successful somebody who wasn't who I saw as Rick. There was no middle ground. I had to choose myself.

I have two choices now, two paths in life that I can choose to walk.

The first is to work, to improve, and to grow. I can be healed and work toward a healthy, happy mind. I can take control. I can complete an IT course and eventually get a job. This won't be easy. My mental health is a barrier that makes everything that much harder. I'll still deal with social anxieties, panic attacks, paranoia, and a lack of self-confidence.

But if I can work through it, learn to live with myself, and adjust to my own issues, I can come out on the other side with a life worth living.

The second choice is to let myself go the way Karl did, allowing my mental illness to overpower me and refusing to fight back. That path will also end in peace of mind but in a much different way. I haven't decided exactly how I feel about that path yet.

Honestly, I don't know which path I will take. For now, I must take each day as it comes. I don't know what the future will bring, and that's okay.

What I do know is that the past is the past. I'm moving forward each day in whatever way I can. I am almost thirty years old. I'm getting closer and closer to the day when I *will* know where I'm headed and what my future will probably hold.

Either way, I am shedding the skin of the last eighteen years. I've been belittled, bullied, and broken. But that is not the end of my story. Day by day, I work with what I have in order to live within the reality that I face. I hope I come out stronger, better, and wiser; I hope I will reach a place of positive growth and healing.

Most of all, I hope anyone reading this knows that if they face similar struggles, if they are being or have been bullied, neglected, and beaten down by family, friends, or strangers and they aren't sure how to go on, they are not alone. You are not alone.

It is not your fault. There is a future for you, just as there is for me.

THE END

AFTERWORD

I am adding this new section as a chance to let you know what happened between my last frightening dream which ended in March 2021 and February 2023 (the time of publishing this Second Edition).

I decided to write this because something unplanned and unfortunate happened right around the time I published the first edition of this book. Three incidents occurred because I lost my own focus while trying to finish and publish my book.

I also wanted to clear up several things I thought you would like to know after the fact.

Before I get into it, I will explain a little bit background information after the dream part in my last chapter…

After getting discharged from the hospital in Desoto due to the 9-1-1 incident which I caused, I was mostly stable, and experienced a new, strange feeling that I was finally at a new beginning.

After only taking a one-week break, I decided to rework and expand my original 65,000-word book and to add Part Five ("The Inevitable Big Bang") to the existing book to detail what happened during those intense and crazy moments. My priority was making my book into a reality at all costs and then to return to a normal life after publishing within six to twelve months. I felt this would finally restore my credibility in front of everybody once and for all. I would be redeemed.

Around the same time, my first ever face-to-face therapy with a case worker/therapist from another Desoto mental facility also started. By court order, she came to my home every two weeks to make sure that I felt well and could return to a normal state and become a productive citizen. With proper treatment, I wouldn't cause any more trouble/headaches for the law and others, and I would *not* end up in jail or worse.

During the whole of 2021, I generally did fine. I managed to finish my book, which felt nothing short of a miracle. Everything was going well as I had hoped.

But in December, I became very unstable after a bad interaction with my parents and my brothers. I realize that this instability was due to the heavy stress that I put myself through while trying to publish my book. The overload on my brain further destabilized my mind which led to three incidents and a bad situation.

I didn't want to say what actually triggered me or describe the specific details. I am focusing on myself for now, instead of my parents or brothers or others. I honestly don't want to make them look bad. I realized in the end that I could have avoided these three incidents pretty easily if only I had waited ten more seconds to think before I acted erratically and irrationally.

The three incidents happened due to me losing my own focus. I hadn't finished my book as early as I wanted, which led to more frustration. I was always thinking about how I was going to make everything work out in the end. My energy was draining and I was exhausted. I felt that time was my enemy.

The first incident happened after I became very unstable for the first time in over a year. Instead of calling 9-1-1 again, I called my officer from my local police department's "Mental Health Response Team."

It was the middle of the night when I called to ask him to put me in jail or someplace safe where I could get away from my family. But I didn't get a response since he wasn't working at that time of day and was very likely sleeping at that time.

I also sent a disturbing-sounding message to all of my writers and editors who had worked on my book, telling them everything was over—including my life—and I was canceling my book because of my dad and my brothers. My message sounded like it came from someone planning to commit suicide, but that wasn't really my plan at all. I only mentioned that everything was over, but I over-dramatized my statements to the point of causing worry.

The next night, two police officers came to my home and put me back in the same hospital in Dallas for an evaluation. After the hospital staff checked me out, they talked to my parents over the phone and decided to let me go the next morning.

The nurse who told me I could go home seemed like an angel who God sent to save me. I felt lucky and miraculous to be back in my home the next day without any other problems. I did feel a little stupid because I just lost my credibility for the first time since the 9-1-1 incident. I never thought another incident would occur because I had decided to move forward very carefully. But at least this new incident would be the very last one.

Or so I thought.

The second incident happened in March 2022. I had finally published the first edition of my book in the middle of February 2022. But then I became unstable again, not three months since the last incident. This happened at night too. Only this time I actually decided to end my life by swallowing 50 tablets of Hydroxyzine meds. I thought it was a sleeping pill because whenever I took it I felt calm and sleepy.

I thought that taking all those meds would make me very sleepy and I just wouldn't have to wake up anymore. It seemed a peaceful way to die. It seemed a fitting way to go, due to raging anger toward my parents and my brothers. I felt like they hadn't learned *anything* from the latest incident, and I had finally had enough...again.

My suicide was undertaken in a revenge-like state. I quickly swallowed those 50 tablets. I wasn't thinking straight (as usual), and my intensely high stress caused me to make the dumbest move that I had ever made in my life.

Instead of going to bed after taking the pills, I decided to confront my family and tell them what I had just done. I told them I would die within two or three hours, just to see how they would react. My family was surprised, though my dad told everybody that the hospital personnel would surgically rip open my stomach and take all out the meds. After that, he said I would be fine.

I was surprised at that statement and realized that my suicide attempt had failed.

My family called the police, and the ambulance took me to a different hospital where medical staff observed me for the remainder of the day. But they didn't really open up my stomach to retrieve those 50 pills. They knew what I did not—that those pills wouldn't cause any lasting health problems and I wouldn't pass out or anything like that. So, they put me in a bed for observation. I had thought something serious would happen if I took all those pills...but no.

Nothing big really happened other than me being so completely tired that I couldn't even walk.

The next day, an American psychiatrist of Indian origin talked to me through a robot-like stand with the monitor.

She asked me why I had decided to do this. I said, "It's because of my family. They destroyed my life and won't listen to me!

She tried to tell me in a calm, gentle fashion—taking care not to be offensive—that I am an almost 30-year-old man and not a kid anymore. That was completely true, and I didn't know how to react.

So, as usual, I got a little embarrassed, but tried not to show it. I didn't tell her about my book for some reason.

After that conversation, they transferred me to a ward for people who tried to harm themselves. It was night when I arrived there and one of the personnel told me straight away that if I didn't want to stay then I could leave for home. That was surprising.

I told him that I would like to leave for home and promised that I wouldn't try to kill myself again.

Luckily, I had Chris' cell phone number and I called him so he could pick me up. He and my mom drove me back home. I felt like a lucky punk again and thought there would definitely be no more incidents.

Unfortunately, that wasn't the case either.

The third and final incident happened one month later in April. To put it simply, Chris made me feel like a fool. A few days after that, I woke up late, around two in the afternoon. My mood was already foul because of a bad dream combined with my anger toward Chris, which was still in my mind. I decided to storm downstairs without thinking straight and confronted my mom. No other family members were at home.

I quickly became enraged, and things got out of control (as usual). I scratched our TV, and my mom called the police when she found out. They came quickly.

This time, I decided to pick up a paperback copy of my book so I could show them just in case they took me to a hospital where I had stayed for several days. I could use my book to show to one of the mental health professionals once I got there, although I hadn't caused this situation with any plan to do that. The "Mental Health Response Team" from my local police department also arrived and witnessed inside our home and the scratched television.

One of the lady officers told me in a friendly way that I had to stop doing this and needed to seriously get things under control. She pointed out that it's not a good thing for me to continuously act like this.

While there, another officer checked out my book for a second and gave it back to me. They were confused by my actions. For some reason they didn't take me anywhere like jail or a hospital. Instead, they decided to just let me go back inside since I had calmed down and wasn't acting erratically in front of them.

Then the police and the other team simply left. I was surprised and lucky again. I thought for sure they would take me somewhere and lock me away.

I felt stupid that this incident and the two previous incidents had happened within such a short amount of time, even though I had promised several people that I wouldn't let these problems start again. I had no idea what the fudge was going on with me. I realized that I had completely lost all credibility. I was truly appearing like someone with behavioral issues, and someone was going to put me down or separate me from my family. The police or the court would have enough of me causing these situations.

All I had been planning was to ditch my old life and return to a normal setting in a very credible way. That was one of the main reasons why my book even existed.

But in the end, I continuously made a fool out of myself, turning into a real joke to everybody. I may accidentally have become a criminal like I predicted previously if I continued on this track.

If I allowed one more bad event to happen, then they would have no other choice but to put me in a jail or somewhere worse, just as I had said in my last few chapters. I wanted to prevent that from happening at all costs. I needed to fully get things under control.

No more messing things up. I realized that I live a life of luxury, even now, despite my mental situation and anything that happened to me in my past. I didn't want to allow these sorts of things and cause more embarrassing scenes. This was getting out of hand, even by my own standards. I was becoming someone who I didn't want to be.

My plan was to personally be doing good after I published the First Edition of my book; otherwise, all the effort would become a real waste.

I didn't want to let this happen again, so I decided to stop everything and take the second choice at the conclusion of my book: not doing anything to get my new life or new future. The last thing I want is to lose everything and become someone that I never wanted. People will assume I am a bad guy with not just mental issues but with some bad behavioral issues as well. I don't know whether I am taking the second choice temporarily or long-term, but I am making this choice in order to stop further bad situations.

Once I got past these bad episodes, I realized that Chris' marriage was coming up. Within the next few months everybody would leave for India. I decided I would go back with them to India in July 2022. So, two months after the last incident. I returned to my childhood home again for three and a half months; my plan was to take a small break, get some fresh air, and rest. I wanted to just get a chance to breathe and restore my mental health.

Now, I have returned to the US feeling very fresh and new. The last three or four years had clearly been very rough, and I wanted to get away from those bad memories.

As long as I don't go back to my old ways then everything should be alright.

Let's see how my future will turn out.

The major thing I wanted to say to the readers in this afterword was about what happened after the book's story was over and to give a small glimpse into what my future may hold. I have ended everything else once and for all, again. I have no desire to repeat any of the bad events that happened in the past. My hope, my goal, my *plan* is that everything will be peaceful for me in the future! I truly believe it.

***

But before I go, I want to say a few other things regarding my other life situations. I wanted to clarify these once and for all for all readers who may still have some doubts.

First, I wanted to say that my dad is *not* a bad guy. He never was. I honestly believe he is a very credible and legit person.

But for whatever mysterious reasons, he just didn't want me to go back to India back in 2014 after Jack's funeral. That decision negatively affected my life for sure.

I felt there was no future for me in America at that time. I had tried to have one for six years after I got bullied in eighth grade, but obviously that failed badly—as you can see from this book. For me, there was always no other real choice but

---

to go back to India temporarily and rediscover my true self. That, too, unfortunately failed because my dad turned his back on me. The result was tragic.

In the end, I paid the ultimate price by becoming a man with a serious mental health disorder. Even as I say this, I don't want to make my dad look bad in front of others.

I have somehow forgiven him, even after all the chaos. I saved both of our lives by not making the wrong or dumb decision during a critical and dangerous time.

In the end, I had no choice but to be angry and frustrated with him throughout my story after learning that he wasn't planning to continue the mission. I wasn't really "fighting" him even though that was what readers may have felt when reading those parts of my life.

All I was trying very hard was to "convince" him instead of "fighting" him before everybody else joined in to stop my mission in its tracks before it really got started. Everything went to crap. And most, if not all of my family, sadly, had turned against me. I became the bad guy because I wasn't doing what they all wanted or expected from me.

Only now do I understand why he didn't let me go back to India back in 2014.

I will repeat, though, that my dad is not a bad guy. I don't want to treat him like a bad guy. Our situation is a little complicated. We have a special relationship, different than my two brothers. That will never change, no matter how others try to make me look bad or divide us. He is my father. I will accept the consequences of his past decisions even if I lose my way of life.

Secondly, I would like to remind readers that the younger cousin I talked about in the preface *really* affected my way of writing my book and telling the full story in a proper and professional way. That is why the tone of the book occasionally got a little more aggressive than usual. That is why I decided to tone down some of the harsher things I said about my dad without changing the truth. I mention this cousin again here in case readers have forgotten about him and the influence he had on me. He is called "Ken" during the times in which he appears in the book.

Readers may think that I said something harsh to him which led him to have such a wrong attitude towards me but that is not true. I had given him full freedom and control, but I never disputed or got angry with him. In fact, I barely spoke to him during those times.

The freedom that I gave him didn't work out well for me in the end because he already was making wrong assumption that I am a bad guy because of the way I interacted with my dad. He tried to fight me just like my brothers (and others) did because they honestly thought I was intentionally destroying my dad.

Ken had plenty of chance and opportunities to not believe that. I can't make excuses for him.

For some reason, he always loved to smirk at me right under everybody's nose without any shame whenever he came to my home. That deteriorated my inner peace while I was working on my autobiography. He would always make funny remarks or gestures, even when someone was around. I tried to ignore him, but I was losing my precious morale every time he came to my home.

He knew about my life's situation and what my book was all about. But still, all he ever did was making fun of me indirectly and directly in cheap ways at my own home.

I tried to tell all the family members on my contact list (except his parents) about him, but it seemed like they don't really care what he did to me or how he acted toward me. What can I say? Ken appears like a cheap narcissist based on his behavior; some might say he acted like a bully wannabe, even though he was several years younger than me. His behavior is both sad and embarrassing.

I could have avoided this situation if I had responded to him, but I had no time for that mind games bullcrap because I was focusing on building my book and ended up giving him a free pass instead.

I allowed his rude behavior to happen while I tried to ignore him. In my determination to finish my book, I didn't learn from similar experiences with bullies and domineering family members in the past. Ken continued his behavior as he realized that I was weak and wouldn't fight back. I wished I never included him; I only did so in the first place because he was an actor/model who I thought could help me with my Hollywood idea.

By the time he was banned from coming to my home on my 29th birthday, it was already too late. That is why the events in Part Five ("The Inevitable Big Bang") had happened. In the end, he made me look bad in front of others and I lost my credibility and my mental health over time.

I also lost most, if not all, of any credibility on Facebook because I made some unnecessary posts during bad moods because of him. Otherwise, I would never have made such posts.

It's safe to say that now he is forever banned from my life for screwing me and jeopardizing my book's existence.

Third, to address something a little controversial that I said in the book: I never really tried or even had serious thoughts about shooting up my former middle school while

I was angry at everything and everyone, and while other school shootings were happening around that time.

Maybe someone else in my shoes might have become a real school shooter. I don't want to appear like I'm bragging that I didn't go down that dark, fatal path. Maybe I am, I don't know, but I never let myself become that person. I also knew, deep down, that the FBI would have caught me anyway because I suspected they were watching me at that time. But still, I don't want any bullied victims to have those kinds of thoughts in the first place or have to go through tough times; many school shooters have a history of abuse by their fellow students or others.

Luckily for me, I know where I came from, and I know who I am. I just never forgot or abandoned my own personal identity. I am grateful and lucky to have had a good childhood that others may not have gotten.

It doesn't matter whether you have an unfair life caused by others or not; in the end, if you commit evil things your life will get thrown away and your legacy will be lost forever...possibly at the expense of innocent lives.

I wanted to say that no matter my mental health state or how upset I may become, I would *never* turn against anyone or become a menace to society. I can guarantee you that.

Fourth, for some miraculous reasons, I no longer have panic attacks. Why? Because I saw a tweet made by Elon Musk about hyena cubs getting infected by toxoplasmosis (mind-controlling parasites) which led them to get killed by lions if they approach them—unlike those hyenas cubs who are not infected.

Mr. Musk was trying to say something about AI (artificial intelligence), but I clearly noticed the hyena part. That tweet made me seriously think about my own life's situation and my book's future.

Coincidence or not, I was having the biggest panic attack when I saw this tweet while I was in my bed.

It turned out to be a godsend.

This tweet really saved me. It completely removed my panic attacks/thoughts/situations in one day without the need for any meds or therapy. I am very grateful for that. That opened a door that had been shut for a long time. I am glad that he made that tweet at that moment. Perfect timing!

I am using this chance in this book to thank Elon Musk for that tweet. He unknowingly gave me a chance to move forward with my life. My panic attacks were a pain in the butt I thought I would never get rid of. But luckily I did because of that tweet. I no longer have panic attacks, which had first started back in 2015 or 2016!

I took a screenshot of his tweet around July 2021, on my cellphone, before I published my first edition of this book. The panic attack was just gone forever, just like the agoraphobia that I had back in 2018 after seeing my online crush. Otherwise, my life would have been doomed. I don't want to lose the ability to play video games or live a normal life because of panic attacks.

Now I have the chance to live and enjoy life again.

Lastly, I want to reiterate that my antagonist Jith is believed to have Narcissistic Personality Disorder but on a high-functioning level. He is highly intelligent, motivated, confident, ruthless, and charming.

He is self-centered, all-knowing, and calculated. He only cares about himself and his social status, success, and power. Plus, some of his relatives and friends are still very supportive of him, even after learning what he did to me. (Although

I won't judge or turn against his parents or his sibling, whatever happens.)

He didn't just "hurt" my feelings, he mentally "disabled" me by continuously and discreetly abusing me over the course of time, so I couldn't operate at a high-functioning level socially among people or genuinely enjoy my life.

Jith has forgotten where he originally came from and who he once was. Sadly, he clearly knows that being a bully is a real key to his own success and helped him rise to the top of the food chain.

He is aware of this book. He may retaliate, discredit me, or try to come after me directly or indirectly to get his "last word." No one has ever stood up to him and tried to make him accountable. He is a highly dangerous individual with a wicked personality that all types of people need to watch out for.

That is why I am avoiding him at all costs both for my own safety and because my own family members are not willing to defend me from him, even after they know everything. I am not going to confront him personally or digitally ever again, but I will let readers know about his character through this book.

Dear vulnerable people, avoid these types of narcissistic characters at all costs.

Please identify them early as you can. Stay away from these characters for your own sake, especially if you are on your own like I was.

These are all the things that I wanted to share in this afterword. Hopefully, it didn't get too long but what I needed to say here was worth it!

Rick Pallattumadom
(Accidental Author)

ACKNOWLEDGMENTS

Even after finishing this book, I truly have no idea how I managed to make my dream a reality. It's still hard to believe. It feels like a miracle because I am the least likely person to do something like this and finish this long, crazy journey. It wasn't without its ups and downs, but here I am at the finish line. Mission accomplished!

I am very proud of myself. My thirteen-year-old self would be very proud too. I did this for him. Without his spirit, I wouldn't have had the willpower to finish my book. Somehow, I always knew he was still there inside me, rooting me on!

When I look back on my journey, I realize there is no way I could have pulled this off by myself. There would be no book at all if it weren't for my three ghostwriters and the seven writers who critiqued my manuscript.

I'd like to thank my very first writer who first helped to develop my book in 2019. She edited my 43,000-word manuscript and helped me to realize I had a real story to tell, even though back then it was far from over. I was still learning how to be professional and hoped she would understand my mental state. I like to think we're still on good terms. I am incredibly grateful for all her hard work.

I'd like to thank my second writer, Marlyse Goodroad. After working with my first writer, I worked on writing the rest of the book with Marlyse's help. She critiqued my work as well as helped with the writing process. She was the main writer to help make my book and my dream a reality.

My English isn't great. I'm not a native speaker, and I lack knowledge and experience about the language. Despite that,

Marlyse did a great job understanding what I meant. She fixed and overhauled my work, added emotion based on my content, and helped tell my story in a way that readers could understand and relate to.

She did a good job understanding my life's story despite our cultural differences, and she took good care of my manuscript. I have no doubt that she helped me move on with my life by helping to reduce my panic attacks along the way which, for a while, were becoming more frequent as my book became more and more real. It was a pleasure having her work on my book!

I'd like to thank R. Lee Brown who edited and proofread the whole manuscript based on Marlyse's work. He also critiqued my storytelling, which resulted in changes that greatly enhanced the final version of my autobiography. Because of him, I became more confident on my work, and I was able to prepare myself for launch day. I'm really lucky to have him on my side.

Next, I'd like to thank several writers who critiqued my work during development: Alexandria Cline, Kathleen Salidas, Megan Stott, Sean Mascarenhas, Jessica Wright, Jordan Iles, and Sarah Lamb.

Their professional second opinions improved my book and helped me to seriously step up my game to create a positive experience for my readers. When I was in a very bad mood toward the end of development, I told them that I was going to quit writing. They encouraged me to keep working, giving me a morale boost and helping me face my fears. Without their support, I may have given up on my book when it was nearly finished.

I'd like to thank my Pallattumadom and Padapurackal family members, as well as other friends and family who have heard about my book and have supported and believed in me, even when my idea seemed a little strange at first.

I don't have to name each of them. They already know who they are and that I am very thankful for them. I will never forget their support. They all gave me a boost of confidence, and their excitement kept me going each time the writing process became difficult.

I'd like to thank my father Joy, my mother Ancy, my older brother Jef, and my younger brother Chris for giving me the funds to develop my book. I know it may seem weird because of the development of these relationships in the book. However, I needed their help, and they were willing to assist me.

Despite what happened between us, I want to use this opportunity to thank them for supporting my book becoming a reality. They knew what was at stake and that my book was an outlet to avoid dangerous situations and difficult days. I am blessed to have had their support despite our rocky history. If there was any chance we could peacefully coexist, creating this book with their involvement was the only way. Whatever happens as a result of publishing this book, I hope it benefits us.

I would like to thank Dr. Jacqueline Burnett-Brown (PhD) for writing the foreword for me for this book. She was able to genuinely understand my story and was willing to write her honest and professional opinions about my story. And also for talking and bringing awareness about my mental illness for my readers in advance before they read my story. Her foreword gave me more mental strength and courage to publish my book, so there would be less chance of me having panic attacks or other bad situations afterward. I am very grateful and truly appreciate her for accepting my invitation.

Finally, I'd like to thank God. I admit I've lost most, if not all, of my faith many times since eighth grade. My faith is still not as strong as it was when I was younger. Luckily, I still have some faith in Him inside me. It's good to have someone watching over me, and I think He was there while I wrote my book. He played a part in the behind-the-scenes events without my knowledge, and I am grateful for that.

With that, I think it is time for me to go. Publishing this book officially marks the end of a crazy and a wild journey. This has been a once-in-a-lifetime experience that I know I will never have again. This will be my first and last book ever. I wrote this one for my own survival and a chance at a peaceful future. I am very glad that I had the opportunity to write my autobiography so I can move on. Without it, I would have been in deep trouble. I'm beyond thankful I was ever inspired to write my story.

I am using this book as a foundation to start a new life. I hope that I can still become who I've wanted to be. I'm thirty years old! It is time for me to leave my troubled past behind and move into a new, calmer age with good spirits. It can't get much better than this.

POSTSCRIPT

I'm going to take the time to read a <u>lot</u> of books so I can improve my life without the need for too many social interactions. I only wish I had done this <u>a long time ago</u>!

GAWKY
Signing out!

RESOURCES

https://www.nami.org/About-Mental-Illness/Mental-Health-Conditions/Schizophrenia/Support

https://www.psychiatry.org/patients-families/schizophrenia

https://www.mayoclinic.org/diseases-conditions/schizophrenia/symptoms-causes/syc-20354443

https://www.academia.edu/65183190/Racial_Dialogues_A_Phenomenological_Study_of_Difficult_Dialogues_from_the_Perspective_of_High_School_English_Teachers

ABOUT THE AUTHOR

Rick Pallattumadom is an Indian immigrant, who settled in the US in 2005 at the age of thirteen with his parents and two brothers. Shortly after he moved to America, he experienced bullying for the first time. He has struggled with Post-Traumatic Stress Disorder and mental health issues because of multiple instances of bullying, but has found his own path toward healing.

Rick enjoys working with computers and playing war-related video games online. He hopes to bring awareness to others by sharing his life story and the impact bullying had on his life. Rick currently lives in Irving, Texas.

CPSIA information can be obtained
at www.ICGtesting.com
Printed in the USA
BVHW090232130123
656164BV00021B/1136

9 798218 104528